Applying
Case-Based
Reasoning:

Techniques for Enterprise Systems

Applying Case-Based Reasoning:

Techniques for Enterprise Systems

Ian Watson

University of Salford, U.K.

Morgan Kaufmann Publishers, Inc.
San Francisco, California

Sponsoring Editor	Michael B. Morgan
Production Manager	Yonie Overton
Production Editor	Cheri Palmer
Editorial Coordinator	Marilyn Alan
Cover Design	Carrie English, canary studios
Text Design and Composition	Sybil Ihrig, VersaTech Associates
Illustrations	Cherie Plumlee
Copyeditor	Sharilyn Hovind
Proofreader	Jennifer McClain
Printer	Edwards Brothers, Inc.

Morgan Kaufmann Publishers, Inc.
Editorial and Sales Office
340 Pine Street, Sixth Floor
San Francisco, CA 94104-3205
USA
Telephone   415 / 392-2665
Facsimile   415 / 982-2665
E-mail   mkp@mkp.com
Web site   http://www.mkp.com

Order toll free 800 / 745-7323

© 1997 by Morgan Kaufmann Publishers, Inc.

Library of Congress Cataloging-in-Publication Data

Watson, Ian D. (Ian Duncan) date.
    Applying case-based reasoning : techniques for enterprise systems
  /   Ian Watson.
        p. cm
    Includes bibliographical references and index.
    ISBN-1-55860-462-6
    1. Expert systems (Computer science)   2. Case-based reasoning.
  I. Title.
  QA76.76.E95W39   1997
  006.3'3--dc21   97-14546
                                          CIP

To Heather

Contents

Preface

This book has taken me about two years to write, on and off. During that time, case-based reasoning (CBR) has grown from a little-known branch of artificial intelligence to a subject of major influence. The purpose of this book is to widen the audience for CBR still further.

Until this book, all the publications on CBR have been intended for a research audience, that is, people with a solid background in artificial intelligence, computer science, or cognitive science. This book, however, is an introductory text suitable for general software and programming professionals, MIS managers, and those responsible for corporate IT thinking and implementation. As an introductory text, undergraduate and master's students from any discipline—not necessarily computing—will find the book of value.

The book, as its title implies, is distinctly applications oriented. Only 4 of the 10 chapters deal with theory, while the remainder deal with practical case studies of commercially fielded applications, detailing the considerable benefits these systems have brought. IT professionals will also find details of tools and methods for building successful CBR systems. Consequently, this book will be of interest and practical use to people from industry who are thinking of building a CBR system.

As I explain further in Chapter 9, CBR is different from many hyped technologies. Unlike an infamous predecessor, rule-based expert systems, CBR's hype has followed its successful commercial application, rather than preceded it. In Chapter 4 I unashamedly list more than 130 companies, many of them household names (e.g., American Express, Apple Computer, British Airways, Dun & Bradstreet, Microsoft, Xerox Corp.) who are already using CBR. True, the majority of these are using CBR to support customer help-desks. But isn't it just typical of artificial intelligence to overlook success and move heedlessly on to new intellectual challenges! One of the purposes of this book is to consolidate the success of CBR. As you will see, CBR is above all a very simple technique, one that can be easily applied to solve relatively simple, yet common problems, such as technical support.

Consequently, if you are a graduate student or postdoctoral researcher, you will not find descriptions here of cutting-edge research. There is no discussion of issues like hierarchical case representations, complex model-based adaptation, or novel algorithms for clustering cases or assessing similarity. You will, however, find the most up-to-date bibliography of CBR research currently in print. The extensive bibliography is intended to provided a resource, both to students, researchers, and commercial developers who wish to delve deeper into CBR. It is structured to help you find those papers that are of interest to you and your individual needs.

The book sets out in Chapter 1 to introduce readers to data processing and knowledge representation, in the form of logic programming and rule-based expert systems. I do not assume that a reader necessarily has any prior background in computing, consequently I make no apologies for the introductory nature of this chapter (if you are familiar with the content of Chapter 1, by all means skip it). It introduces the weaknesses of these techniques and concludes by introducing the concept of successfully recalling solutions to previous problems. That is, case-based reasoning.

Chapter 2 introduces the *CBR-cycle,* a common way of conceptualizing CBR, and briefly recounts the history of CBR. This starts with the work of Schank and dynamic memory and continues with the early work of Kolodner and Hammond and the prototypical CBR systems, such as CHEF. The main body of the chapter describes the techniques that make up CBR. That is, case representation, indexing, retrieval, and adaptation. In particular, the two most widely used retrieval techniques, nearest neighbor and inductive retrieval, are described in detail using simple examples.

Chapter 3 divides CBR applications into *classification problems* and *synthesis problems,* a common division in artificial intelligence. It advises that classification problems are easier to solve using CBR. CBR is compared with other decision support technologies, such as information retrieval, statistics, rule-based reasoning, machine learning, and neural networks. Advice is given on when, and when not, to use

CBR. The chapter concludes by briefly describing some influential academic applications of CBR.

Chapter 4 starts to look at the industrial application of CBR. Four commercially fielded application case studies are described. The CLAVIER system at Lockheed is the classic CBR system. CLAVIER shows that for this particular problem, Lockheed did not have a theoretical model of how to solve it. Consequently, they could not implement a rule-based system. They wanted a means of archiving best practices and comparing new situations to previously successful ones. To dispel the misconception that CBR might only be applicable to high-tech companies, such as Lockheed, the next case study takes place in a small aluminum die-casting plant in Wales. Wayland, as you will see, is a very simple application, well within the budget and skills of even the smallest company. The third case study, at British Airways, shows how CBR can be used to support complex diagnoses. It also discusses the advantages the CBR tool has for British Airways over conventional diagnostic tools. The final case study in this chapter introduces an entirely different class of problem, the detection of top management fraud at Deloitte & Touche. This problem is highly judgmental and is based on opinion and subtle observation. Deloitte & Touche uses CBR in a very mature way to help confirm and question the company's own assumptions.

Chapter 5 continues with application case studies, but this time that of customer support and help-desks. This application area is CBR's bread and butter, and the chapter begins by showing why CBR is so appropriate for this activity. The first case study is of the classic CBR help-desk at the Compaq Computer Corp. It describes how the system was implemented and shows how nontechnical staff using the CBR system can now handle over 90% of the routine technical queries, leaving more experienced staff to handle more difficult issues. It also demonstrates the learning ability of CBR. This case study is followed by a brand-new innovation, providing case-based customer support on the World Wide Web. The Broderbund case study shows how this was almost a natural progression, and I'm confident that many readers will be excited by the possibilities of this approach. Finally, the chapter concludes with a case study that describes a methodology for building case-based help-desks. As you will learn throughout the book, CBR systems are dynamic, they learn, and consequently particular attention must be made to their maintenance and support.

Chapter 6 provides a comprehensive review of 10 commercially available CBR tools and several public domain tools. The review highlights the significant features of each tool and will provide you with a guide to the tool that may be most suited to your needs.

Chapter 7 then takes one of these tools, Inference Corp.'s CBR3, and shows how you might build a simple diagnostic case-base. The application chosen is that of solving problems with laser printers and is exactly the sort of case-base you would develop if you were supporting an IT help desk. The step-by-step guide shows you how easy it is to build this type of case-base.

Chapter 8 takes a more theoretical view of building a CBR system and discusses some of the issues you should consider when building, testing, and maintaining a case-base. The chapter contains many guidelines that will help you to develop more successful case-bases.

Chapter 9 reviews what you have just read. It outlines the key assumptions of CBR and reaffirms that CBR is about similarity and should be kept simple. The advantages that I believe CBR has over conventional expert system techniques are discussed, and the chapter concludes with a look ahead at some of the challenges and opportunities for CBR.

Chapter 10 provides a structured bibliography of CBR research papers, books. and reports. Instead of simply providing an alphabetically sorted bibliography, the chapter is divided into subsections, each of which deals with a specific topic. Works are assigned to more than one topic if they deal with more than one issue. I hope that this will make it easy for the reader to identify works of interest to them even if they are not very familiar with the CBR literature. The chapter concludes with a short list of Internet information sources of relevance to CBR, including AI-CBR, that I maintain.

There are many people to thank for helping me, either directly or indirectly. Firstly, I would like to thank Lawrence Poynter of Inference Ltd. Many years ago he showed me an early beta version of a new product called CBR Express that Inference was working on. The simplicity of this tool impressed me so much, I started looking into this interesting new technique called CBR. Since then, Lawrence has kept me up to date with the stream of new products Inference has produced. In particular, he and others at Inference provided me with the beta version of CBR3 (that is reviewed in Chapter 6), and with details of the Compaq and Broderbund case studies. I would also like to thank all the other companies that provided me with evaluation copies of their software. I hope you all feel I have been fair with your products. Each has its strengths, but, sorry guys, none of them is perfect!

I would also like to thank Chris Price of the University of Wales, who provided me with the material for the Wayland case study; Oliver Curet of Deloitte & Touche, who provided me with details of the top management fraud system; and Rick Magaldi of British Airways, who provided me with details of the CASELine system. Rick also reviewed a draft of this book—thanks for your enthusiastic comments. Thanks also to the other reviewers who spent so much time on the first draft. Some of you I know, but others preferred to remain anonymous. I hope that you'll see I have made many of the changes you suggested, and that you will recognize you sometimes had contradictory views. This book would have been worse without your input—any flaws are now mine alone.

I would not have had the time to write this book if it were not for support from the U.K. Engineering and Physical Sciences Research Council. In particular, the three grants they have awarded me in recent years (GR/J42496, GR/J43660, and GR/L16330) have helped to give me the time (and money) to pursue my research interests. However, their funding would have been useless without the support of my university. Sadly, Salford University seems to be a rarity in the United Kingdom in that it rewards successful researchers by significantly reducing their teaching loads. Thanks are therefore due to Peter Barrett, Roger Baggott, and Peter Brandon for implementing this policy. I should also thank my research students and research fellows for so enthusiastically embracing CBR and keeping me on my toes by asking challenging questions. You've all helped me to clarify my views. (You've also sometimes frustrated me, by often forgetting that CBR should be kept simple. Hopefully, this book will remind you!)

At a general level, I would like to thank the CBR community (you know who you are). Many of you I have met at conferences and workshops, but some I have only met through e-mail. Your warmth, acceptance, and openness encouraged me that CBR was an area I could work in. I hope you will feel that this book makes a valuable contribution to promoting CBR. If I have misrepresented or misinterpreted your work, please excuse me.

Finally, I would like to thank my wife, whose love and support makes me happy and whose high standards have helped me to achieve more than I would have in other company.

What Is
Case-Based Reasoning?

This chapter introduces the way in which computers represent data and how we draw meaning or information from that data. It introduces the concepts behind relational and object databases and shows how these can be used to support simple queries. It then briefly describes logic programming and introduces the concepts behind rule-based reasoning and expert systems. The problems and limitations of rule-based expert systems are discussed and contrasted to the way in which we routinely solve problems. The essential characteristics of case-based reasoning (CBR) are then introduced. By the end of this chapter, you should have an understanding of how computers represent data and how they can reason with that information. You will see why existing computing technologies are not always sufficient and how CBR may offer a solution.

1.1 Representing Information

Computers are used to manipulate information, be it a payroll program, a word processor, a game, or a decision support system. Computer programs process data in one form or another, and current tools are the result of continuous attempts to improve and extend the ability of computers to automate information processing.

Computers perform simple transformations on symbols. The primitive transformations are defined by the electrical circuits in the chips that make up the central processing unit. In binary terms, these primitive transformations perform functions like adding two sequences of binary numbers together, subtracting them, shifting patterns left or right, and comparing sequences.

It is important to realize that a computer does not "know" what it is doing. Its programs are designed to mimic how we perform and represent tasks. For example, if you write a letter using a word processor, the computer does not know what any of the words mean, it does not even know they are words. The keys on the keyboard are translated into binary sequences, manipulated, and then translated back for display on the monitor.

Because of the design of its circuits, the computer has to use an internal representation for letters and words that it can manipulate. It must translate inputs into a representation *it* can manipulate and outputs into a representation *we* can understand (Figure 1-1). Developing a computer program that can manipulate data in a meaningful way involves the following steps:

1. First, define a scheme for presenting data symbols to the computer that faithfully represents what we intend.
2. Next, define the transformations that are permissible on the data and are meaningful to us.
3. Finally, define a formalism that lets the computer present the result to us in a meaningful way.

Fortunately, most of this groundwork has already been done, and many codes and international standards have already been defined. For example, ASCII (the American Standard Code for Information Interchange) is an international standard code for representing alphanumeric characters and certain other special symbols. Moreover, there are numerous high-level computer languages that provide a wide range of functions that can transform symbols for us. Thus, data processing is helped by the definition of appropriate representations for the data and for the transformations upon that data.

Figure 1-1.
Translation to and from a computer's internal representation

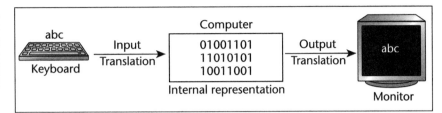

However, it is vital to understand that the choice of representation defines what types of transformations are ultimately possible. Consider the following analogy: Golf players have many ways of describing how a golf ball has been hit. These include words like "sliced," "hooked," "squarely," "top-spin," "pitched," and so on. The richness of their language for describing the hitting of the ball means that golf players can describe this vital aspect of their sport in a way that people who do not play golf cannot understand. Thus, our understanding is restricted by our language, or representation.

1.2 Representing Data in a Computer

Databases impose structure on the data they store. This is a reflection of the realization that the meaning of data does not reside at an atomic or unitary level. The meaning (i.e., the information) we draw from data is contained in the relationship between data items.

Thus, in Figure 1-2 it is not the elementary data items themselves that convey any meaning, but the relationship between them when they are placed into a structure (a record). We recognize that they are addresses and we can see that John Martin lives at 16 Elm Street in New Town. Database systems define high-level representations of the relationships between data items. The relational and object-oriented approaches to databases are different methods of solving the problem of structuring data in a meaningful way.

In a relational database, partially to reduce data storage space but also to help maintainability, data items are only stored once. Relationships between items are defined using relational tables and identifying codes called *keys*.

Figure 1-2.
Meaning and relationships

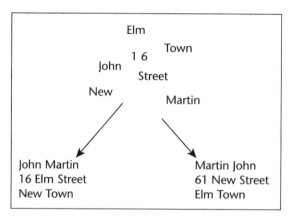

Figure 1-3.
Relational tables

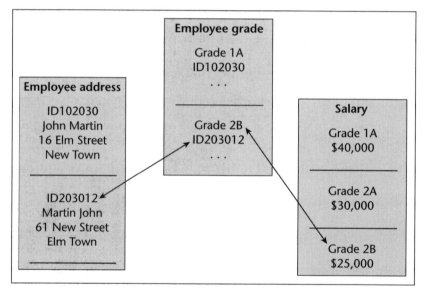

Thus, from Figure 1-3 we can determine that Martin John's salary is $25,000 through the Employee grade relational table. If this data were implemented in a relational database, a query language would let us ask for Martin John's salary. Moreover, if salaries in this company were all increased by 5%, we could apply a function to increase all the salaries in the Salary table without having to alter any other data in any other table.

1.3 Object Databases

An alternative way of representing data and one that is currently popular is by the use of object-oriented techniques. In an object database, individual records are stored as *instances* of classes. Thus, as shown in Figure 1-4, Martin John and John Martin are represented as instances of the class of employees.

The class "employee" defines all that is common to all employees. That is, they all have a name, social security number, address, department, and salary grade. The object hierarchy can be expanded to classify certain grades of employee as in Figure 1-4. The instance that represents Martin John is classified as being of employee grade 2B. Through a process known as *inheritance,* Martin John will "inherit" the salary from the class "Grade 2B." The classification of real-world entities into object hierarchies and the use of inheritance provide object databases with greater representational power than that of relational databases.

Figure 1-4.
An object hierarchy

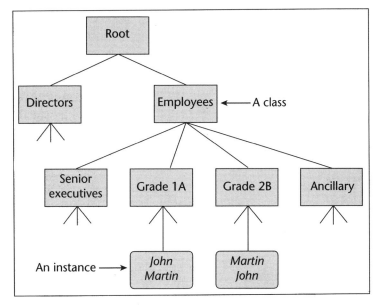

1.4 A More Powerful Representation

Although there is a relationship between Martin John and his salary, it is implicit in the structure of the relational tables. The object database explicitly categorizes Martin John as an instance of an employee of Grade 2B. Any changes to the salary of that grade will be inherited by all instances of the class. An alternative approach to representing such information is through the use of declarative logical statements; commonly a predicate calculus notation is used. This book is not the place for a full explanation of logic programming, but in essence a relationship between entities is defined by a relation name (a predicate) followed by a list of the related entities.

For example, the fact that a company—let's call it Big Co.—employs Martin can be represented in Prolog (**Pro**gramming in **Log**ic) as

        employs (big_co, martin)
or   employs (martin, big_co)

The interpretation of the order of the arguments of the predicate is left to the programmer. The fact that Martin, John, Bill, and Peter are all employees of Big Co. can be represented as

        employees (big_co,[martin, john, bill, peter])

Logic programming becomes more expressive by using variables as arguments to predicates (variables usually start with a capital letter) and logical operators such as AND, OR, and NOT, and IF-THEN statements. This enables rules to be defined; for example the rule that a person (A) usually earns more than an employee (X) they manage can be represented as follows:

        earns_more(A,X) IF manages(A,X)

Thus, if we assert the facts that Bill manages Martin and John, and that Bill is managed by Peter

        manages(bill,martin)
        manages(bill,john)
        manages(peter,bill)

we can infer, by applying the rule defined above, that

earns_more(bill,martin) is *true*, while
earns_more(bill,peter)   is *false*

In this representation, the knowledge of who manages whom is explicitly stated as declarative facts or assertions. Moreover, the rule for determining who earns more is also explicitly defined. Importantly, it is possible using this representation to infer new facts from our existing data and rules, such as the fact that Bill earns more than Martin.

1.5 Rule-Based Expert Systems

The ability to define rules in an IF-THEN format as described above has several advantages:

- Rules can be easily understood by programmers and experts alike.
- Rules can encapsulate small chunks of knowledge that collectively can model a complex problem.
- Rules are independent of each other.
- Rules can be placed in any order in a program.

More fundamentally, rules have enabled artificial intelligence (AI) researchers to represent problem-solving knowledge as models that could be implemented computationally. In rule-based systems, knowledge is represented as facts about the world (i.e., relationships between entities) and rules for manipulating the facts. This apparent simplicity is complicated by the problems that at any one time more than one rule may apply and that as each rule is applied many more may become applicable. Therefore a rule-based program needs a control structure to decide which rule to apply next and how to chain rules together.

Consider the following simple rules:

IF A THEN B
IF B THEN C
IF C THEN D

If A is true, we can logically infer that D is true by applying the three rules. This can be represented diagrammatically as in Figure 1-5.

Figure 1-5.
*Graphical
notation for rules*

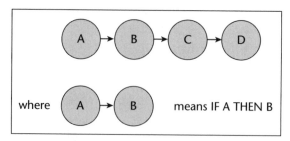

A more complex set of rules such as

    IF A THEN B & C
    IF B THEN D
    IF C THEN E
    IF D THEN G

can be represented as in Figure 1-6.

The problem here is the order in which the inference takes place—unless the computer has parallel processors, a decision must be made as to which rule to "fire" first. If A is true, is it better to make B true before C or vice versa? In fact, it is up to the programmer to decide, but a commonly used control structure called *depth-first search* would mean that inferences would be made in the order indicated by the numbers in Figure 1-7.

Thus the system would infer that G was true before it inferred that E was true. Indeed, if G was a solution, it may not need to infer that E was also a potential solution. This control structure is more correctly known as *depth-first forward chaining. Forward* indicates that new facts are being inferred from existing facts. It is also possible to use the same set of rules in reverse (i.e., *backward chaining;* see Figure 1-8) to find out what *needs* to be true for a premise to be true. For example, using the same set of rules we could ask the question "What needs to be true for G to be true?"

The answer of course is "A." Backward chaining is commonly used in rule-based expert systems to enable a hypothesis to be tested. This mimics human problem-solving strategies, as for example, in medical diagnosis. When you are sick, your doctor often hypothesizes using knowledge of what the possible cause of your illness may be. Doctors then try to confirm their hypothesis by looking for characteristic symptoms or by performing certain tests. If these do not confirm their hypothesis, they will think of another illness and test that hypothesis. This problem-solving strategy is often referred to as *generate and test* and has been used successfully by many expert systems, particularly in diagnosis.

Figure 1-6.
A more complex rule tree

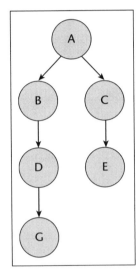

Figure 1-7.
Depth-first forward chaining

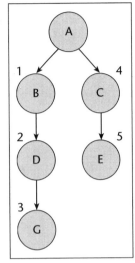

Figure 1-8.
Backward chaining

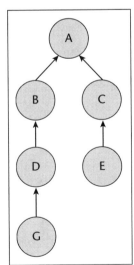

1.6 The Limitations of Rules

Rule-based expert systems have arguably been the most successful product of AI research to date. Many successful systems have been implemented and are in regular beneficial use. Their success is due to several factors:

- The control structure seems to mimic some human problem-solving strategies.

- The control structure is relatively simple and can be understood by people other than computer scientists.

- Rules are a part of everyday life, and so again people can relate to them.

- Importantly, there are many commercially available tools (called *expert system shells*) that make it relatively easy to build a rule-based system.

However, there are some significant limitations to rule-based systems. It is often extremely difficult to obtain a correct set of rules. This problem has dogged the development of rule-based expert systems for the last two decades and is often referred to as the *knowledge-elicitation bottleneck*. This bottleneck has several causes, any of which can make it extremely difficult to elicit knowledge in nontrivial domains:

- An expert may be too busy (often solving the problem full-time) to spend the amount of time the knowledge engineer requires to elicit their knowledge and code it.

- The expert may have the expertise and the time but be unable to articulate it to the knowledge engineer. This is surprisingly common and can force experts to attempt to falsely postjustify their reasoning.

- The knowledge engineer may not be able to understand the problem fully, due to its specialized nature, and therefore may have difficulty in producing a correct model.

- The knowledge representation chosen may not be able to represent the elicited knowledge fully.

Finally, there is the problem at the heart of rule-based systems, namely the knowledge itself. The rule-based approach assumes that there is a generally accepted body of explicit knowledge that most practitioners in the domain can agree upon. At this point it is worth considering the heritage of rule-based systems. Most of the pioneering systems (e.g., MYCIN, DENDRAL, PROSPECTOR, etc.) came from university research laboratories, and in particular from collaborations between computer scientists and other scientists (doctors, chemists, geologists, etc.). It is no surprise therefore that such people, who are used to using models, believed that rule-based reasoning could solve so many problems. Their academic disciplines are founded on explicit rules, and reasoning from first principles is second nature to them.

However, in many other walks of life, there are no underlying causal models and no generally agreed-upon first principles on which to build a model. So, given either the absence of an explicit model or the extreme difficulty in eliciting the model, how can you create useful decision support systems?

1.7 Elephants Never Forget!

Some biologists have suggested that elephants' longevity and success in harsh environments may be due to the memories of herd members, in particular the memory of the oldest female, who leads the herd. The matriarch's memory of where water or food can be found or where danger exists helps the herd survive. The herd retains a *collective memory* of problems and their solutions. For example, a herd of elephants probably do not have an explicit model of the geology and drainage of the area they live in, but during a drought they remember that water can usually be found if they dig holes in a certain place in a dried-up riverbed. So, the matriarch leads them there and they start digging. The message is that they almost certainly do not infer where the water is by reasoning from first principles, they *remember* where water can usually be found during a drought.

Thus, elephants can solve problems like these without using models or rules (see Figure 1-9). To build a rule-based system, you must first know how to solve the problem. A system can then be built that resolves the problem each time it is run. But why resolve a problem each time if someone has already solved it? Would it not be simpler to remember the solution? In terms of computational efficiency the answer is often yes.

Thanks to magnetic storage and newer storage media such as compact discs, computers are very good at remembering (i.e., storing and retrieving) data. Indeed, that is an important function of most computer systems. Therefore, if you could store problem descriptions in a database along with their solutions, you theoretically could build an expert system even though you had no explicit model. All you need are simple relationships linking problems to solutions as shown in Figure 1-10.

Figure 1-9.
Where's the water?

Figure 1-10.
Relating problems to solutions

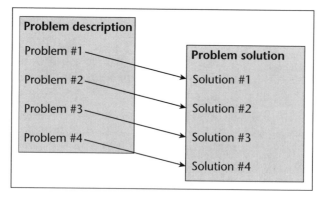

1.8 I've Got the Answer, What's the Question?

Database technology would seem ideally suited to the task of retrieving known solutions to problems: databases can store large quantities of information, maintain relationships between items, and access information rapidly. Unfortunately, it's not quite so simple. Before we can retrieve a solution, we have to identify what the problem is. It is at this point conventional database technology lets us down.

To find the correct problem and thus its known solution, we have to match our current problem against the problems stored in the database. However, "real-world" problems are often fairly complex with many contributing features. The current problem may not present itself in exactly the same manner as the problem stored in the database. Databases are excellent at finding exact matches but are poor at near or fuzzy matches.

Let's take a simple example: Suppose you call the phone directory information service to find a telephone number for a company called Kwik-Tyre in Newton. You tell the operator that the town is "Newton" and the company is "Kwik-Tyre." The operator types "New Town" in the Town field and "Quick Tire" in the Company field. The search fails. Eventually after trying "Quick Tyre," "Kuick-Tyre," "Kwik Tire," and "Newtown," you both give up the search. This is because most conventional database searches use the following search techniques:

- Keyword searches that must match exactly
- Wildcards such as WEST* matching to WESTMINSTER and WESTON
- Wildcards such as ?EST matching to WEST and NEST
- Logical operators such as AND, OR, and NOT

While these methods are useful and efficient at retrieving known information, they are very susceptible to retrieval problems like simple spelling errors and often result in searches returning no matches at all.

To retrieve a matching problem, which may be much more complex than the telephone number example, we need a more flexible method that will

- Let us describe the problem how we see it, perhaps even using natural language.

- Find the nearest matching problem description in the database, or even a set of similar problems.
- Perhaps ask several questions to confirm the matching problem or focus in on the best match.
- Then offer the known solution to the best match.
- Maybe even adapt the retrieved solution to account for differences between the retrieved problem and our current one.

This functionality is what characterizes case-based reasoning.

1.9 Summary

This chapter has introduced you to the concepts behind representing data or information in a computer. It is the structure of the data representation that enables us to draw meaning or information from data. It is possible to define rules that let a computer perform inferences on data, and rule-based systems have become a major success for artificial intelligence. However, rule-based reasoning is certainly not what people do when we solve problems. We usually try to remember if we've ever met a similar problem in the past and reuse the solution we used then—providing it was successful.

This chapter has shown that associating solutions with problems seems ideally suited to computers but that current database technology is not sufficient for this task. What is needed is case-based reasoning. The next chapter introduces the concepts and technology of case-based reasoning.

1.10 Further Reading

There are many excellent textbooks providing a general introduction to artificial intelligence. I recommend

Ginsberg, M. (1993). *Essentials of Artificial Intelligence*. San Francisco: Morgan Kaufmann Publishers.

2

Understanding CBR

The previous chapter outlined the need for case-based reasoning. This chapter introduces you to the CBR-cycle. It then describes the development of CBR in the United States in the 1970s and 1980s and describes the main techniques used in the CBR-cycle, in particular *nearest-neighbor retrieval* and *inductive indexing*. By the end of this chapter, you should understand the concepts used in CBR and how they are implemented.

2.1 The CBR-Cycle

A case-based reasoner solves new problems by adapting solutions that were used to solve old problems.

—Riesbeck and Schank, 1989

Understanding how CBR works is very simple and is one of the reasons why it has been adopted so readily. Let us consider what a CBR system should do, using a simple example: Assume you work for a bank and have to advise on the suitability of a person for a loan. As a banker, you do not want to lend money to people who will be unable to repay it. But your caution must be balanced against a desire not to turn people down needlessly. After all, the bank makes its profit from the interest people pay on loans.

One way of solving your problem is to compare each new loan application against your knowledge of loans you have granted in the past (let's also assume you've worked for the bank for many years and have an exceptionally good memory!). If a person's circumstances are similar to those of someone who successfully repaid a loan in the past, then you would grant the loan. Conversely, if their circumstances are similar to those of someone who defaulted on a loan, then you wouldn't grant the loan.

Let us examine what mental tasks you perform in solving this problem:

1. You search your memory of previous loans and make an assessment of similarity.

2. You attempt to infer an answer from the most similar loan you remember.

3. You may have to make allowances and adjustments for changes in circumstance over the years—for example, $15,000 is a small salary in 1995 but was not such a small salary in 1965.

4. If you grant the loan, you will monitor and record the outcome of the loan for future use.

We can simplify this mental process to describe CBR typically as a cyclical process comprising the *four REs*:

1. REtrieve the most similar case(s).
2. REuse the case(s) to attempt to solve the problem.
3. REvise the proposed solution if necessary.
4. REtain the new solution as a part of a new case.

A new problem is matched against cases in the case-base, and one or more similar cases are *retrieved*. A solution suggested by the matching cases is then *reused* and tested for success. Unless the retrieved case is a close match, the solution will probably have to be *revised*, producing a new case that can be *retained*. (See Figure 2-1.)

This cycle rarely occurs without human intervention. For example, many CBR tools act primarily as case retrieval and reuse systems, case revision (i.e., adaptation) often being undertaken by users of the case-base.

This is how CBR works at a conceptual level, and as you can see it very closely matches how we routinely solve problems. Consequently, you should have no trouble understanding how a CBR system works conceptually. Fortunately, to use CBR, it is not essential that you have a detailed understanding of how this conceptual cycle is actually implemented.

Figure 2-1.
The CBR-cycle

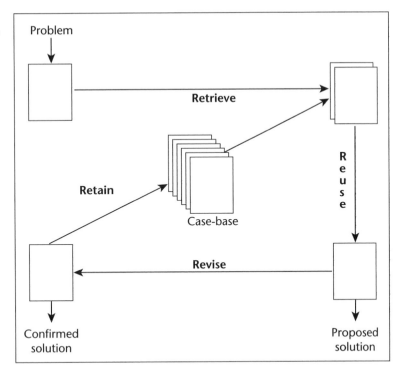

The rest of this chapter provides an overview of the history of the development of CBR and gives a more detailed description of the processes involved in each stage of the CBR-cycle.

2.2 A Short History of Case-Based Reasoning

CBR came from research into cognitive science: the work of Schank and Abelson in 1977 is widely held to be the origins of CBR. They proposed that our general knowledge about situations is recorded in the brain as *scripts* that allow us to set up expectations and perform inferences. Scripts were proposed as a structure for conceptual memory, describing information about stereotypical events such as going to a restaurant or visiting a doctor. However, experiments on scripts showed that they were not a complete theory of memory representation—

people often confuse events that have similar scripts. For example, a person might mix up room scenes from a visit to a doctor's office with a visit to a dentist's office.

Roger Schank continued to explore the role that the memory of previous situations (i.e., cases) and situation patterns, or *memory organization packets* (MOPs), play in both problem solving and learning. Perhaps with the benefit of hindsight it is also possible to find references of significance to CBR in Wittgenstein's observation that natural concepts such as tables and chairs are in fact polymorphic and cannot be classified by a single set of necessary and sufficient features but instead can be defined by a set of instances (i.e., cases) that have family resemblances.

While the philosophical roots of CBR could perhaps be claimed by many, what is not in doubt is that it was the pioneering work of Roger Schank's group at Yale University in the early 1980s that produced both a cognitive model for CBR and the first CBR applications based upon this model. Janet Kolodner developed the first CBR system, called CYRUS, in 1983. CYRUS contained knowledge, as cases, of the travels and meetings of former U.S. Secretary of State Cyrus Vance and allowed users to ask questions about these events. CYRUS was an implementation of Schank's *dynamic memory model*. Its *case-memory model* later served as the basis for several other influential CBR systems, including MEDIATOR, CHEF, PERSUADER, CASEY, and JULIA.

An early alternative approach came from Bruce Porter's work, at the University of Texas in Austin, into heuristic classification and machine learning and resulted in the PROTOS system. PROTOS combined general domain knowledge and specific case knowledge into a single case-memory model.

In the late 1980s, the U.S. DARPA program funded a series of workshops on CBR and the development of a CBR tool. This tool became Cognitive Systems' ReMind and marked the transition of CBR from purely academic research in cognitive science and artificial intelligence into the commercial arena. ReMind was joined in the marketplace almost immediately by several other tools.

The history of CBR is not a long one compared to other decision support technologies such as rule-based system or neural networks. I believe that its rapid uptake is because of its intuitive nature and the relative simplicity of its implementation. The next section describes in more detail how CBR is implemented.

2.3 Case-Based Reasoning Techniques

This section describes in some detail how CBR is implemented computationally and shows how each stage of the CBR-cycle is supported.

2.3.1 *Case Representation*

A case is a contextualized piece of knowledge representing an experience. It contains the past lesson that is the content of the case and the context in which the lesson can be used. A case can be an account of an event, a story, or some record typically comprising

- The *problem* that describes the state of the world when the case occurred

- The *solution* that states the derived solution to that problem

One way this is often visualized is in terms of the *problem space* and the *solution space*. In Figure 2-2, you can see that an individual case is made up of two components: a problem description and a stored solution. These reside respectively in the problem space and the solution space. The description of a new problem to be solved is positioned in the problem space. Retrieval identifies the case with the most similar problem description (the arrow labelled "R" in Figure 2-2), and its stored solution is found. If necessary, adaptation occurs (the arrow labelled "A") and a new solution is created. This conceptual model of CBR assumes that there is a direct one-to-one mapping between the problem and solution spaces. In other words, if a new problem is "down and to the left" of a known problem, then the new solution will also be "down and to the left" of the retrieved problem's solution.

Within a case you can store most types of data that you would expect to be able to store in a conventional database, such as names, product identifiers, values like cost or temperature, and textual notes. An increasing number of CBR tools also support multimedia features, such as photographs, sound, and video.

There is a lack of consensus within the CBR community as to exactly what information should be in a case. However, two pragmatic measures can be taken in the account to decide what should be represented in cases: the functionality of the information and the ease of acquisition of the information.

Figure 2-2.
*The problem
and solution
spaces (after
Leake, 1996)*

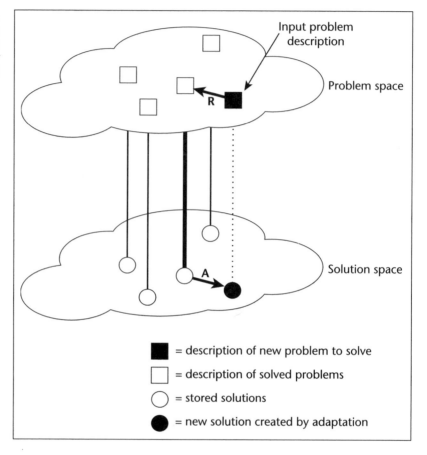

2.3.2 *Indexing*

Most database systems use indexes to speed up the retrieval of data.
For example, an index may be created to the family names of records
about people in a database. An index is a computational data structure that can be held in memory and searched very quickly. This
means the computer does not have to search each record stored on
disk, which would be much slower. CBR also uses indexes to speed up
retrieval. Information within a case is of two types:

1. Indexed information that is used for retrieval
2. Unindexed information that may provide contextual information of value to a user but is not used directly in retrieval

Figure 2-3.
Indexed and unindexed case features

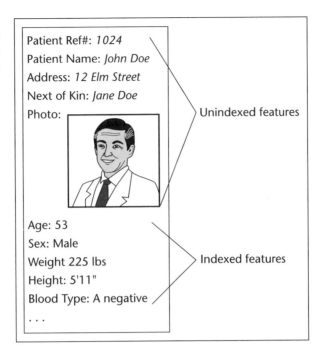

Patient Ref#: *1024*
Patient Name: *John Doe*
Address: *12 Elm Street*
Next of Kin: *Jane Doe*
Photo:

Unindexed features

Age: 53
Sex: Male
Weight 225 lbs
Height: 5'11"
Blood Type: A negative
. . .

Indexed features

For example, in a medical system you may use a patient's age, sex, height, and weight as indexed features that can be used for retrieval and you may include a photograph of the patient as an unindexed feature (see Figure 2-3). The photograph cannot be used for retrieval, but may be useful in reminding doctors who the patient is.

As a guideline, indexes should

- Be predictive
- Address the purposes the case will be used for
- Be abstract enough to allow for widening the future use of the case-base
- Be concrete enough to be recognized in the future

Let us use the bank employee example again. Some information provided by prospective clients, such as their name or telephone number, is clearly not predictive of their likely success at repaying a loan. Some information, such as their address, *may* be predictive—if they live in an upmarket suburb, for example, you might assume they are financially stable. However, certain information is clearly predictive of their ability to repay a loan, namely, their income and their existing financial commitments, such as home loans, car payments, life insurance, and so on. Thus, in this instance you may choose to use their income and financial commitments as your indexes since they are predictive, they address the purpose of the case-base, they could be used for other purposes in the future, and they are easily recognized.

Both manual and automated methods have been used to select indexes. Choosing indexes manually involves deciding a case's purpose with respect to the aims of the system and deciding under what circumstances the case will be useful.

There is an ever-increasing number of automated indexing methods cited in the literature, including

- Indexing cases by features and dimensions that tend to be predictive across the entire domain. For example, MEDIATOR, a system that resolves disputes between people or countries that covet each other's property, uses this method by indexing on the type and function of disputed objects and the relationship between disputants, while CHEF, a system that can create new recipes from existing ones, indexes on features like texture and taste.

- Difference-based indexing, which selects indexes that differentiate a case from another case as in CYRUS.

- Similarity- and explanation-based generalization methods produce an appropriate set of indexes for abstract cases from cases that share some common set of features, while the unshared features are used as indexes to the original cases.

- Inductive learning methods identify predictive features that are then used as indexes.

Several of the CBR tools presently on the market support the automatic identification of case indexes, and therefore, for practical applications, indexes can be chosen automatically, manually, or by both techniques.

2.3.3 *Storage*

Case storage is an important aspect in designing efficient CBR systems in that it should reflect the conceptual view of what is represented in the case and take into account the indexes that characterize the case. The case-base should be organized into a manageable structure that supports efficient search and retrieval methods. A balance has to be found between storing methods that preserve the richness of cases and their indexes and methods that simplify the access and retrieval of relevant cases. These methods are usually referred to as *case-memory models*. The two most influential academic case-memory models are the *dynamic-memory model* of Schank and Kolodner, and the *category-exemplar model* of Porter and Bareiss. These techniques are still widely used by the cognitive science community, but none of the commercially available CBR tools use these techniques. Instead they either store cases as simple flat file data structures, or within conventional relational database structures, and use indexes to reference the cases.

2.3.4 *Retrieval*

The retrieval of cases is closely related and dependent on the indexing method used. In general, two techniques are currently used by commercial CBR tools: *nearest-neighbor retrieval* and *inductive retrieval*.

2.3.4.1 Nearest-Neighbor Retrieval

At a conceptual level, *nearest neighbor* is a very simple technique. Let us use the bank manager example we introduced earlier—namely, how to decide if a new client should be granted a loan. In this domain, a case is a previous loan. First, let's decide on the case features we want to use as indexes. In a previous section I said that case indexes should

- Be predictive
- Address the purposes the case will be used for
- Be abstract enough to allow for widening the future use of the case-base
- Be concrete enough to be recognized in the future

Two specific features immediately fit these criteria:

1. A person's net monthly income—that is, the money they have left after taxes and other financial commitments
2. The monthly repayment on their loan

For the time being, let's use just these two features as indexes. Thus, our cases will comprise the information shown in Table 2-1.

As you can see in Figure 2-4, the two indexes can be used as axes for a graph, with net monthly income on the *x*-axis and monthly loan repayments on the *y*-axis. A past case, for example someone with a relatively high net monthly income and a relatively low loan repayment, can be plotted on the graph.

In a similar way, other past cases can also be plotted as points on our graph (Figure 2-5). Now, we said that our indexes should be predictive, and common sense tells us that people with relatively low net monthly incomes and relatively high loan repayments are more likely to default on the loan than those with high incomes and low repayments. Thus, it is no surprise if one of our clusters of cases represents those who successfully repaid their loans and the other represents those who defaulted.

We can now use this graph as a decision support tool. If a prospective client walks through the door, all we have to do is ask for their net monthly income, calculate their loan repayment, and plot this on our graph. If they fall in or near the good cluster, we should grant them the loan. If they fall in or near the bad cluster, we should refuse the loan.

Table 2-1.   A simple case representation

Case indexes
Net monthly income in dollars
Monthly loan repayment in dollars
Case result
Good or bad loan

Figure 2-4.
A simple graph

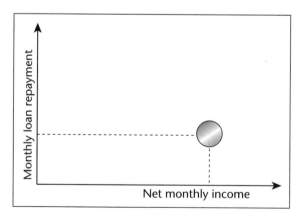

Figure 2-5.
*Clusters of good
and bad loans*

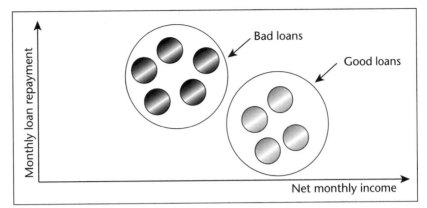

Figure 2-6.
*A new case on
the graph*

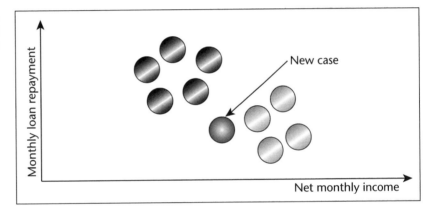

Now in the graph shown in Figure 2-6, it is easy to see that our new client is nearest the good loans. However, to be certain, we should use the graph to calculate the distances. All we need to do is to calculate the relative *x* and *y* distance of the new case (the *target case*) to the other cases (the *source cases*). Let's simplify the graph and consider just three cases: two existing source cases called A and B and a target case called T. Let us also state that Case A was a good loan and Case B was a bad loan. We can now easily obtain an *x* and *y* distance of T from each of the source cases A and B.

As you can see in Figure 2-7, the *x* distance of T from A is 3 units, and the *y* distance is 0, while the *x* distance of T from B is 1 unit and the *y* distance is 3 units. Thus,

The distance of T from A: $d_A = X_A + Y_A$
The distance of T from B: $d_B = X_B + Y_B$

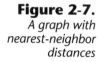

Figure 2-7.
A graph with nearest-neighbor distances

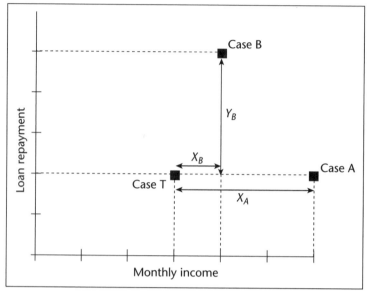

Whichever gives the smallest value is the nearest neighboring case to T. So in our example the distance of T from A equals 3 (i.e., 3 + 0), while the distance of T from B equals 4 (i.e., 1 + 3), and therefore A is T's nearest neighbor. You should recommend the loan. Although the target has a low income, the loan is also low. Our decision is supported by the nearest neighboring case (Case A) being a good loan.

The concept of nearest-neighbor is basically that simple. But we can make this more realistic by *weighting* the attributes. From your years of experience as a bank employee, you believe that a person's net monthly income is more predictive of their ability to repay a loan than the relative size of the monthly loan repayment. Perhaps this is because people on high salaries tend to have more job security and financial stability than those on lower incomes. Let us say that we will weight the person's income as twice as important as the size of the loan repayment. We can still use the same graph, but our simple nearest-neighbor formula changes to:

The distance of T from A: $d_A = (X_A \times W_x) + (Y_A \times W_y)$
The distance of T from B: $d_B = (X_B \times W_x) + (Y_B \times W_y)$

where W_x is the weight of the attribute X and W_y is the weight of the attribute Y.

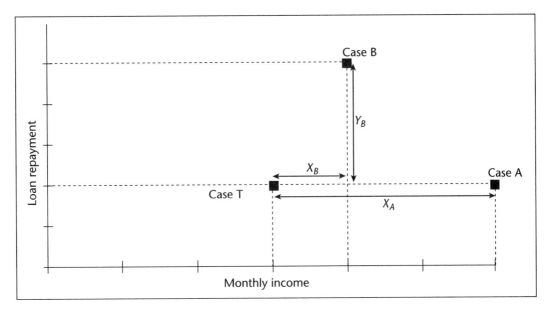

Figure 2-8.   *A graph with a weighted x-axis*

We will state that $W_x = 2$ and $W_y = 1$. Thus,

The distance of T from A: $d_A = 6$ (i.e., $(3 \times 2) + (0 \times 1)$)
The distance of T from B: $d_B = 5$ (i.e., $(1 \times 2) + (3 \times 1)$)

Consequently, using our weighted nearest-neighbor formula, Case B is now the nearest neighbor to Case T and you should refuse the loan because Case B was a bad loan. A way of visualizing this is to redraw the previous graph with the *x*-axis at twice the scale of the *y*-axis (Figure 2-8). This now more clearly shows that T is closer to B than A. Thus, you can see how adding background knowledge to our nearest-neighbor formula in the form of relative importance, or weightings, on each attribute dramatically altered which case was retrieved as a best match.

This example is very simple. In reality, cases may have 10, 20, or more attributes, each with their own weighting. Thus, instead of using a two-dimensional space, as in our example, cases are plotted into an *n*-dimensional space. Moreover, we are not restricted to simple numerical comparisons of similarity. Some case features may hold symbolic values (e.g., colors such as red, green, and blue), Boolean values (e.g., true, false, or unknown), and textual values.

Nonetheless, despite this increase in complexity, nearest-neighbor algorithms all work in a similar fashion. The similarity (i.e., the proximity) of the target case to a source case for each attribute is determined. This measure may be multiplied by a weighting factor. Then the sum of the similarity of all attributes is calculated. This can be represented by the relatively simple equation

$$\text{Similarity}(T,S) = \sum_{i=1}^{n} f(T_i, S_i) \times w_i$$

where

> T is the target case
>
> S is the source case
>
> n is the number of attributes in each case
>
> i is an individual attribute from 1 to n
>
> f is a similarity function for attribute i in cases T and S
>
> w is the importance weighting of attribute i

Algorithms similar to this are used by most CBR tools to perform nearest-neighbor retrieval. Similarities are usually normalized to fall within a range of 0 to 1 (where 0 is totally dissimilar and 1 is an exact match) or as a percentage similarity where 100% is an exact match.

2.3.4.2 Inductive Retrieval

An alternative retrieval technique used by many CBR tools involves a process called *induction*. Induction is a technique developed by machine learning researchers to extract rules or construct decision trees from past data. In CBR systems, the case-base is analyzed by an induction algorithm to produce a decision tree that classifies (or indexes) the cases. The most widely used induction algorithm in CBR tools is called ID3. The way in which this works is outlined conceptually below.

Once again we will use the bank loan example. For simplicity's sake, let's say we only have experience of four loans, two of which were successful and two of which were not. These are classified as *good* (the bank made a profit); *very good* (the bank made a large profit); *bad* (the bank lost some money); and *very bad* (the bank lost a lot of money). We've also decided that a third case feature is sometimes predictive of the ability to repay a loan: whether a person is paid an hourly rate for a job (i.e., waged) or paid an annual salary (i.e., salaried). See Table 2-2.

Table 2-2. **Four loan cases**

	Loan status	Monthly income	Job status	Repayment
Case 1	good	$2,000	salaried	$200
Case 2	very bad	$4,000	salaried	$600
Case 3	very good	$3,000	waged	$300
Case 4	bad	$1,500	salaried	$400

ID3 builds a decision tree from the database of cases. It uses a heuristic called *information gain* to find the most promising attribute on which to divide the case-base. ID3 requires a target attribute whose value the tree will predict. In this example we will become the ID3 algorithm. First let us state that our *outcome* value (i.e., the one we want to predict) is the status of the loan (i.e., very good, good, bad, or very bad).

We want to study our cases to see which features are predictive of the outcome. Since the outcome is likely to be influenced by a combination of features (i.e., the variables are not independent), we should look for a feature and value that best divides our set of cases in half while still predicting the outcome.

From the table we can see that we cannot use monthly income as a predictor, since the highest income ($4,000) and the lowest income ($1,500) both resulted in bad or very bad loans. Similarly, we can't use a person's job status (i.e., waged or salaried), because salaried cases resulted in both good and bad loans. Consequently, the attribute that best divides the set of cases into two (i.e., best discriminates between the cases) is the loan repayment size. In this example, all repayments equal to or greater than $400 resulted in bad or very bad loans. Thus we can create our first division and hence the first node in our decision tree (Figure 2-9).

Having discovered the first node in the decision tree, we can now try to discriminate between good and very good loans. Let's try to discriminate between Case 1 and Case 3. Cases 1 and 3 have relatively similar loan repayments and incomes, but their job status discriminates them well. So we have the next node in our tree (Figure 2-10).

Figure 2-9.
The first node in a decision tree

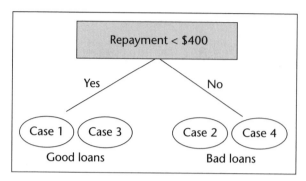

Figure 2-10.
The second node in a decision tree

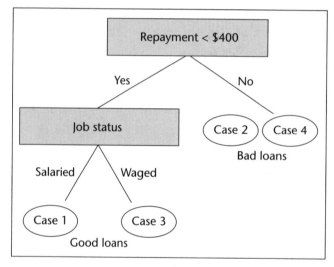

We must now proceed to discriminate between Case 2 and Case 4. These have the same job status and large repayments but very different incomes. So income is used to discriminate between Cases 2 and 4 to produce our finished decision tree (Figure 2-11).

Our completed tree can then be used for retrieval in the following manner. Assume a new client arrives with the details shown in Table 2-3.

Figure 2-11.
*The completed
decision tree*

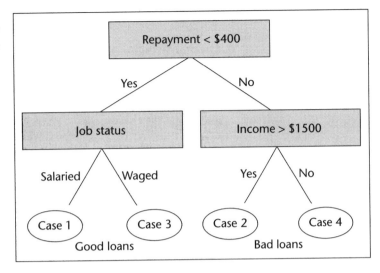

Table 2-3. A target case

	Loan status	Monthly income	Job status	Repayment
Case X	?	$2,500	salaried	$250

Table 2-4. The target case with loan prediction

	Loan status	Monthly income	Job status	Repayment
Case X	*good*	$2,500	salaried	$250

To find the best matching case in our case-base, we walk the decision tree asking the question at each node in Figure 2-11.

1. Is the loan repayment less than $400? Answer *yes*, therefore take the left branch.
2. Is the person salaried or waged? Answer *salaried*, therefore Case 1 is the best match.

We can therefore predict that the loan will be a good one because Case 1's outcome was good (Table 2-4).

Table 2-5. Another target case

	Loan status	Monthly income	Job status	Repayment
Case X	?	$3,500	salaried	$500

Similarly, if you were presented with a different client, who had the details shown in Table 2-5, you could easily determine, by following the tree in Figure 2-11, that the best matching case is Case 2. This suggests the loan prospect is *very bad*. You would therefore reject that loan application.

As you can see, induction is a relatively straightforward process. However, it becomes very complex when there are several hundred or even several thousand cases. As you have seen, induction and nearest neighbor use very different ways of retrieving similar cases. The following section compares and contrasts the two approaches.

2.3.4.3 **Nearest Neighbor vs. Inductive Retrieval**

Now that you understand the principles behind the two techniques of case retrieval that are most widely used in CBR tools, it is worthwhile comparing and contrasting them.

As you saw, nearest neighbor is a simple technique that provides a measure of how similar a target case is to a source case. Nearest neighbor has one major weakness, namely, retrieval speed. To find the *best* matching case, a target case must be compared to *every* source case in the case-base. Moreover, a similarity (i.e., distance) comparison must be calculated for every indexed attribute. Thus, if there were 100 source cases with a single indexed feature, 100 similarity calculations would be required. If the cases had 10 indexed features, then 10×100 or 1,000 similarity calculations would be required. If the case-base grew to 10,000 cases, then 100,000 similarity calculations would be required every time a new target case had to be matched against the cases in the case-base. Thus, retrieval effort has increased from 10,000 to 100,000 calculations.

This problem means that nearest neighbor can become inefficient as either the size of a case-base increases or the number of indexed attributes increases. A partial solution to this problem is to compute a position in the *n*-dimensional space for each source case in the case-base off-line and to use this as an index. At runtime all that is required is to calculate the position of the target case in the n-dimensional space and then apply a test to identify all source cases that fall within a certain distance of the target case. This can produce retrieval times that remain nearly constant despite the size of the case-base. The drawback of this preindexing approach is that developing the index is time consuming. Moreover, a new index has to be made every time a new case is added to the case-base.

On the other hand, inductive retrieval obviously depends on preindexing, since the decision tree is made off-line before retrieval can start. This is also a time-consuming process for a large case-base, and it has to be redone every time a new case is added to the case-base. However, retrieval times using inductive index trees are extremely quick and only increase slowly as the number of cases in the case-base increases.

Inductive retrieval does, however, have one major disadvantage: If case data is missing or unknown, it may not be possible to retrieve a case at all. In the loan example we used earlier, consider a person who does not yet know what the loan repayment is because they haven't decided on the size of the loan. In that situation, we could not answer the first question in the decision tree we created to index the cases, and therefore we could not retrieve any cases at all. Nearest-neighbor retrieval is much less sensitive to missing, or noisy, case data. In this example, nearest-neighbor retrieval would still work and might be able to recommend that a person with a certain high salary should be allowed loans up to a specified amount. There are ways around this problem with inductive retrieval by dynamically building the inductive index tree at runtime, thereby avoiding questions to which data is not currently available. However, this method will slow down retrieval times.

In conclusion, you can see that the two alternative techniques most widely used in CBR tools have different strengths and weaknesses. To decide which is better for any particular application may require experimentation and will certainly require experience. In general, I would advise using nearest-neighbor retrieval without any preindexing until retrieval time becomes an important issue. If speed is an issue, then preindex your case-base or consider using inductive retrieval. However, these two techniques need not always be used in isolation. It is possible, with some CBR tools, to use inductive indexing to retrieve a set of matching cases and then use nearest neighbor to rank the cases in the set according to their similarity to the target case.

2.3.5 *Adaptation*

Once a matching case is retrieved, a CBR system will attempt to reuse the solution suggested by the retrieved case. In many circumstances the solution may be sufficient. However, in other instances the solution from the retrieved case may be close to the required solution, but not close enough. The CBR system must then adapt the solution stored in the retrieved case to the needs of the current case. Adaptation looks for prominent differences between the retrieved case and the current case and then applies formulas or rules that take those differences into account when suggesting a final solution. In general, there are two kinds of adaptation in CBR:

- *Structural adaptation* applies adaptation rules or formulas directly to the solution stored in cases.

- *Derivational adaptation* reuses the rules or formulas that generated the original solution to produce a new solution to the current problem. In this method, the planning sequence that constructed that original solution must be stored as an additional attribute of the case. Derivational adaptation can only be used for domains that are well understood.

Several techniques, ranging from simple to complex, have been used in CBR for adaptation. These include the following:

- *Null adaptation* uses no adaptation at all. It just applies whatever solution is retrieved to the current problem without adapting it. Null adaptation is useful for problems involving complex reasoning but with a simple solution. For instance, in the bank loan example we have been using, the final answer we require from the decisions support tool is very simple: either grant the loan, reject the loan, or possibly refer the loan application to a superior for a decision.

- *Parameter adjustment* is a structural adaptation technique that compares specified parameters of the retrieved and current case to modify the solution in an appropriate direction. This technique was used in a CBR system called JUDGE, which could advise on sentencing for criminals. For example, JUDGE would increase the sentence given to a robber if the robbery was with violence.

- *Reinstantiation* is used to instantiate features of an old solution with new features. For example, the CBR system CHEF can reinstantiate *chicken* and *snow peas* in an existing Chinese recipe with *beef* and *broccoli,* thereby creating a new Chinese recipe. CHEF can do this because it knows that *chicken* and *beef* are both types of meat and that *snow peas* and *broccoli* are both types of crispy green vegetables.

■ *Derivational replay* is the process of retracing the method used to arrive at an old solution (or solution piece) to derive a solution in the new situation. For example, the CBR system BOGART can replay stored electrical circuit design plans to solve new design problems. An electrical engineer interacts with BOGART, replaying decisions BOGART says are applicable to the new problem. The engineer then completes the circuit design by adding knowledge that is outside BOGART's scope.

■ *Model-guided repair* uses a causal model to guide adaptation. This technique also requires a good understanding of the problem domain. The CBR system CASEY makes use of causal rules to diagnose heart problems. CASEY can substitute its own knowledge that irregular heart rate suggests arteriosclerosis with a causal link between high blood pressure and arteriosclerosis.

While adaptation is useful in many situations, it is by no means essential. Many of the most successful commercial CBR systems do not perform adaptation at all. They either simply reuse the solution suggested by the best matching case (i.e., null adaptation) or they leave adaptation to people. In other words, they are primarily case-retrieval systems. Unless adaptation can be done easily using simple and well-understood parameter adjustments or reinstantiations, my advice would be to avoid it. Case adaptation is in many ways the Achilles' heel of CBR. Complex adaptation is knowledge intensive, and since CBR is often applied to problems that are not well understood, complex knowledge-intensive adaptation will not be possible.

One interesting possibility suggested by some researchers is to use CBR itself for case adaptation. Thus, when adaptation (or revision, using the four-REs terminology discussed in Section 2.1) is required, CBR is used to see if a similar adaptation has been done in the past. If so, the adaptation is retrieved and reused (or even possibly revised itself). If not, a person is asked to perform the adaptation. Once the adaptation has been done successfully, either by the program or the person, it is stored for future use. In this way, a CBR system could continually improve its adaptation ability and hence its overall problem-solving ability.

2.4 Summary

This chapter has introduced you to the concept of the CBR-cycle. It has outlined the historical development of CBR and, from a more technical viewpoint, described how CBR is implemented computationally. It is not necessary that you fully understand all the techniques in order to apply CBR successfully. However, it is important that you are familiar with the underlying concepts of the process. In particular, it is important that you can follow the CBR-cycle and see the significance of each stage. Later chapters in this book will refer back to this cycle and will help you understand each process within it. It is now time to see how CBR can be applied.

2.5 Further Reading

This book provides a description of the early development of CBR at Yale University:

Riesbeck, C.K., and Schank, R.S. (1989). *Inside Case-Based Reasoning.* Northvale, NJ: Lawrence Erlbaum Associates.

Undoubtedly the most comprehensive account of the history and development of CBR is to be found in this book by Janet Kolodner. The book also describes in detail the *dynamic-memory* model and the *category-exemplar* model. Adaptation and other issues are also very well covered.

Kolodner, J. (1993). *Case-Based Reasoning.* San Francisco: Morgan Kaufmann Publishers.

Two recent review papers describe the CBR-cycle and the processes that implement each part of the cycle:

Aamodt, A., and Plaza, E. (1994). Case-Based Reasoning: Foundational Issues, Methodological Variations and System Approaches. *AI-Communications* 7(1), 39–52.

Watson, I., and Marir, F. (1994). Case-Based Reasoning: A Review. *The Knowledge Engineering Review* 9(4), 355–381.

This report on CBR tools has several chapters that describe nearest-neighbor and inductive retrieval in a more rigorously mathematical way:

Althoff, K-D, Auriol, E., Barletta, R., and Manago, M. (1995). *A Review of Industrial Case-Based Reasoning Tools*. Oxford: AI Intelligence.

The ID3 induction algorithm is described in

Quinlan, J.R. (1986). Induction of Decision Trees. *Machine Learning*, 1(1), 81–106.

A comprehensive study of various machine learning techniques is given in

Weiss, S.M., and Kulikowski, A. (1990). *Computer Systems That Learn: Classification and Prediction Methods from Statistics, Neural Nets, Machine Learning and Expert Systems*. San Francisco: Morgan Kaufmann Publishers.

A comprehensive review of adaptation techniques is given in

Hanney, K., Keane, M.T., Smyth, B., and Cunningham, P. (1995). What Kind of Adaptation Do CBR Systems Need? A Review of Current Practice. In *Adaptation of Knowledge for Reuse: Proceedings of the 1995 AAAI Fall Symposium,* edited by D.W. Aha and A. Ram. AAAI Technical Report FS-95-04. Cambridge, MA: AAAI Press / MIT Press.

The early CBR systems mentioned in this chapter are described in the following papers:

Bain, W.M. (1986). *Case-Based Reasoning: A Computer-Model of Subjective Assessment*. Ph.D. thesis, Yale University.

Bareiss, E.R. (1988). *PROTOS: A Unified Approach to Concept Representation, Classification, and Learning*. Ph.D. thesis, Dept. of Computer Science, University of Texas. Technical Report CS 88-10, Dept. of Computer Science. Nashville, TN: Vanderbilt University.

Hammond, K.J. (1986). CHEF: A Model of Case-Based Planning. In *Proceedings of AAAI-86, August 1986*. Cambridge, MA: AAAI Press / MIT Press.

Hinrichs, T. (1989). Strategies for Adaptation and Recovery in a Design Problem Solver. In *Proceedings of the DARPA Case-Based Reasoning Workshop,* edited by K.J. Hammond. San Francisco: Morgan Kaufmann Publishers.

Koton, P. (1988). Reasoning About Evidence in Causal Explanations. In *Proceedings of the DARPA Case-Based Reasoning Workshop,* edited by J.L. Kolodner. San Francisco: Morgan Kaufmann Publishers.

Mostow, J., Barley, M., and Weinrich, T. (1992). Automated reuse of design plans in BOGART. In *Artificial Intelligence in Engineering Design*, edited by C. Tong and D. Sriram. San Diego: Academic Press.

Simpson, R.L. (1985). *A Computer Model of Case-Based Reasoning in Problem Solving: An Investigation in the Domain of Dispute Mediation.* Georgia Institute of Technology, School of Information and Computer Science Technical Report No. GIT-ICS-85/18.

Sycara, E.P. (1987). Finding Creative Solutions in Adversarial Impasses. In *Proceedings of the Ninth Annual Conference of the Cognitive Science Society.* Northvale, NJ: Lawrence Erlbaum Associates.

3

The Application of CBR

The previous chapter introduced the concepts and processes that underlie CBR. I hope you found that CBR is not too difficult to understand. I believe that it is both the intuitive nature of the CBR process and the relative simplicity of its implementation that has led to its rapid uptake and success.

This chapter will now place the theory into context by describing some influential applications of CBR. It is divided into three sections. The first section provides a categorization of CBR applications. The second section compares CBR with a range of alternative decision support techniques and advises when to consider using CBR. The final section describes some influential CBR applications that are the product of academic research. These systems, mostly developed in the United States, demonstrate certain key features of CBR. They should be viewed as technology demonstrators, since there is little evidence they have been used in commercial situations. (The following chapters describe influential commercial CBR applications in more detail.)

3.1 A Classification of Applications

The classification of CBR applications used in this section has been adapted from a report by Althoff et al. (1995) and is laid out in Figure 3-1.

Being able to classify your problem into a certain category of problem types is useful in helping you decide if CBR is appropriate and what type of CBR system may be required.

CBR applications can be broadly classified into two main problem types:

1. *Classification tasks*

2. *Synthesis tasks*

Classification tasks cover a wide range of applications that all share certain features in common. A new case is matched against those in the case-base to determine what *type*, or *class*, of case it is. The solution from the best matching case in the class is then reused. For example, consider the problem of identifying the best food for a pet. The first task is to classify the pet into an animal class; that is, is it a horse, dog, cat, bird, rodent, reptile, or fish? If it's a reptile, is it a turtle, snake, or lizard? If it's a lizard, then the best food might be insects.

Most commercially available CBR tools support classification tasks well and are primarily concerned with case retrieval. Classification tasks come in a wide variety of forms, such as

- *Diagnosis.* For example, medical diagnosis or equipment failure diagnosis

- *Prediction.* For example, the forecasting of equipment failure or stock market performance

- *Assessment.* For example, risk analysis for banking or insurance or the estimation of project costs

- *Process control.* For example, the control of manufacturing equipment

- *Planning.* For example, the reuse of travel plans or work schedules

Synthesis tasks attempt to create a new solution by combining parts of previous solutions. An example would be designing a new house by combining parts of other houses: the kitchen and living room from one house, with the basement and garage from another, combined with the bedrooms and bathrooms from a third. Synthesis task are inherently complex because of the constraints between elements used during synthesis. CBR systems that perform synthesis tasks must make use of adaptation and are usually hybrid systems combining CBR with other techniques. There are fewer of these systems, but they involve such tasks as:

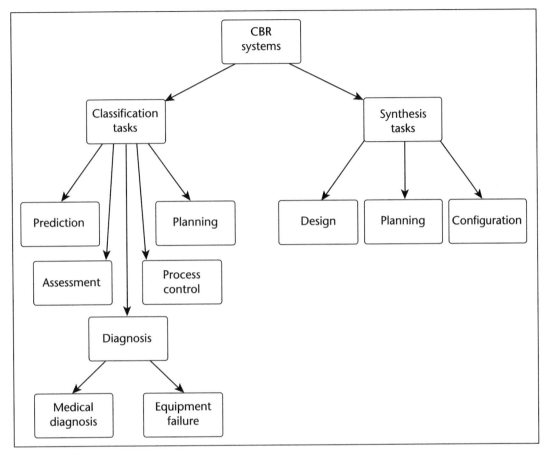

Figure 3-1. *A classification hierarchy of CBR applications after Althoff et al. (1995)*

- *Design.* The creation of a new artifact by adapting elements of previous ones
- *Planning.* The creation of new plans from elements of old ones
- *Configuration.* The creation of new schedules from old schedules

Since classification is well supported by CBR tools, the rest of this chapter will primarily focus on these tasks. If you decide that a system you want to implement is a synthesis task, you should be warned that it will be harder to implement.

3.1.1 *Classification Tasks*

Classification tasks are very common in business and everyday life. They can be recognized by the need to match an object or event against others in a library from which an answer can be inferred. Very often the objects or events that make up the case-library can be classified into groups that are predictive of the outcome. For example, the following business problems are all classification tasks (possible classifications are indicated):

- What type of house is this? [luxury, executive, midrange, blue-collar]

- What treatment should the patient be given? [observation, antibiotics, steroids]

- Should I grant a loan? [yes, no, refer]

- Is there oil below this land? [very likely, possible, unlikely, impossible]

- How long will this project take to complete? [three months, six months, one year]

It should be noted, though, that classification may not result in discrete values such as luxury or executive homes, but is, rather, indicative of ranges such as "$150,000 to $250,000" and "over $250,000."

You will probably have noticed that the possible classifications given to each of the questions above refer to outcomes. The outcome is usually an attribute of each case and is commonly how we tend to classify cases. However, it is perfectly possible to classify cases in different ways. Thus, one doctor may classify cases according to the age of patients and another according to the treatment they receive.

CBR can be applied easily to classification problems, since classification becomes a simple task of

1. Retrieving the set of broadly similar cases, such as those where antibiotics were the treatment.

2. Retrieving a best match from within this set, perhaps to suggest penicillin as the specific antibiotic.

3. Adapting the suggested solution, for example, by altering the dosage for differences in weight or age.

4. Retaining the outcome of the new case for future use.

Classification tasks are often easy to implement, because 1) they match the CBR-cycle well, 2) cases tend to be easier to represent and easy to collect, and 3) the retrieval algorithms used by most CBR tools are classifiers. Typically, organizations keep records that detail much of the information the CBR system will require. One field or attribute of each record will almost certainly be the outcome or classifier of each case, and many of the other attributes in each record will be predictive of the outcome. It is, however, dangerous to assume that all the attributes required are necessarily recorded or to assume that they are in an appropriate format. Implementing a successful CBR system is rarely as simple as using existing records intact, and some elicitation of new case features and preprocessing of existing data is often required.

There are other reasons why classification tasks are more suitable for CBR. Many of these are computational—such as the suitability of the machine learning algorithms used in inductive retrieval to classification tasks—and will not be dealt with further here.

3.1.2 *Synthesis Tasks*

Tasks requiring synthesis are common in commerce but are harder to implement. This is because it is generally easier to match an artifact against a set of prototypical artifacts than it is to construct an artifact from a specification. The classification task merely requires recognition of features while the synthesis task requires placing the correct features in the correct places in the correct order.

Case-based synthesis systems operating in the domains of design or planning generally tend to try to simplify the creative process by producing a known-to-be-good design or plan from which the final plan can be produced. This is likely to be quicker than starting a design or plan with a blank sheet of paper. It is assumed that modifying a good initial design or plan will be easier than creating a new one from scratch. In many circumstances, this assumption is likely to be true. However, there are examples where new solutions must be created from scratch without reference to past examples. For example, NASA would not have been able to adapt the design of the Saturn 5 moon rockets to design the Space Shuttle. A radically new approach was required.

There are several reasons why case-based synthesis systems are hard to build:

- The case representation of a plan or design is often complex and highly structured with many interdependent features.

- Cases are not usually stored in a single homogenous media, and thus case collection becomes more difficult.

- CBR tools do not tend to support indexing or retrieval of highly structured case representations.

- Adaptation is often a major requirement in synthesis tasks.

However, in defense of CBR, it must be said that synthesis tasks also pose difficulties for other techniques and consequently there are fewer intelligent synthesis systems compared with classification systems.

Having characterized the types of tasks for which CBR is appropriate, I will now compare CBR with a range of alternative decision support technologies.

3.2 CBR vs. Other Techniques

This section is intended to provide an understanding of the strengths and weaknesses of CBR compared with other computational techniques, including information retrieval, statistical analysis techniques, rule-based techniques, machine learning, and neural networks. It is not the role of this book to provide a detailed description of each of these techniques.

3.2.1 *CBR and Information Retrieval*

Chapter 1 introduced the concepts of *information retrieval* (IR) from databases and claimed that CBR had advantages in that it could handle "fuzzy" matching. An example of a phone directory information service was used. However, CBR and IR have many features in common. IR can use techniques other than standard database queries, in particular when retrieving information from large textual information sources such as compact discs or the Internet. An increasingly popular retrieval technique is *concept-based retrieval*. This uses a thesaurus to find similes for words in a query to widen the scope of the query. Thus, a query such as "remedies for colds" would include words such as *cure* and *treatment,* which are synonymous with *remedy,* and *flu* and *influenza,* which are synonymous with *cold.*

In this context, IR and CBR both support flexible querying and both will retrieve a set of potentially relevant, but possibly inexact, matches. However, there are differences between the two techniques:

- IR methods are mainly focused upon retrieving text from large document sources, whereas CBR methods can deal with a wider range of data types (e.g., numbers, symbols, and Booleans, as well as text).

- IR systems do not tend to use background knowledge about the information being retrieved that CBR systems can use, for example, by weighting attribute values.

Thus, CBR differs in that it tends to be used on richer information sources than IR techniques, which tend to be used only on textual databases. However, this distinction is being blurred, and CBR techniques are increasingly being used on large textual information sources. For example, Microsoft is using a CBR retrieval engine within the help system of their Microsoft Office for Windows 95 product.

3.2.2 *CBR vs. Statistical Techniques*

Several comparative studies of CBR and various statistical techniques have been reported in the literature. In 1995, a comparison of nearest-neighbor case-based approaches and linear discriminant analysis (a widely used statistical technique) was carried out by Wolverhampton University and the Heartlands Hospital (Musgrove and Davies 1995). The data concerned the treatment of patients with the blood-thinning agent Warfarin. More than 1,200 patient consultations were used, with three possible outcomes: raise the patient's dosage of Warfarin, decrease the dosage, or leave the dosage unchanged. A nearest-neighbor CBR system correctly classified treatments 87% of the time, compared to 67% for discriminant analysis.

In 1993, Daimler-Benz carried out a comparative study between linear discriminant analysis and CBR (Nakhaeizadeih 1993). The domain was the quality control of gearboxes. They had more than 7,000 cases, each of which was described by 57 attributes or features. An inductive CBR algorithm was applied to the cases to partition them into 91 different diagnosis classes. The results of the CBR system in correctly assigning a case to a diagnosis class were compared to a linear discriminant analysis.

Table 3-1. Percentage accuracy of CBR versus linear discriminant analysis

Tests	Case-based induction	Linear discriminant analysis
1	93.4%	61%
2	93.4%	60%
3	92.6%	62%
4	93.2%	61%
5	93.5%	62%
Average	93.2%	61%

Table 3-1 summarizes the results of Daimler-Benz's experiments, showing that the case-based induction algorithm was around 30% more accurate at successfully classifying diagnoses than the statistical method. These results are more spectacular than those from the Heartland Hospital, but both show an improvement over linear discriminant analysis. Interestingly, taken together both results indicate that CBR, either by induction or nearest neighbor, can outperform the statistical technique.

While these two studies might suggest that CBR performs better than linear discriminant analysis, it would be unwise to overlook the success of statistics. The two should be seen as complementary techniques; statistical techniques are usually applied to large volumes of well-understood data to test well-formed hypotheses. Techniques such as discriminant analysis are not suited to exploratory analysis, where the independence of variables may not be known. Thus, CBR can be seen as being of particular value in analyzing less well-understood data sets.

3.2.3 *CBR vs. Rule-Based Expert Systems*

In Chapter 1, rule-based systems (i.e., those using IF-THEN rules) were introduced. You were shown that a rule-based system breaks a problem down into a set of individual rules that each solves part of the problem. Rules are combined together to solve a whole problem. To create these rules by hand, you have to know *how* to solve the problem, and this task can be extremely complex and time consuming.

CBR systems differ fundamentally in that to use them, we do not need to know *how* to solve a problem, only to recognize if we have solved a similar problem in the past. As with statistical techniques, it would be wrong to underrate the success of rule-based systems. During the last 20 years, hundreds of rule-based systems have been built and used very profitably in industries from agriculture to space exploration.

However, both rule-based reasoning and CBR techniques are often used to solve similar problems such as fault diagnosis. The last chapter of this book will return to the benefits of CBR, but they can be summarized as follows:

- A reduction in knowledge-elicitation effort, since CBR systems do not require an understanding of how to solve the problem. That is, to build a CBR system you only have to obtain past cases and their solutions; you do not have to elicit rules from experts.

- The ability to learn by acquiring new cases over time without having to add new rules or modify existing ones.

- The ability to provide justification by offering past cases as precedence rather than justifying a solution by showing a trace of the rules that led to the decision.

Rather than stating that CBR is better than rule-based techniques, it is perhaps more appropriate to show how the techniques differ (Table 3-2).

Table 3-2. **Rule-based reasoning versus CBR**

	Rule-based systems	CBR
Problem area	narrow, well understood, strong domain theory, stable over time	wide, poorly understood, weak domain theory, dynamic over time
Knowledge representation	facts and IF-THEN rules	cases
System provides	answers	precedents
Explanation by	trace of fired rules	precedents
System can learn	no, usually requires manual addition of new rules	yes, by case acquisition

Thus, if one has a narrow, well-understood problem that does not change with time, it may be sensible to use a rule-based system. Where a problem is less well understood or is dynamic, CBR may be better. Interestingly, an increasing number of hybrid systems are being developed that use rule-based techniques for areas that are well understood and CBR to handle less well-understood problems.

3.2.4   *CBR vs. Machine Learning*

It is perhaps misleading to caption this section as one technique versus another, since the induction algorithms used in CBR are derived from machine learning research. However, there is a distinction in how the techniques are applied. In general, machine learning involves analyzing past cases to derive rules that apply to the set of cases. These rules may then be applied to solve new problems. Machine learning clearly separates the processes of *learning* rules and *solving* problems.

CBR uses induction algorithms, such as ID3, to classify existing cases ("training examples" in machine learning terminology). The result of this process is an index tree that is used to match a new case against existing cases. Thus, the distinction between learning and problem solving is less clearly separated.

Another important distinction is in the justification for a decision or answer. Machine learning problem solvers will justify a decision by quoting the rules that were induced from the training examples; however, any link or reference to individual training examples is completely lost. A CBR system will use the retrieved cases as precedents to support a decision. This is an important distinction, since in general people understand and trust precedents but are less comfortable with abstract rules.

3.2.5   *CBR vs. Neural Networks*

Superficially, there are some similarities between CBR and neural networks (NNs). Both techniques rely on past cases with known outcomes to inform their decisions, but there the similarities end. NNs are good in domains where data cannot be represented symbolically, such as voice recognition and interpreting signal data from scientific instruments. Conversely, CBR is less good with purely numeric data and much better with complex, structured symbolic data.

The group at Wolverhampton University and the Heartlands Hospital also compared CBR (a nearest-neighbor system) to an NN (a multilayered perceptron trained by back propagation). The NN system could correctly advise on the dosage of Warfarin in 79% of cases compared to 87% for the CBR system. The NN system therefore outperformed the linear discriminant analysis (67% accuracy) but was less accurate than CBR. However, we would expect NN technology to perform much better on data that was better suited to it, such as signal processing.

The major disadvantage of NN technology compared with CBR is that an NN system functions as a "black box." The answer given by an NN is a function of the weighted vectors of its neurons. No explanation or justification of any sort can be given by an NN. This is therefore even worse than rule-based or machine learning systems, which can at least quote the rules used to justify a decision. For this reason, NNs are unsuitable in many application domains. For example, in Europe it is illegal for a bank to refuse a customer credit without giving an explanation of why the decision was made. Consequently, NNs cannot be used for credit approval, even though they might be suitable, because they cannot explain how a decision was reached.

3.2.6 *Summary of Technology Comparisons*

Table 3-3 is a guide to when you should and should not use each of the technologies discussed. In general, I believe that CBR should be used if it can be used. I believe that you will often obtain an adequate solution faster through implementing a CBR solution than you will by using any alternative technique. The major limitations of CBR are that it may not handle large volumes of purely numeric data as well as statistical or neural network techniques, and that if complex adaptation is required to provide a precise or optimum answer, you may have to use another technique anyway to perform adaptation. Remember that CBR retrieves the most *similar* case and attempts to reuse the solution from that case. CBR does not, therefore, provide precise, exact, or optimum solutions. If your system requires an exact solution, CBR may not be for you, but it may help you provide a quick ballpark answer from which you could develop an exact solution.

Table 3-3.   Technology comparisons

Technology type	When to use	When not to use
Databases	well-structured, standardized data and simple precise queries possible	Complex, poorly structured data and fuzzy queries required
Information retrieval	large volumes of textual data	nontextual complex data types, background knowledge available
Statistics	large volumes of well-understood data with a well-formed hypothesis	exploratory analysis of data with dependent variables
Rule-based systems	well-understood, stable, narrow problem area and justification by rule-trace acceptable	poorly understood problem area that constantly changes
Machine learning	generalizable rules are required from a large training set and justification by rule-trace is acceptable	rules are not required, and justification by rule-trace is unacceptable
Neural networks	noisy numerical data for pattern recognition or signal processing	complex symbolic data or when a justification is required
Case-based reasoning	poorly understood problem area with complex structured data that changes slowly with time and justification required	when case data is not available, or if complex adaptation is required, or if an exact optimum answer is required

Sycara (1992) identified characteristics of domains where CBR is most applicable. I have slightly adjusted some of these characteristics to give the following list:

1. An expert (i.e., the person who solves the problem) knows what they mean by a case.

2. Domain experts routinely compare a current problem to past cases.

3. Experts adapt cases to solve new problems.

4. Cases are available in bibliographic sources and in experts' memories, and can be recorded as new solutions are generated.

5. There are means in the domain to assign an outcome to a case, explain it, and deem it a success or a failure.

6. Cases can be generalized to some extent. Features that make them relevant can be abstracted.

7. Case comparisons and adaptations can be done effectively.

8. Cases retain currency for relatively long time intervals.

9. The domain may, or may not, have a strong model.

10. Cases are used in training professionals in the domain.

If the problem you are attempting to solve satisfies most of these features, then CBR is probably suitable.

3.3 Academic Demonstrators

In the relatively short time since the first CBR systems were implemented, there have been numerous academic CBR demonstrators. The following subsection presents a selection of some of the better known ones, classified according to tasks. This section as a whole is included to give you an idea of the range of problems to which CBR can be applied. Perhaps your organization has a problem similar to one of the systems described here.

3.3.1 *Diagnosis*

The diagnosis of disease has been one of the most popular problem domains for artificial intelligence since the early days of MYCIN (a classic rule-based expert system that diagnosed bacterial infections). However, diagnosis need not be restricted to medicine. Auto mechanics perform in a very similar way to a doctor when they work out why your car won't run. Moreover, it has been demonstrated that even experienced physicians rely heavily on their memory of past cases when performing a diagnosis. After all, this is why (given the choice) you would prefer your family doctor to be a person with a lifetime experience of medicine to a graduate fresh from medical school.

■ PROTOS (Porter and Bareiss 1986) was developed in the domain of clinical audiology. It learned to classify hearing disorders from descriptions of patients' symptoms, histories, and test results. PROTOS was trained with 200 cases in 24 categories from a speech and hearing clinic. After training, PROTOS had an absolute accuracy of 100%.

- CASEY (Koton 1989) is a system that diagnoses heart failure. As input, it uses a patient's symptoms and produces a causal network of possible internal states that could lead to those symptoms. When a new case arises, CASEY tries to find cases of patients with similar but not necessarily identical symptoms. If the new case matches, then CASEY adapts the retrieved diagnosis by considering differences in symptoms between the old and new cases.

- CASCADE (Simoudis 1992) is a system for diagnosing the causes of crashes to the VMS computer operating system to suggest a solution. Although this system is purely a retrieve-and-suggest system (i.e., there is no adaptation), it assists effective recovery from a system crash.

- PAKAR (Watson and Abdullah 1994) is a system that identifies possible causes for building defects and suggests remedial actions. Developed in CBR Express, PAKAR is able to combine textual information and CAD drawings to advise on possible causes of defects and their potential solutions.

3.3.2 *Planning*

Planning is yet another area where we commonly rely on our experience. If today you were told you had to go to London for a business meeting, you might plan your trip from scratch. That is, book the flights to London, find a good convenient hotel, and even plan a visit to a museum or show. If next month you had another trip to London and your previous trip was a success—that is, the flights were on time and the hotel was comfortable—you might simply reuse the majority of your previous plan by reusing the same airline and hotel. However, you would probably adapt the old plan by visiting a different museum or going to a different show.

- BATTLE (Goodman 1989) projects the results for plan evaluation in the domain of land warfare planning. The system was built from an existing database of 600 cases. The user describes a battle situation and chosen battle plan. BATTLE retrieves cases that are composed of pieces of battles and experts' evaluations to predict the outcome of the battle plan.

■ BOLERO (Lopez and Plaza 1993) builds a diagnostic plan according to information known about a patient. BOLERO combines CBR with a rule-based system. The rule-based component has knowledge about specific diseases, while the CBR component has planning knowledge particular to patient care.

■ TOTLEC (Costas and Kashyap 1993) was developed to solve complex manufacturing planning problems such as the detection of errors during the design phase, and warning and advising the user about nonmanufacturable designs.

3.3.3 *Legal Reasoning*

Since the legal systems of many countries are based on the concept of precedent and case law, it is no surprise that CBR has been widely applied to support legal reasoning.

■ JUDGE (Bain 1986) represents a case-based model of criminal sentencing. The program starts with a simple set of strategies for forming sentences and then begins to retrieve remindings of cases for developing new sentences. JUDGE reasons about murder, manslaughter, and assault cases. JUDGE has five stages of operations: interpretation, retrieval, differential analysis, application, and modification and generalization. JUDGE uses its case-base to maintain a consistent sentencing pattern.

■ HYPO (Ashley 1988) does case-based legal reasoning in the area of patent law. Centered on cases claiming violation of a patent, such as the release of a trade secret, HYPO uses its case-base of precedents to generate plausible arguments for both the prosecution and defense.

■ KICS (Yang and Robertson 1994) operates in the domain of building regulations. This system accumulates case histories of interpretation of regulations used to establish precedents. These precedents can be used when revising statutory regulation and enrich the resulting new versions of regulations. They also provide relevant information for the experts to interpret and make decisions about cases coming to appeal.

3.3.4 *Design*

Despite what designers might say, it has been proved that designers in all walks of life (from architects to software engineers) reuse past designs. An architect may never reuse a whole design, although there are certainly many very similar buildings around, but they will use parts or snippets of a design. This is also true of other designers and is even enshrined in software engineering under the term *reuse*. Consequently, despite the fact that design is a synthesis task, it is no surprise that design has been an important growth area for CBR.

- CYCLOPS (Navinchandra 1988) solves design problems in the domain of landscaping. It is focused on finding potential problems when designing new amenities.

- JULIA (Hinrichs 1989) is a case-based designer that works in the domain of menu design. It uses cases to propose solutions, decomposing the problem as necessary and posting constraints to guide synthesis. It exploits a repertoire of adaptation methods to transform previous dishes in order to meet the constraints of the current problem. These adaptation methods are used both to modify previous cases and repair previous decisions that have been invalidated by constraints.

- CADET (Sycara 1992) is a case-based design system that functions as a designer's assistant for mechanical design. It retrieves previous successful designs while avoiding previous failures such as poor materials or high costs. CADET transforms abstract descriptions of the desired behavior of the device into a description that can be used to retrieve relevant designs and generate a variety of equivalent alternative designs for a given set of design specifications.

- ARCHIE (Pearce et al. 1992) is implemented using ReMind and helps architects in the high-level task of conceptual design. It gives architects access to office building designs created by other architects and points to factors that should be considered in solving a given problem. Each case in ARCHIE contains several types of information, including design goals, design plans, descriptions of how well the design satisfied its goals and constraints, and lessons to be learned from the case.

- NIRMANI (Perera and Watson 1995) is implemented using ART*Enterprise* to assist developers of light industrial warehouse units. The system contains a library of designs and their construction costs stored in a hierarchical case representation. Cases include two-dimensional and three-dimensional CAD drawings, specifications, photographs, and even video tours of completed buildings. From an initial client's requirements, a design can be quickly retrieved and costed. The use of past cases augmented with multimedia helps the clients refine their requirements and so improves the resulting design brief.

3.3.5 *Analogous Reasoning*

A characteristic of human intelligence is our ability to identify analogies between different situations. Indeed, we often use analogies to inform our decisions. For example, the United States is reluctant to put its troops into an overseas conflict if the situation is in any way analogous to the Vietnam War. A CBR system that uses analogy is SWALE (Kass 1989), which has a library of cases of stories about animals and people dying in strange circumstances. For example, if SWALE is given an anomalous event such as the death of a healthy, young racehorse, it searches for explanations of death in other analogous contexts, such as a basketball player dying from a drug overdose. SWALE will then suggest that perhaps the racehorse died from an illegally administered drug.

3.3.6 *Arbitration*

Arbitration is a skilled task and often relies on the arbiter and the disputing parties making use of precedence.

- MEDIATOR (Simpson 1985) works in the domain of dispute resolution. Given a conflict between several parties, it proposes possible compromises. If one proposal fails to satisfy all the parties involved, it generates new proposals and records the failure, thus avoiding a similar failure in the future.

- PERSUADER (Sycara 1987) proposes resolution of disputes between labor and management. The input is a description of a dispute between management and labor over wage-benefit packages and the output is a compromise package adapting contracts that have been used by similar companies. The existence of a backup planner makes it unlike other CBR systems, since it can generate new contracts when no existing ones can be found or adapted.

3.3.7 *Adaptation*

An important aspect of CBR is the ability to adapt or repair solutions to past problems, so they can be more successfully reapplied. Many CBR systems do not use adaptation at all, whereas the systems described below specifically focus on adaptation.

- CHEF (Hammond 1986) creates new recipes from old ones. CHEF begins planning by finding a recipe that satisfies as many of its active goals as possible. It uses a set of object critics and modification rules to change the old recipe and satisfy the goal of the new one. One of the important aspects of CHEF is explanation of failures through a causal description of why they occurred. CHEF links recipes to a failure's explanation to predict the failure in similar circumstances.

- PLEXUS (Alterman 1986) is a planner that adapts old plans to new situations. This system is designed to compare two plans, by, for example, adapting a plan for riding San Francisco's subway system into a plan for riding New York's subway system. It has a mechanism for comparing the similarity—and dissimilarity—of two cases in the adaptation process.

- COACH (Collins 1987) is a program that works in a football domain. COACH generates new football plays by improving on old plays. COACH has relatively few plays in its library, but it has many strategies for adaptation to form new plays.

3.3.8 *Tutoring*

CBR has many parallels in education. We often learn by being shown how to solve a problem and then being given a similar problem to solve ourselves. It is perhaps surprising therefore that there are not more case-based tutoring systems. One reason is perhaps a feeling among educators that CBR does not support understanding since it does not rely on any first principles, but rather encourages mindless repetition akin to rote learning. CBR systems are sometimes called "lazy learners" (Aha 1996), since they may know how to solve a problem but do not bother to find out why the solution works.

- DECIDER (Farrel 1987) is a system that helps students understand or resolve a pedagogical problem by selecting and presenting appropriate cases from a database that respond to the student's goal.

■ HYPO, a case-based tutoring system for law students, is described in Aleven and Ashley (1992). The system is used to generate fresh cases for analysis in response to a particular issue of interest as identified by a tutor. In this system, the tutor enters as input the theme to be taught, and the system presents a set of pedagogically related cases that are used by the tutor to teach that particular theme to students.

3.4 Summary

This chapter has presented a classification of problem domains suitable for CBR. In general, those problems that broadly fall under the banner of classification tasks, such as diagnosis and prediction, are easier to implement than tasks that require synthesis, such as design. This chapter has also contrasted CBR with alternative, or in some instances, complementary technologies. Thus, you should now be in a position to both understand how CBR works and have an idea of when to consider applying it. The chapter concluded by introducing you to several influential academic CBR demonstrators. The following chapters will describe some commercially fielded CBR applications in more detail.

3.5 Further Reading

A classification of CBR tasks according to Chandrasekaran's *generic task analysis* is given in the following CBR review paper:

Aamodt, A., and Plaza, E. (1994). Case-Based Reasoning: Foundational Issues, Methodological Variations and System Approaches. *AI-Communications* 7(1), 39–52.

Further information on generic task analysis may be found in

Chandrasekaran, B. (1988). Generic Tasks as Building Blocks for Knowledge Based Systems: The Diagnosis and Routine-Design Examples. *The Knowledge Engineering Review*, 3, 183–219.

A classification of CBR tasks and a comparison with other technologies is given in the following report:

Althoff, K-D, Auriol, E., Barletta, R., and Manago, M. (1995). *A Review of Industrial Case-Based Reasoning Tools*. Oxford: AI Intelligence.

The comparisons of CBR with statistical and neural network techniques are given in

Musgrove, P., and Davies, J. (1995). A Comparative Study of Three Machine Learning Approaches to the Treatment of Patients of Anticoagulant Out-Patient Clinics. *Applications and Innovations in Expert Systems III*, edited by A. Macintosh and C. Cooper. Oxford: SGES Publications.

Nakhaeizadeh, G. (1993). Learning Prediction of Time Series. A Theoretical and Empirical Comparison of CBR with Some Other Approaches. In *Proceedings of EWCBR'93*, edited by M.M. Richter et al. Berlin: Springer-Verlag.

A comprehensive discussion of machine learning can be found in

Weiss, S.M., and Kulikowski, A. (1990). *Computer Systems That Learn: Classification and Prediction Methods from Statistics, Neural Nets, Machine Learning and Expert Systems*. San Francisco: Morgan Kaufmann Publishers.

The list of features that characterize a suitable problem for CBR are detailed in

Sycara, K. (1992). A Case-Based Synthesis Tool for Engineering Design, *International Journal of Expert Systems* 4(2), 157–188.

The following references describe the CBR systems mentioned in this chapter:

Aleven, V., and Ashley, K.D. (1992). Automated Generation of Examples for a Tutorial in Case-Based Argumentation. In *Proceedings, Second International Conference on Intelligent Tutoring Systems (ITS 92)*, edited by C. Frasson, G. Gauthier, and G.L. McCallan. Berlin: Springer-Verlag.

Alterman, R. (1986). An Adaptive Planner. In *Proceedings of AAAI-86*. Cambridge, MA: AAAI Press / MIT Press.

Ashley, K.D. (1988). Arguing by Analogy in Law: A Case-Based Model. In *Analogical Reasoning: Perspectives of Artificial Intelligence, Cognitive Science, and Philosophy*. Norwell, MA: D. Reidel.

Bain, W.M. (1986). *Case-Based Reasoning: A Computer-Model of Subjective Assessment*. Ph.D. thesis, Yale University.

Collins, G. (1987). *Plan Creation: Using Strategies as Blueprints*. Ph.D. thesis, Department of Computer Science, Yale University.

Costas, T., and Kashyap, P. (1993). Case-Based Reasoning and Learning in Manufacturing with TOTLEC Planner. *IEEE Transactions on Systems, Man, and Cybernetics,* 23(iv) July/August 1993.

Farrel, R. (1987). Intelligent Case Selection and Presentation. In *Proceedings of the Tenth International Joint Conference on Artificial Intelligence, IJCAI-87,* 1, 74–76.

Goodman, M. (1989). CBR in Battle Planning. In *Proceedings of the DARPA Case-Based Reasoning Workshop,* edited by K.J. Hammond. San Francisco: Morgan Kaufmann Publishers.

Hammond, K.J. (1986). CHEF: A Model of Case-Based Planning. In *Proceedings of AAAI-86, August 1986.* Cambridge, MA: AAAI Press / MIT Press.

Hinrichs, T. (1989). Strategies for Adaptation and Recovery in a Design Problem Solver. In *Proceedings of the DARPA Case-Based Reasoning Workshop,* edited by K.J. Hammond. San Francisco: Morgan Kaufmann Publishers.

Kass, A. (1989). Strategies for Adapting Explanations. In *Proceedings of the DARPA Case-Based Reasoning Workshop,* edited by K.J. Hammond. San Francisco: Morgan Kaufmann Publishers.

Koton, P. (1989). *Using Experience in Learning and Problem Solving.* Ph.D. thesis, Laboratory of Computer Science, Massachusetts Institute of Technology. MIT/LCS/TR-441.

Lopez, B., and Plaza, E. (1993). Case-Base Planning for Medical Diagnosis. In *Methodologies for Intelligent Systems, 7th International Symposium, ISMIS-93.* Lecture Notes in Artificial Intelligence 689. Berlin: Springer-Verlag.

Navinchandra, D. (1988). Case-Based Reasoning in CYCLOPS, a Design Problem Solver. In *Proceedings of the DARPA Case-Based Reasoning Workshop,* edited by J.L. Kolodner. San Francisco: Morgan Kaufmann Publishers.

Pearce, M., Ashok, K.G., Kolodner, J.L., Zimring, C., and Billington, R. (1992). Case-Based Support—A Case Study in Architectural Design. *IEEE Expert,* October 1992.

Perera, R.S., and Watson, I. (1995). A Case-Based Design Approach for the Integration of Design and Estimating. In *Progress in Case-Based Reasoning,* edited by I. Watson. Lecture Notes in Artificial Intelligence 1020. Berlin: Springer-Verlag.

Porter, B.W., and Bareiss, E.R. (1986). PROTOS: An Experiment in Knowledge Acquisition for Heuristic Classification Tasks. In *Proceedings of the First International Meeting on Advances in Learning (IMAL),* 159–174. Les Arcs, France.

Simoudis, E. (1992). Using Case-Based Retrieval for Customer Technical Support. *IEEE Expert,* 7(5), 7–13.

Simpson, R.L. (1985). *A Computer Model of Case-Based Reasoning in Problem Solving: An Investigation in the Domain of Dispute Mediation.* Georgia Institute of Technology, School of Information and Computer Science Technical Report No. GIT-ICS-85/18.

Sycara, E.P. (1987). Finding Creative Solutions in Adversarial Impasses. In *Proceedings of the Ninth Annual Conference of the Cognitive Science Society.* Northvale, NJ: Lawrence Erlbaum Associates.

Sycara, K. (1992). CADET: A case-based synthesis tool for engineering design. *International Journal for Expert Systems,* 4(2), 157–188.

Watson, I.D., and Abdullah, S. (1994). Developing Case-Based Reasoning Systems: A Case Study in Diagnosing Building Defects. In *Proceedings of the IEE Colloquium on Case-Based Reasoning: Prospects for Applications,* Digest No: 1994/057, 1/1–1/3.

Yang, S., and Robertson, D. (1994). A Case-Based Reasoning System for Regulatory Information. In *Proceedings of the IEE Colloquium on Case-Based Reasoning: Prospects for Applications,* Digest No: 1994/057, 3/1–3/3.

Janet Kolodner provides a very complete description of many other influential academic CBR demonstrators in

Kolodner, J. (1993). *Case-Based Reasoning.* San Francisco: Morgan Kaufmann Publishers.

David Aha has edited a special issue of the *AI Review* on lazy learning:

Aha, D., ed. (1997). *Artificial Intelligence Review* (special issue on lazy learning). Norwell, MA.: Kluwer.

4

Industrial Applications of CBR

The previous chapter outlined a categorization of CBR domains, discussed when CBR should be used, and described some influential academic CBR demonstrators. Although CBR is a young discipline in comparison to, say, rule-based expert systems or neural computing, there are already a surprising number of commercially successful applications. Below, I list more than 130 major companies using CBR for a range of tasks.

Technology—Hardware
Apple Computer: corporate memory of troubleshooting events
ATT Bell Laboratories: customer support
Cisco Systems: customer support
Compaq Computer Corp.: customer support
Conner Peripherals: customer support
DEC: hard-disk failure recovery in VNS operating system
Epson America: customer support
Gateway 2000: customer support
Groupe Bull: customer support
Hewlett-Packard Co.: customer support
IBM: customer support
Intel Corp.: customer support

ITT: process quality control of electronic circuits
NCR Corp.: customer support
NEC Technologies: customer support
Philips: configuration of X-ray control systems
Siemens AG: customer support
Texas Instruments: troubleshooting support
Xerox Corp.: customer support

Technology—Software
Artisoft: customer support
Autodesk: customer support
Broderbund Software: customer support
Dun & Bradstreet Software Services: customer support
Intergraph Corp.: customer support
J.D. Edwards: customer support
Lucas Arts Entertainment Co.: customer support
Microsoft Corp.: customer support
NEC: corporate memory of software quality issues
PeopleSoft: customer support
Sterling Software: customer support
Symantec: customer support

Finance and Insurance
Abbey National PLC: customer support
American Express: credit card risk assessment
Anderson Consulting: property and casualty underwriting
Charles Schwab & Co.: customer support
Chase Manhattan Bank: classification and routing of interbank
    financial telexes
Chubb & Son: customer support
Compagnie Bancaire: credit assessment
Deloitte & Touche: fraud assessment
Halifax Building Society: customer support
Legal & General: computer purchasing support tool
Liberty Mutual Insurance Group: customer support
Mellon Bank, N.A.: customer support
National Westminster Bank PLC: customer support
Principal Mutual Life Insurance: customer support
Prudential: life and motor insurance underwriting
Rabobank: customer support
Reuters Ltd.: customer support
Roussel Uclaf: data analysis

Swiss Bank: financial information retrieval
VISA International: customer support

Telecommunications
AT&T Corp.: customer support
British Telecommunications PLC: customer support
Mercury Communications Ltd.: customer support
Nokia Telecommunications: customer support
Orange Personal Communications Services Ltd.: customer support
SITA: telecommunication network management

Manufacturing and Transportation
Air Products and Chemicals: customer support
American Airlines: technical support of ticket reservation system
American Standard Companies: customer support
Beckman Instruments: customer support
British Airways: aircraft maintenance
British Petroleum: gas-oil separation for oil-drilling platforms
Caledonian Paper: fault diagnosis of electrical drives
Cfm International: maintenance of aircraft engines
Chrysler Corp.: customer support
Cincinnati Milacron: troubleshooting milling equipment
Daimler-Benz: quality control of Mercedes gearboxes
Elf Acquitaine: classification tasks
Enginetics: bid preparation for process engineers
Freightliner Corp.: customer support
General Dynamics: submarine fault diagnosis
General Electric: maintenance of mission-critical equipment
General Motors: car maintenance
Institut Français du Pétrol: selection of lubricants
Kaye Presteigne: pressure die casting
Lockheed Martin Corp.: layout of composite materials in an
    autoclave
Matra Space Corp.: satellite fault diagnosis
Mitsubishi Electric Corp.: plant information management
Naheola Mill: process control
NASA: process planning and Space Shuttle landing decision support
Nestlé: process control
Nippon Steel: process configuration
Sepro Robotics: diagnostics for plastic-injection-press robots
Shai: architectural engineering
Siemens: selection of synthetic materials

SINTEF: mud drilling for the oil industry
VINITI: chemical safety
Volkswagen: quality assurance
Westinghouse: nuclear fuel refinement

Utilities

Commissariat à l'Energie Atomique: information retrieval
Duke Power Co.: customer support
Electricité de France: information retrieval
London Electricity PLC: customer support
Oglethorp Power Corp.: customer support
Reliance Electric Industrial Co.: customer support
Scottish Hydro Electric: customer support
South Western Electricity PLC: customer support
Southern Electric PLC: customer support
U.K. Electric: maintenance of electrical turbines
United Utilities: customer support
Yorkshire Water Services Ltd.: customer support

Retail/Consumer

Argos Distributors Ltd.: customer support
Bass Brewers Ltd.: customer support
Black & Decker Corp.: customer support
Canon U.S.A.: customer support
Circuit City Stores: customer support
FTD: customer support
Holiday Inns: customer support
J Sainsbury PLC: customer support
Marriot International: customer support
Woolworth PLC: customer support

Outsourcing

ICL Sorbus U.K. Ltd.: customer support
Innovative Services: customer support
MCI Telecommunications Corp.: customer support
McQueen: customer support
National Electronics Warranty: customer support
Vanstar Corp.: customer support

Miscellaneous

Amdahl Corp.: customer support
Blue Cross: medical diagnosis

Buena Vista Home Video: customer support
Dow Chemical Co.: customer support
French Ministry of Defense: command and control systems
GTE: health care, network traffic control and monitoring
Honeywell: training U.S. Air Force pilots
Los Angeles Times: customer support
MicroAge: customer support
Mitre: air traffic control
Olsten Kimberly Quality Care: customer support
Ordnance Survey: customer support
Paris' Hospitals: epidemiology
Raychem Corp.: customer support
SEI Corp.: customer support
U.K. Department of Social Security: technical support
University Hospital Munich: medical diagnosis and personnel
   scheduling

As can be seen, there is already an impressive number of major companies using CBR for a wide variety of tasks. In some companies, such as Apple Computers and Texas Instruments, CBR is being used as a *corporate memory*, providing a shared resource where employees can record their problems and solutions and access the experience of others. In many of the companies (e.g., American Airlines, J Sainsbury, and Reuters), CBR is being used to provide in-house technical support, whereas in the majority of companies (e.g., Black & Decker, Compaq, and London Electric), it is being used to assist customer service centers. Some firms, such as Compaq, are including CBR in their products, and Microsoft has embedded CBR technology within the intelligent help system of its Microsoft Office for Windows 95 product.

The use of CBR within customer service centers is the predominant use of CBR and is dealt with in detail in the next chapter. The remainder of this chapter will focus in some detail on four of the industrial systems mentioned above. The first, at Lockheed, was one of the first commercial CBR systems and deals with a complex planning problem. The second, at Kaye Presteigne, shows how a very simple CBR system can bring real business benefits. The third, at British Airways, is a diagnostic problem, while the last, at Deloitte & Touche, shows how CBR can be used to tackle an otherwise insoluble problem within the finance sector.

4.1 Lockheed—CLAVIER

One of the first commercially fielded CBR applications was the CLA-VIER system at Lockheed Missiles and Space Company in Sunnyvale, California. Modern aircraft and missiles contain many elements that are made up from composite materials. These are made from layers of carbon-fiber products, such as Kevlar, that are formed into single laminated components by curing in a large oven, called an autoclave. Lockheed produces many such parts because of the exceptional strength and light weight of the composites.

Individual composite parts are very expensive and can cost many thousands of dollars for the materials alone. If a manufactured part has even the slightest fault, it cannot be melted down or recycled—it must be discarded. Each part has its own curing characteristics and must therefore be cured correctly. If curing is not correct, the part will have to be discarded. Unfortunately, the autoclave's heating characteristics are not fully understood (i.e., there is no physical model that operators can draw upon to predict its performance). This is complicated by the fact that many parts are fired together in a single large autoclave and the parts interact to alter the heating and cooling characteristics of the autoclave. A schematic diagram of the autoclave is shown in Figure 4-1.

Many parts are placed in the autoclave simultaneously (some autoclaves measure 20 feet wide by 50 feet long); smaller parts rest on tables and larger parts are unsupported, resting directly on the floor. Correctly selecting and positioning parts in the autoclave so that they all heat up and cool down correctly is an art rather than a science and is almost entirely based on experience of successful loadings.

Operators of Lockheed's autoclaves relied upon drawings of previous successful layouts to inform how to layout the autoclave. However, this was complicated by the fact that layouts were rarely identical because parts were required at different times and because the design of the composite materials was constantly changing. Consequently, operators had to select a successful layout that closely matched the list of parts waiting to be cured and adapt it to the current situation by substituting parts that had similar characteristics.

Figure 4-1.
An autoclave load

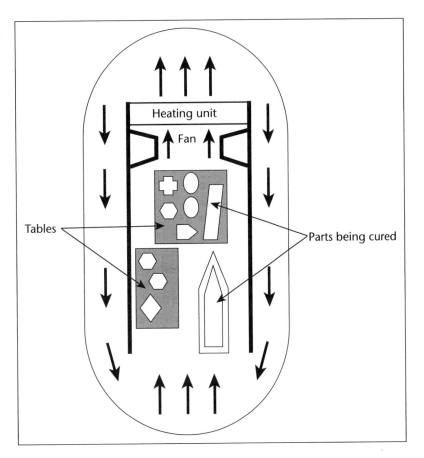

This closely resembled the CBR paradigm, so when Lockheed decided to implement an expert system to assist the autoclave operators, they decided upon CBR (a previous attempt to build a rule-based system had failed because operators were unable to articulate good rules). Their objectives were

- To reuse previously successful loadings
- To reduce the pressure of work on one or two experts
- To secure the expertise of the experts as a corporate asset
- To help train new personnel

The development of CLAVIER started in 1987, and it has been in regular use at Lockheed since fall 1990.

4.1.1 *Case Representation*

Each layout case in CLAVIER is described in terms of

- The names of parts
- The tables (or otherwise) on which parts were placed
- Where the parts were located
- The relative positions of other parts
- Production statistics such as start and finish times, pressure, and temperature

This information was sufficient for performing efficient retrieval. It is worth noting that information on the geometry, density, or constitution of parts was not required as might have been expected.

4.1.2 *Case Retrieval*

Autoclave operators have a prioritized list of parts waiting to be cured. For any given list of parts, CLAVIER seeks to retrieve a past layout that successfully cured the greatest number of high-priority parts on the waiting list. The highest scoring historic case is returned to the operator for approval or adaptation.

4.1.3 *Case Adaptation*

When the best matching case is not completely filled by parts on the waiting list, CLAVIER can substitute a nonmatching part with a similar part as shown in Figure 4-2. This adaptation strategy is based on the idea that if a similar part were in a similar place in a similar layout, it could safely be substituted. Although this line of reasoning is intuitively valid, operators were not happy with CLAVIER automatically adapting cases. They preferred to do the task themselves, so a graphical case editor was provided to let them do this. Once they have adapted a case, CLAVIER can critique their change and warn them if there was a similar layout in the past that turned out unsuccessfully.

After the layout is run through the autoclave, it is added to the case-base, either as a successful layout for future layout configuration, or as an unsuccessful layout to ensure that mistakes are not repeated.

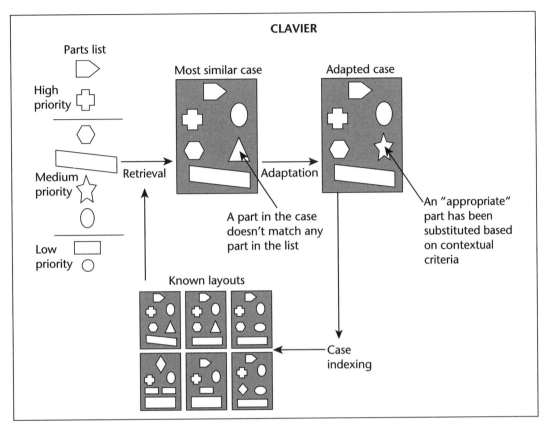

Figure 4-2. *A schematic of CLAVIER's adaptation process*

4.1.4 *Implementation*

CLAVIER was implemented in about nine person-months on a Macintosh using Common Lisp. The first version was delivered in September 1990. It started with a library of only 20 successful cases, could configure individual loads, and provided an editor for user adaptation. CLAVIER Version 2 was delivered in November 1991 after a further 15 months of programming. The new version provided a multiload scheduler whose goal is to find the smallest number of layouts that will complete all the parts on the waiting list. CLAVIER Version 2 also provides validation of adapted layouts (by checking to see if they are similar to unsuccessful layouts), as well as various reporting and administrative functions.

4.1.5 *Impact*

CLAVIER acts as a collective memory for Lockheed and as such provides a uniquely useful way of transferring expertise between autoclave operators. In particular, the use of CBR made the initial knowledge acquisition for the system easier (remember that Lockheed had tried and failed to implement a rule-based system). CLAVIER also demonstrates the ability of CBR systems to remember. The system has grown from 20 to several hundred successful layouts, and its performance has improved, such that it now retrieves a successful autoclave layout 90% of the time. Interestingly, although CLAVIER can adapt layouts, this facility was not liked by the engineers. Consequently, they now adapt layouts themselves and use CLAVIER to check that their adaptation will not repeat a failed layout. A recent article by David Hinkle and Christopher Toomey of the Lockheed AI Center (Hinkle and Toomey 1994) described the tremendous success of CLAVIER and its benefits to Lockheed's composite manufacturing process:

> Clavier has been in continuous daily use at Lockheed's Composites Fabrication facility in Sunnyvale, California, since September 1990. Two or three autoclave loads are cured per day in this facility, all of which are selected through operator consultations with CLAVIER. CLAVIER also generates hard copy reports of the autoclave loads that are used for record-keeping purposes. The system has recently been expanded for use in other Lockheed manufacturing facilities, and negotiations are under way for licensing the software to other aerospace companies. . . . Since CLAVIER came on line, discrepancy reports due to incompatible loads have virtually been eliminated, saving thousands of dollars each month.

4.2 Kaye Presteigne—Wayland

Wayland is a CBR system that advises on the setup of aluminum pressure die-casting machines. In some ways, Wayland is similar to CLAVIER, but in other ways it differs. First, it performs approximate numerical matching of case features, whereas CLAVIER uses textual matching. Second, adaptation of the result is an important part of Wayland, whereas, as discussed in the previous section, it was dropped from CLAVIER. Third, Wayland was implemented using a very simple CBR shell that was devised specifically for this project.

The shell, called CASPIAN, is in the public domain and can be downloaded from the Internet for you to experiment with (www.aber.ac.uk/~cjp/getting-caspian.html). (CASPIAN is reviewed in Chapter 6.)

Wayland has been deployed for two years in the United Kingdom and demonstrates the clear benefits that CBR systems can provide. This case study will describe the mechanics of the Wayland system and the foundry's experience with it.

4.2.1 *The Pressure Die Design Problem*

Pressure die casting involves injecting molten metal at very high pressure into a mold (a die), where it cools to make a casting. Figure 4-3 illustrates the main components involved in the process.

Some of the key components and processes of die casting:

- *Gate.* The hole through which the molten metal enters the impression part of a die. The gate is usually kept to a narrow slit to reduce the cost of the casting. It has to be removed from the casting, and if the gate is more than about 3 millimeters deep, the excess has to be sawn off rather than clipped. Consequently, both the gate depth and the gate cross-sectional area are of interest.

- *Sleeve.* The tube into which the molten aluminum is poured so that it can be pushed by the plunger into the die.

- *Tip.* The end of the plunger by which the metal is pushed into the die. Smaller tips allow higher pressures to be exerted on the die. Larger tips allow quicker filling of the die.

- *Number of impressions.* Some dies make more than one component per casting. For example, a die that makes four components from a single casting is referred to as a "four-impression die."

- *Cycle time.* The total time to make a casting, from one injection of metal to the next. It includes filling the casting (cavity fill time), cooling time, and extraction of the component from the die.

Machine settings are critical for successful pressure die casting, and there will always be a compromise between such factors as the cost of producing the casting, maximizing the die life, and the quality of the final product. If the machine settings for a new die are badly off, this can become dangerous. For example, the combination of small tip size, high pressure, and small casting can cause the die to splash, that is, the die opens momentarily, spraying molten aluminum at temperatures in excess of 1300°F (500°C).

Figure 4-3.
Schematic of a pressure die-casting machine

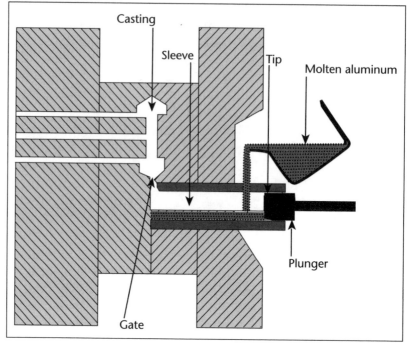

The ability to calculate values for machine settings during die design also has commercial implications when bidding for a new casting contract. There are no generally applicable formulas for calculating values for pressures on the molten metal, gate velocity, cycle time, and so on for a given set of conditions, although different professional bodies have attempted to present formulas to rationalize the process. The different formulas, however, give vastly differing results, even for identical operating conditions, so there is no agreed mathematical model for calculating results.

The reason for the discrepancies between these formulas is that there are several sets of conditions under which a casting can be made. The die parameters are strongly interrelated, making the problem nondecomposable. A change in one parameter can be compensated for by altering another.

CBR is an appropriate technology for this problem, because a foundry will tend to have a particular way of working. Engineers will refer to records of previous dies with similar input requirements, and adjust the parameters for a similar die to reflect the different requirements of the new die being built. The records of previous dies are good examples of working compromises between the different operating requirements: such compromises might well have been found by costly adjustments performed in the foundry after the die was built.

Wayland automates the identification of past dies with similar characteristics, alters the die settings to take into account the differences between the past die and the new one being designed, and validates that the new solution is within design limits.

4.2.2 *Implementation*

Wayland was implemented using a CBR shell called CASPIAN. This shell is implemented in C, and cases are represented as structured ASCII text (CASPIAN is an acronym for CASe Parser by IAN). The Windows interface of Wayland was also written in C. CASPIAN provides two functions, case retrieval and adaptation, using adaptation rules. Each of these is described below.

4.2.3 *Case Retrieval*

Wayland has a case-base of some 200 previous die designs, extracted from records of actual die performances in a database maintained at the foundry. Only dies with satisfactory performances have their values entered into the case-base, so foundry personnel are confident that each case provides a good basis for calculating new solutions. Cases are fixed-format records, with a field for each of the values shown below. Some of the fields may be blank, if complete records for a die have not been available. A typical case representation in Wayland is shown below:

```
CASE INSTANCE die_no_5014 IS
        weight_of_casting = 240.00;
        weight_of_casting_and_overflows = 310.00;
        weight_of_total_shot = 520.00;
        no_of_slides = 0.00;
        projected_area_of_casting = 19.50;
        total_projected_area = 35.50;
        average_no_of_impressions = 1.00;
        machine_type = t400;
        metal_type = lm24;

SOLUTION IS
        imagefile = 'dn5014.gif';
        gate_velocity = 6414.09;
        cavity_fill_time = 13.77;
        length_of_stroke = 3.10;
```

```
                    percentage_fill = 16.24;
                    gate_area = 135.00;
                    gate_width = 90.00;
                    gate_depth = 1.50;
                    plunger_velocity = 225.00;
                    pressure_on_metal = 8000.00;
                    tip_size = 70.00;
                    cycle_time = 35.00;
        END;
```

Notice that the case is divided into two sections: a problem description and a solution. Retrieval is restricted by pruning the case-base so that only cases for the same type of die-casting machine (e.g., only dies used on the 400-ton machine) are retrieved. Each of the retrieved cases is then assigned an overall *match value*. This is done by assigning a match score to each field and summing the total. Each field is given a weight that expresses its significance (e.g., the number of impressions is an important field to match, because it specifies how many of the parts are made at once in the die). Matches can be specified as *exact* (e.g., for number of impressions) or *approximate* (for items such as weight of casting), where the score awarded will depend on how close the match is. The case with the highest overall mark is the best match. The formula used is similar to that described in Chapter 2. After a case is retrieved, it will then have adaptation rules applied to it in order to produce the correct machine settings.

4.2.4   *Case Adaptation*

Adaptation rules are applied to the specification values and to the answers from the past case in order to

- Calculate further information from the specification
- Take account of the differences between the past case and the new problem
- Change parameters when safety criteria are violated
- Decide whether the final result is good enough

This section explains what each kind of rule does and gives an example of each adaptation rule in Wayland.

The simplest type of rule calculates a required value directly from the information that the user has already given. For example, the total volume of the metal in the casting and overflows is needed in order to calculate other values. It can be calculated by the following rule:

```
REPAIR RULE find_volume_of_casting_and_overflows IS
        WHEN volume_of_casting_and_overflows IS UNDEFINED
        THEN
        EVALUATE volume_of_casting_and_overflows TO
        weight_of_casting_and_overflows / 0.0026;
END;
```

Other simple adaptation rules take results from the retrieved case and adapts them to the differing circumstances of the new die. For example, the following rule uses the length of the plunger stroke for filling the new die and the value for plunger velocity taken from the past case, and calculates the time it takes to push the metal into the die:

```
REPAIR RULE find_cavity_fill_time IS
        WHEN cavity_fill_time IS UNDEFINED THEN
        EVALUATE cavity_fill_time TO (length_of_stroke /
        plunger_velocity) * 1000;
END;
```

Some of the rules check whether operating values are within safe boundaries and change them if they are not. The following example checks that the velocity of the metal through the gate is not too high. If it is, then it increases the size of the gate, so that the velocity will be reduced. The command *REPAIR* causes all adaptation rules to be reevaluated in light of this safety-critical adaptation. This enables adaptation rules to fire more than once if the gate velocity is still too high, thereby reducing the velocity in increments until a safe velocity is reached.

```
REPAIR RULE gate_velocity_too_big IS
        WHEN gate_velocity >= 5000 THEN
        EVALUATE gate_area TO gate_area + 10;
        EVALUATE gate_depth TO (gate_area / gate_width) /
        no_of_impressions;
        pr(['Warning: changed gate depth: gate velocity too
        big']);
        REPAIR;
END;
```

However, some problems caused by the difference between the past case and the new die are too complex for the Wayland program to deal with in the way shown above for gate velocity. In those cases, the user is warned about the problem. The following example warns that the job is too large to run on any of the machines in the foundry:

```
REPAIR RULE no_machine_big_enough IS
        WHEN total_projected_area >= 160 THEN
        pr(['Warning: projected area too big for 700-ton
        machine.']);
END;
```

Once a case has been accepted, and the die casting has been found to be successful in practice, the case is entered into Wayland's case-base by an engineer, thus completing the CBR-cycle.

4.2.5 *Benefits of Wayland*

Wayland has been available at the foundry for more than two years and is used by several different kinds of foundry personnel. They are interested in different information from the case-base. For some users, the information that they actually want is not held on-line in the case-base, but the best matching case can be used to index further information held in manual files. Such users still find this much faster and more effective than browsing through paper records of past dies to find relevant information. The main users of Wayland are sales staff, die designers, and foundry engineers.

- *Benefits to sales staff*: Wayland is in daily use to provide estimates of the cost of producing a new component. Sales staff are most interested in cycle time, although close matches in the case-base are also used to access off-line information such as the cost of building the die to manufacture such a component. Before Wayland was available, sales staff had either to obtain an accurate estimate from an experienced engineer (this would take several hours), or simply guess an estimate, which is very unsatisfactory in the highly competitive foundry industry.

- *Benefits to die designers*: A close match with an existing die design can be helpful when designing a new die. It enables the designer to reuse an existing design for running and gating (the critical layout for metal feeding into and overflowing from a die). This can save several days of work. More importantly, it bases the new design on a previous design known to be successful and so minimizes the risk that the new design will not work properly or will have a short life span.

- *Benefits to foundry engineers*: These were the people for whom Wayland was originally intended. By providing the most accurate available values for parameter settings, it can save significant setup time when a new die is first being installed. Previously, several days might have been spent experimenting with settings such as plunger velocity, in order to produce acceptable castings. In some cases, the physical shape of the die needed to be altered in order to produce acceptable results, causing further expense and loss of production. The use of Wayland has significantly reduced this time. The Wayland case-base is maintained by one of the foundry engineers, and perhaps the best measure of its success is that he is happy to have the task of maintenance. The amount of time it saves him and his colleagues far outweighs the effort of adding new cases.

The engineers are imaginative in their use of Wayland and produce new ways in which it can help them. One of the most recent innovations was using Wayland in troubleshooting. The engineers had problems with one particular die for some time and were unable to make it work consistently. An engineer decided to enter its parameters to Wayland. There was a good match on an existing case, and Wayland recommended a larger gate area than there was on the problem die. The gate on the problem die was altered accordingly, and the problems went away.

4.2.6 *Summary of Benefits*

The benefits of Wayland can be broken into four main areas:

1. *Wayland replaces opinion with reference to actual experience.* In the troubleshooting example just described, different engineers had different opinions of how to fix the problems. Wayland referred to a good previous solution and used that as a basis for its recommendations.

2. *Wayland saves engineers' time.* Less time needs to be spent altering dies or changing parameters.

3. *Wayland reduces scrap.* Fewer bad castings are made, because the parameters are more often correct.

4. *Wayland produces accurate estimates.* This could be done before, but only by expending engineers' time on a very speculative exercise. The foundry can now produce more competitive tenders in a fiercely competitive market.

Perhaps the most telling item in favor of the system is that the benefits were clear enough to persuade the company to use Wayland elsewhere. The foundry where the system was first deployed is part of a group of three foundries, and the system has now been deployed in the other two. This has been done using each foundry's own case-base, as their methods of working and typical dies are different.

4.3 British Airways—CASELine

CASELine is a first-generation technology demonstrator used by British Airways (BA) to assess the potential of CBR (Magaldi 1994). CASELine assists Boeing 747-400 technical support engineers with aircraft fault diagnosis and repair between aircraft arrival and departure. It advises on past defects and known successful recovery and repair procedures.

4.3.1 *The Problem*

Commercial aircraft spend the majority of their time in service, since it is only when in flight that they are earning money. Airline schedules are very tight, and a typical turnaround time (i.e., the time it takes a plane to land, unload passengers, refuel, take on new crew and passengers), even for long-haul flights, may only be one hour. If a plane's takeoff is delayed because of a fault, it can cost the airline $1,500 per minute. For lengthy delays, all the passengers may have to be put up in a hotel or even be offered alternative flights on competing airlines. Consequently, management wants to minimize any delays caused by maintenance requirements. This is, however, balanced against the overriding safety responsibility the airline is under.

When a fault in a Boeing 747-400 is detected or suspected, either by automatic monitoring equipment or the pilots, details are transmitted to ground staff (Figure 4-4). The plane may only be scheduled to be on the runway for one hour, during which time engineers have to identify the cause of the fault and effect repair. This is complicated, because defects are often obscure and have complex and inconsistent causes. To delay the plane will disrupt schedules and cost thousands of dollars per minute. To let the plane take off with an unresolved fault could potentially have catastrophic consequences.

4.3.2 *Implementation*

CASELine is implemented in Cognitive Systems' ReMind (this software is described in Chapter 6). Users can input diagnostic information and control the search for available repair and recovery information. In early 1994, the system contained around 200 cases describing previous failure instances and details of successful recovery actions.

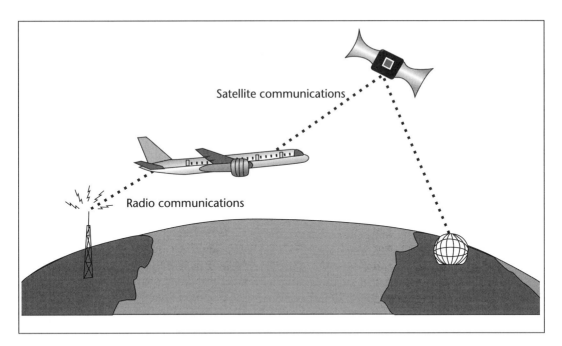

Figure 4-4. *Fault descriptions are relayed to the ground*

Three main search modes are provided by CASELine:

1. *ATA Chapter.* A simple two-digit number referring to a fault in the plane's maintenance manual
2. *EICAS Message.* A precise but variable-length alphanumeric text indicating a fault
3. *Reported Defect.* A variable-length string describing a fault

These can be used alone or together for case retrieval using either nearest-neighbor or inductive retrieval. CASELine helps engineers identify procedures that have the highest likelihood of success. The engineer is still obliged to use the aircraft maintenance manuals as a final authority and to follow approved procedures. But CASELine does reduce costly delays by cutting out less productive routes to fault finding and analysis.

4.3.3 *Impact*

Initial assessment by BA states:

> CBR has a set of in-built capabilities that complement a specific range of engineering problems. These are by nature, often more than just technical in origin, and require an awareness of many competing human, organizational and operational factors when posing solutions.
>
> —Magaldi 1994

In particular, BA identifies three benefits of CBR:

1. CBR is intuitive to both developers and users.
2. CBR complements human reasoning and problem solving.
3. CBR retains the rich context of a problem situation—it discards nothing but simply indexes on different features of what it stores.

The latter point is of particular legal interest. If a rule-based diagnostic system were developed, its rules would represent distilled abstract knowledge. The original reasons why a rule was created may become obscured with time. However, cases are always heavily contextualized. If, following an accident, BA were sued for negligence, the company could, using CASELine, demonstrate that engineers had followed procedures that had proved successful in a past case—a simple and honest defense. However, if BA used a rule-based system, expert witnesses would have to prove that each rule in the system was *theoretically* correct. This is a much more complex legal defense, because other expert witnesses would be found who would counter and question the evidence.

British Airways now reports that CASELine is being extended to cover the maintenance of Concorde. This is a critical system since the Concorde supersonic aircraft is only operated by two airlines (British Airways and Air France), the planes are 20 years old, only a few of the planes were ever built, and consequently expertise in maintaining them is scarce. CASELine will act as a repository of knowledge about known faults of Concorde and their resolution.

4.4 Deloitte & Touche—Top Management Fraud

Deloitte & Touche is a multinational firm of accountants. News headlines over the last decade have been full of instances of senior management defrauding their own companies. Recent figures indicate that fraud accounts for around £25 million ($39.25 million) lost per day in the U.K. economy, while business crime in the United States is predicted to exceed $200 billion by the year 2000. In South Africa, the total estimated losses due to white-collar crime for the year ending October 1994 exceeded R375 billion ($85 billion). This is larger than the gross domestic product of the country. As auditors, Deloitte & Touche may be legally liable if they give a company a clean bill of health only to later have fraud discovered. This section describes the implementation of the Top Management Fraud Diagnostic Tool (TMFDT), a CBR system that helps auditors assess the likelihood of top management fraud occurring within a company.

The TMFDT system was designed to enhance decision making during auditing by acting as a stimulus and counterpoint to the auditors. The system provides auditors with access to cases that have specific similarities to the situation in question. In addition, users can accelerate their learning and gather more experience in making judgments by navigating through individual cases or clusters of cases.

Audit judgment may in part be dependent on specific psychological biases. The fact that auditors' experiences are often different could explain why there are many situations in which auditors have difficulty in making judgments. For example, according to a senior official of the U.K. Serious Fraud Office, in a sample of fraud cases, misstatements were not detected in approximately 90% of instances, mainly because auditors failed to consider a wider and more accurate picture of the businesses concerned. Judgment in auditing is a complex balancing act, aggregating and weighing many pieces of evidence. It is not the application of a set of rules or the result of a series of calculations. For all these reasons, the creation of a CBR system for auditing with particular reference to fraud was challenging.

4.4.1 *Implementation*

The TMFDT system was implemented using ReMind from Cognitive Systems and involved a considerable amount of knowledge engineering. This is an example of where a single database or repository of cases was not available and so could not be simply converted into a case-base. Deloitte & Touche started by issuing a questionnaire to experienced auditors from Europe, America, and the Far East. The questionnaire asked auditors to identify factors that may indicate the likelihood of fraud or that conversely may indicate that fraud was not likely.

The list of factors were collated and presented back to the auditors, to see if they agreed or disagreed with their colleagues' opinions, and to prompt them for more factors. This process continued in iterative cycles until a consensus was reached. This Deloitte & Touche named *feature stabilization*, that is, the feature set of the case-base had ceased to grow and they had found a stable set of case features.

Once around 160 case features were identified, several hundred audit cases were obtained from the company's global business. These were not all cases where fraud had occurred. Many were cases that looked suspicious but were legal. The auditors who dealt with these cases were asked to fill in a questionnaire and rank each case feature from 1 to 6. A score of 1 indicated that they had found no evidence that the feature was true, while 6 indicated they were certain it was true.

Features in the questionnaire asked for value judgments such as

- Is the chief executive officer domineering?
- Does a senior executive have a very expensive hobby (e.g., yacht racing, horse racing, art collecting)?
- Has a senior executive repeatedly transferred funds from account to account or country to country without an obvious business rationale?

Once the questionnaires were completed, the information was entered into ReMind and the system was ready for use. It is important to recognize that TMFDT does not provide the auditor with a probability of fraud, such as "There is a 72.5% probability that fraud has occurred." This would be misleading, so instead the system prompts the auditors for information and encourages them to examine the company more critically. The system then retrieves similar cases, some of which were fraudulent and some of which were not. This questions the assumptions of the auditors, encouraging them to consider different alternatives. Ultimately, the auditors are responsible for making an evaluation of the likelihood of fraud, not the system.

4.4.2 *Evaluation*

Before fielding the system, Deloitte & Touche performed evaluative tests on it. The first of these involved establishing the precision of the system. This used two factors:

precision (proportion of retrieved items that are relevant) $= \dfrac{\text{hits retrieved}}{\text{number retrieved}}$

noise (complement of precision) $= \dfrac{\text{waste retrieved}}{\text{number retrieved}}$

Thus, *precision* was a measure of how many correct cases were retrieved, while *noise* was a measure of how many incorrect cases were retrieved. Since ReMind provides both nearest-neighbor and inductive indexing, both methods were evaluated. The evaluation was performed by removing a case from the case-base and using it as a target case. This was repeated with different cases 100 times.

- *Nearest-neighbor results:* In 79% of cases the first nearest neighbor to the target case was a similar case (either fraud or nonfraud). For all the test cases, at least one similar case to the target case was retrieved among its 10 nearest neighbors. The number of *hits* (i.e., similar cases to the target case within the 10 nearest neighbors) was 65%.

  Noise (i.e., cases that differ in type to the target case within the 10 nearest neighbors) was 35%.

  Thus, using the nearest-neighbor analysis, the auditor would have nearly an 80% chance of finding that the first case retrieved was similar in outcome to the target case.

- *Inductive results:* Since inductive retrieval does not provide a degree of similarity, it was not possible to identify the first matching case. However, the number of hits (i.e., similar cases to the target case) within the set retrieved was 67%. Noise (i.e., the number of misses) was 33%.

  Thus, using inductive retrieval the auditor user has a 67% chance of retrieving a similar case.

4.4.3 *User Evaluation*

Having confirmed in the laboratory that the system could perform
well, the views of auditors were then sought. This involved preparing
a questionnaire that was completed by auditors who used the system.
The questionnaire covered users' views about TMFDT as a technical
system and about TMFDT's impact on people and the organization.

Regarding TMFDT as a technical system, users responded as follows:

- Using cases for fraud detection was considered to be both flexible and appealing.

- The system was seen to help the diagnosis of TMF.

- Decisions taken on the basis of its findings appeared more consistent than in the past. However, users have problems in understanding the technology.

- The system's output was perceived as comprehensive and an appropriate way to justify users' decision making.

- Overall, users felt that the system complemented other existing
  systems in tackling the diagnosis of TMF.

TMFDT's impact on the social system (both people and organization) was judged as follows:

- Both management support and staff involvement in the project
  was felt to be positive and important.

- Users recognized that TMFDT contains expert knowledge.

- TMFDT does not contribute to decreasing the workload and does
  not have any significant impact on people's esteem.

- It was felt that both experienced and novice users could learn
  from the system.

- TMFDT also helps the organization keep up with the changes in
  the TMF field.

- Internally, it was felt that the innovative, or high-tech, corporate
  culture of the company was not significantly affected by TMFDT,
  but the system does reinforce the public image of the firm to a
  large extent.

- Finally, even if users have a modest opinion about TMFDT's impact on the firm's performance in diagnosing top management
  fraud, there was a consensus and a positive feeling that the sys-

tem was worth the investment and has strengthened the firm's competitiveness.

4.4.4 *Summary*

The TMFDT is an interesting system since it attempts to solve a problem that does not have a precise answer. The system emphasizes searching, solving, and learning issues—it is not enough for the user to have access to cases that have specific similarities to the present situation. Users are encouraged to understand the problem by navigating through individual cases or clusters of cases so that learning is supported. Although the system does not identify fraud per se, Deloitte & Touche report that it has successfully helped them identify fraud and thereby avoid potentially damaging litigation.

4.5 Summary

A continual problem in artificial intelligence has been scaling up academic demonstrators into commercial-strength applications. This chapter has shown that for CBR, unlike some techniques, this has not been a problem.

CBR has shown that it has several advantages over other techniques:

- CBR systems can be built without necessarily passing through the knowledge-elicitation bottleneck, since elicitation may become a simpler task of acquiring past cases. This is demonstrated by CLAVIER, Wayland, and CASELine. However, extensive knowledge elicitation is required for TMFDT.

- CBR systems can be built where a model does not exist. This is well demonstrated by CLAVIER, Wayland, and TMFDT.

- Implementation becomes a task of identifying relevant case features (and not necessarily understanding how these are related). This is well demonstrated by TMFDT.

- In many examples, a system can be rolled out with only a partial case-base, as happened with CLAVIER and CASELine. Indeed, with CBR, a system is never *complete,* since it will be continually growing. This removes one of the bugbears of knowledge-based systems: how to tell when a knowledge-base is complete.

- CBR systems can propose a solution quickly by avoiding the need to infer an answer from first principles each time, important in CASELine and in most help-desk situations such as those described in the next chapter.

- Individual or generalized cases can be used to provide explanations that are more satisfactory than explanations generated by chains of rules. This can be important in domains with potential legal implications, as in CASELine and TMFDT.

- CBR systems can learn by acquiring new cases, as is demonstrated by CLAVIER, Wayland, and CASELine.

- Finally, by acquiring new cases, CBR systems can grow to reflect their organization's experience. This is demonstrated by all the systems described in this chapter.

You now should have a good understanding of how CBR can be used for a range of tasks in industry. The next chapter describes three case studies of the most common use of CBR.

4.6 Further Reading

The following report provides an overview of the industrial uses of CBR:

Althoff, K-D, Auriol, E., Barletta, R., and Manago, M. (1995). *A Review of Industrial Case-Based Reasoning Tools*. Oxford: AI Intelligence.

The CLAVIER system is described in detail in the following papers:

Hennessy, D., and Hinkle, D. (1991). Initial Results from Clavier: A Case-Based Autoclave Loading Assistant. In *Proceedings of the DARPA Case-Based Reasoning Workshop*, edited by R. Bareiss. San Francisco: Morgan Kaufmann Publishing.

Hennessy, D., and Hinkle, D. (1992). Applying Case-Based Reasoning to Autoclave Loading. *IEEE Expert* 7(5), 21–26.

Hinkle, D., and Toomey, C. (1994). Clavier: Applying Case-Based Reasoning to Composite Part Fabrication. In *Innovative Applications of Artificial Intelligence* 6, 54–62. Cambridge, MA: AAAI Press / MIT Press.

The Wayland system is described in

Price, C.J., and Peglar, I.S. (1995). Deciding Parameter Values with Case-Based Reasoning. In *Progress in Case-Based Reasoning*, 122–133, edited by I. Watson. Lecture Notes in Artificial Intelligence 1020. Berlin: Springer-Verlag.

The British Airways CASELine system and other applications of CBR to aircraft maintenance are described in

Dattani, I., Magaldi, R.V., and Bramer, M.A. (1996). A Review and Evaluation of the Application of Case-Based Reasoning (CBR) Technology in Aircraft Maintenance. In *Applications and Innovations in Expert Systems IV*, 189–203, edited by A. Macintosh and C. Cooper. Oxford: SGES Publications.

Magaldi, R.V. (1994). Maintaining Aeroplanes in Time-Constrained Operational Situations Using Case-Based Reasoning. In *Advances in Case-Based Reasoning*, edited by J.-M. Haton, M. Keane, and M. Manago. Lecture Notes in Artificial Intelligence 984. Berlin: Springer-Verlag.

The TMFDT system is described in

Curet, O., and Jackson, M. (1995). Tackling Cognitive Biases in the Detection of Top Management Fraud with the Use of Case-Based Reasoning. In *Applications and Innovations in Expert Systems III*, 223–236, edited by A. Macintosh and C. Cooper. Oxford: SGES Publications.

5

CBR and Customer Service

Customer service has become very important in the competitive business environment of the 1990s and is now a multimillion-dollar industry. In increasingly competitive markets, customer satisfaction is a vital corporate objective. Key elements to increasing customer satisfaction include producing consistently high-quality products and providing high-quality customer service.

Unfortunately, as customers come to increasingly demand and expect higher quality service, the profit per unit on, for example, computer equipment is decreasing due to increased global competition. This situation is a manager's nightmare. As profit margins decrease, they are expected to increase the quality of customer service. Many companies, particularly in the computer industry, provide telephone support for their products, often through toll-free 800 numbers. Companies often provide a single national point of contact for customers, and may receive thousands of support requests daily. These telephone service centers, or help-desks (HDs), must be staffed by personnel who can provide the appropriate level of consistent support. Unfortunately, there are several major problems that managers of HDs encounter:

1. *Training.* To be effective, help-desk operators (HDOs) must have considerable knowledge of the products being supported. If a company has many product lines, HDOs must either specialize

in certain products (requiring teams of HDOs for each product line) or must have encyclopedic knowledge of all products.

2. *Retention.* HDs have a high staff turnover. This compounds the training problem, since new HDOs require extensive training but may leave the company after only a few months.

3. *New Products.* When new product lines are released, it is often impossible to train HDOs to deal with the problems of the new products. If the company knew the products had problems, it might have delayed its release. Thus, HDOs will often have to handle entirely new problems that no one in the company has anticipated. Consequently, HDs require a mechanism for retaining knowledge once a new problem has been encountered and solved.

The first two of these problems would suggest that a rule-based expert system would be an essential part of any HD. Most HDs deal with product problems, and expert systems are known to be effective at diagnostic problem solving. Thus, HDOs could use an expert system that would help them diagnose problems. The expert system via the HDO would ask questions of the customer to arrive at a successful diagnosis. The HD could be set up as shown in Figure 5-1.

Unfortunately, the third problem argues against the use of rule-based expert systems. For the expert system to diagnose a fault, it must have *knowledge* of that fault. But, for that knowledge to be included in the system, the designers of the product must already know about the fault. Therefore, it is likely that the fault would be corrected before the product was released. Rule-based reasoning systems cannot deal with unforeseen "teething problems" with new products; they can only deal with known faults.

Figure 5-1.
A help-desk using an expert system

Customer with a problem

Inexperienced HDOs use an expert system

The only way of dealing with teething problems is to let them arise, find a solution, and then update the expert system with this new knowledge. This, therefore, suggests that to support an HD, a type of expert system is required that can support diagnostic problem solving and can be easily updated when new problems and their solutions are encountered. As we have seen from previous chapters, these are exactly the characteristics of CBR. Because cases are independent of one another, whereas rules are chained together, adding a new problem and its solution is as simple as adding a new case to the case-base. Consequently, CBR is potentially an ideal technology to support help-desks and service centers.

This chapter first describes the architecture of help-desks in general, then describes one of the first successful implementations of a help-desk using CBR. The next case study shows how this technology can be automated to provide 24-hour, 365-day customer service through an unmanned help-desk on the Internet. Finally, the chapter describes the implementation of a customer support center for product ordering using CBR.

5.1 Help-Desk Architecture

Help-desks commonly come in two basic forms:

1. *Single point of contact.* All customer support calls are initially handled by a single frontline HD. If the HDO cannot successfully deal with the call, it is referred to one of several second-line HDs staffed by more experienced technical specialists. This process is referred to as *call escalation,* as in Figure 5-2.

2. *Multiple point of contact.* Customers can choose from several HDs, each specializing in a particular product or problem area (Figure 5-3).

Increasingly, there is a trend toward single-point-of-contact HDs. This trend is for two reasons:

■ A single point of contact for all support calls makes it easier for an organization to maintain management statistics on support calls.

Figure 5-2.
Single-point-of-contact help-desk

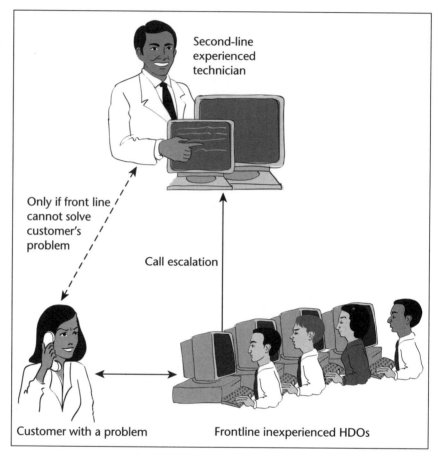

- A frontline HD acts as a filter: less-experienced HDOs can handle relatively simple problems, freeing more-experienced HDOs to deal with more complex problems. This decreases the frustrating hold time for a customer before they can speak to someone who is knowledgeable.

- Customers do not like being passed from one person to another, which is very likely with a multiple-point-of-contact help-desk.

CBR is ideally suited to supporting a single-point-of-contact help-desk, as will become apparent during the following three case studies.

Figure 5-3.
Multiple-point-of-contact help-desk

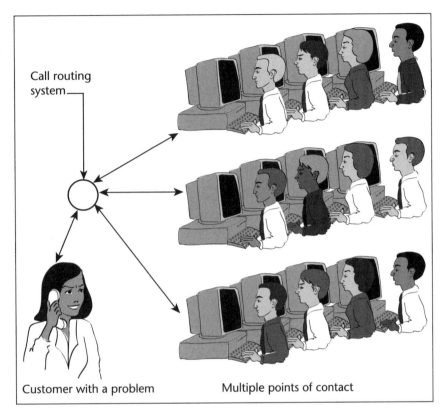

Call routing system

Customer with a problem

Multiple points of contact

5.2 The Compaq SMART System

5.2.1 The Problem

Compaq is a multibillion-dollar Fortune 500 company that manufactures personal computers, ranging from laptops to high-end server systems. Compaq has a reputation for quality, and at one point was in exactly the situation described at the beginning of this chapter, namely, having to provide better customer support while profit margins were falling dramatically due to increasing competition and decreasing margins. The company identified that customer service could differentiate it from its competitors and provide it with a competitive advantage through customer loyalty. The aim of its customer support service was to: "elate every customer by being accessible, responsive, enthusiastic, courteous, helpful, and caring."

In the early 1990s, Compaq had an automatic call-routing system that fed calls to support engineers. Each engineer had to answer the telephone, obtain caller and problem information, analyze the problem, and resolve it as shown by the work-flow diagram in Figure 5-4. To support them, the engineers used a variety of electronic and paper-based resources as well as talking with their peers.

Traditionally, Compaq had provided technical support to its network of dealerships, but not directly to individual customers. To improve its visibility to the customer, Compaq decided to deal directly with its customers. In March 1991, Compaq opened a customer support center that provided customers with direct technical support. This more than doubled the number of support requests received daily to thousands. Despite increasing staffing by 100%, Compaq realized that it needed a new system to support its engineers.

Figure 5-4.
Problem-resolution work flow (adapted from Acorn and Walden 1992)

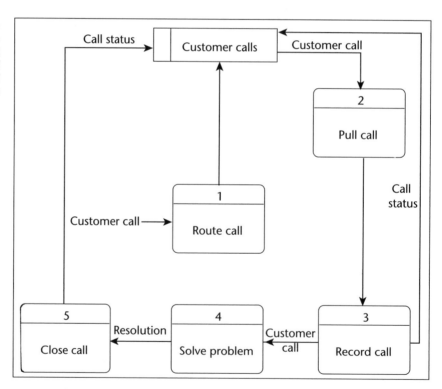

5.2.2 *The Solution*

To satisfy Compaq's strategic business aims, the customer support department had to provide

- Information at the point of need
- Continuous availability of expertise—24 hours a day, 7 days a week, and 365 days a year—regardless of who was staffing the service
- Consistent and accurate answers and responses, regardless of who took a support call
- A reduction in the need to resolve problems many times (i.e., once a new problem had been solved, the solution must be quickly made available to everyone)
- A training aid for new staff
- A method of retaining corporate knowledge

To meet these objectives, Compaq, in collaboration with Inference Corporation, developed a CBR system called Support Management Automated Reasoning Technology (SMART). SMART integrated with the existing call-routing and logging system, but it changed the work flow, as is shown in Figure 5-5. Engineers would now collect basic customer information (name, address, and so on) and log the call. They would then ask for a brief description of the problem, which they would type verbatim into the summary field of the call log. SMART uses this description of the problem to perform an initial search of the case-base. The engineer is then presented with a list of the best matching cases and questions associated with them.

The support engineer uses these questions to request additional information from the customer to define the problem better. As answers are provided, SMART performs a new search of the case-base and returns an increasingly more accurate set of relevant cases and their associated questions. Once a sufficient level of certainty is reached, the engineer can relay a solution to the customer.

Figure 5-5.
Work flow
using SMART

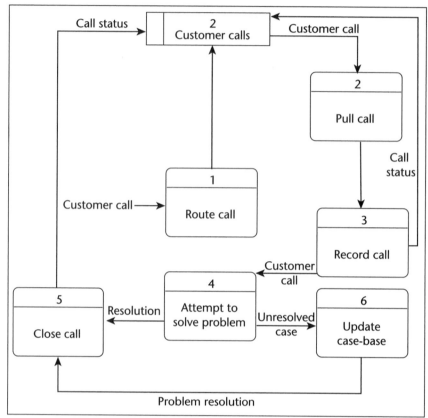

However, the real innovation of SMART was the way in which problems that could not be solved were handled. If SMART was unable to suggest a solution to a customer's problem with a sufficient degree of certainty (usually more than 70%), the call would be logged as an *unresolved case*. The call would be escalated to a second line of more experienced engineers, who would solve the problem. Once they had solved the problem, and had told the customer the solution, they would update the case-base with the new problem and its solution. In this way, problems that SMART had not encountered before could be solved and added to SMART as new cases in a controlled and incremental way. SMART could learn on the job, and knowledge was retained irrespective of which engineer took the call or solved the problem.

5.2.3 *SMART Implementation*

SMART uses a client-server architecture and had to integrate with Compaq's existing software, namely, a VAX-based call-logging system. Implemented on a corporate LAN, SMART used a Windows-based VT220 terminal emulator to move data between the call-logging application and the SMART system with Windows' dynamic data exchange. The graphical user interface was built using Asymetrix ToolBook. Various network drivers were used to exchange data between PCs running Windows, the VAX system, UNIX SCO servers, and a Banyan Vines File Server. A synchronization program, called SYNC SMART, keeps the case-bases in synch and ensures that the system never need go off-line, even when cases are being added or edited. It can be seen from Figure 5-6 that integrating the CBR software (in the top left box) into the entire system was a nontrivial task that required considerable systems-integration skills.

The SMART case-base was populated in a structured way. A decision was taken to divide the problem domain into nine partitions. Each partition was a collection of cases referring to a specific product. These were Novell, LAN Manager, Banyan Vines, UNIX, DOS, Windows, OS/2, hardware, and general software. To ensure consistency between case-bases, focusing questions were established that are used in more than one case-base. These are questions like "What operating environment are you using?"

Each case-base was built in a similar way. Designated senior engineers with different specialties were trained as *case-builders*. The list of unresolved cases was reviewed daily, and cases were assigned to case-builders based on their area of expertise. The assigned case-builder would review the information logged during the call, research the problem, and incorporate the session information into a new case complete with the problem resolution. Once the new case is saved to the case-base, it immediately becomes available to all users of SMART. This development process is very different from that of, for example, a rule-based system, since SMART went live before it had a complete and correct knowledge-base. The knowledge engineering for SMART was undertaken to a large degree while the system was operational. SMART was deployed as shown in Table 5-1.

Figure 5-6.
*SMART system
architecture
(after Acorn and
Walden 1992)*

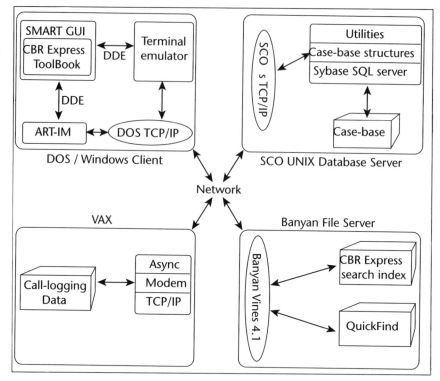

Table 5-1. The SMART rollout program

Date	Activity
August 1991	Development lab on-line to support case building
September 1991	Multiuser access available in lab
November 1991	Case-base moved to relational database; 12 case-builders on-line plus 20 additional users
December 1991	First LAN completed 50+ users
January 1992	Second LAN completed additional 50+ users

5.2.4 *Impact*

Compaq's Human Factors Organization conducted a usability test of SMART in October 1991, during its development. This showed that less than 50% of test problems were solved by engineers on their own, while 87% of these problems were solved when using SMART. Problem resolution took less than two minutes using SMART.

SMART was awarded the AAAI "Innovative Application in Artificial Intelligence Award" in 1992. SMART had increased Compaq's problem resolution from 50% to 87%. This significantly reduced the escalation of calls for support. That is, frontline HDOs were able to deal with the majority of support calls, while better-trained specialists could now deal with a smaller proportion of more difficult requests.

SMART now resolves 95% of support calls successfully, and calls take, on average, less than two minutes. Moreover, SMART has delighted the engineers, since they are proud to offer a better quality of service. Corporate knowledge can now be retained and made available to all engineers.

Compaq now views SMART as a vital part of the service it provides and is planning to release product-specific versions with its new products. This lets customers diagnose common problems without even having to call the HD. In early 1994, the new range of Compaq PCs were released with a utility called Compaq EZSearch. This lets users of Compaq PCs retrieve information from Windows Help Files by entering natural-language queries such as "the battery won't charge." Unlike the Windows Help Engine, EZSearch is not affected by spelling mistakes or typing errors (see Figure 5-7).

A recent study on the reasoning style most suited to HDs concluded that CBR techniques are likely to prove more appropriate as solutions for supporting frontline HDs than model-based systems. They found that

- CBR systems recognize the limits of their scope better than model-based systems.

- Product teething problems were handled better by CBR systems.

- CBR systems allowed the HDO a more active role, which improved the customer's perception of the HDO's competence and hence the quality of the service.

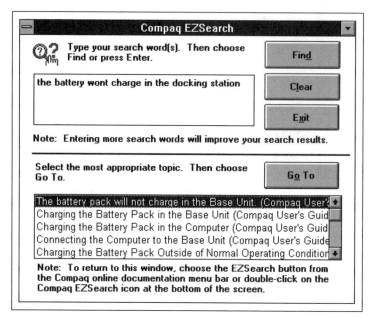

Figure 5-7.
Compaq EZSearch utility

- CBR systems are significantly easier to build and maintain than, for example, rule-based expert systems.
- CBR systems operate well across a broad range of relatively shallow problems.

However, they also concluded that while CBR should be used in preference for frontline HDs, knowledge-based systems with more understanding may be more appropriate to the more specialist work of second-line HDs.

5.3 Broderbund—The GizmoTapper

Broderbund Software is a major supplier of computer games and educational software. Its diverse line of software gives adults new skills, helps children expand their reasoning and creative abilities, and, during the process of learning, entertains users at all levels of experience. Its products include bestselling titles like MYST®, Where in the World Is Carmen Sandiego?® (Figure 5-8), The Print Shop® Deluxe, 3D Home Architect®, and KidPix® Studio. The company has a significant share of the worldwide PC multimedia market, and they recognize that customer service is vital to their continuing success.

Figure 5-8.
*Broderbund's
Carmen Sandiego*

With the launch of each successful new product, Broderbund knows the volume of support calls will rise. Broderbund's entry-level software is marketed to users who are relatively new to computers, and that means that support representatives must be able to provide extra levels of knowledge about hardware, operating systems, drivers, and so on.

5.3.1 *The Problem*

The company's support staff had been using Broderbund's own DOS-based keyword search product, called Memory Mate, as its primary technical support tool. The product had no Windows version, limited ability to accommodate a growing volume of data, and no selectivity. It retrieved every mention of a word in a problem description—whether or not it was relevant to the problem—and placed the burden on the support representative to understand the information, determine whether it was appropriate, and interpret it for the user. Even though Broderbund had abandoned further development on Memory Mate, it was all that technical support had to work with.

Users were frustrated; serious problems often took multiple calls to resolve, and the well-trained technical support staff was irritated by repeated calls about minor problems. After all, these were experienced technologists, not people trained as service representatives. They were surly, short-tempered, and occasionally insulting to the customers. If anyone attempted to manage them, they'd threaten to quit and take all their expertise with them. The company knew something had to be done quickly, because it was launching a major new PC game, called MYST, just in time for Christmas 1995.

Consequently, Broderbund knew that it would receive a large number of technical support calls on and immediately after Christmas day, as presents were unwrapped and eagerly played with. As we all know, there is nothing more irritating to a child (of whatever age) than a toy that doesn't work! This should have meant that Broderbund would need extra staff manning their help-desk during the holiday season. However, once again in collaboration with Inference Corp., they implemented an automated Internet/Web-based, 24-hour customer support center.

5.3.2 *The Solution*

Broderbund reasoned that many of its customers would have a modem and Internet access. They felt that many of these people would choose to access a Web site to obtain troubleshooting help, rather than calling an 800 number. Using Inference's CasePoint Web-Server technology (described in the following chapter), Broderbund could make its problem-resolution case-bases available directly to customers through their Internet browsers. This would be entirely automated and would leave the telephone lines free for other customers (i.e., those without Internet access).

5.3.3 *Implementation*

This groundbreaking service was implemented in December 1995 and went live on Christmas day. The system, with 3,000 cases, was rolled out in less than two months. CasePoint WebServer provides a default HTML interface (HTML is an acronym for HyperText Markup Language and is the language in which Web pages are coded). However, Broderbund felt it was important that its Web service had a look and feel that was consistent with its product range. Consequently, it implemented a graphical interface to CasePoint, called the Gizmo-Tapper™. This is shown in Figure 5-9.

Customers can answer the first question—"Which operating system are you using?"—by clicking on the icon of their OS (i.e., Macintosh, Windows 3.1, or Windows 95). Further questions are then dynamically generated by the GizmoTapper. If relevant, users can enter a description of their problem. This can be freely entered using any words they want, including spelling mistakes and typos. This process is shown in Figure 5-10. The GizmoTapper may ask more questions until a solution is found to the user's problem. In Figure 5-11, a solution to the user's error-message problem is displayed with a certainty of 94%. By following the hypertext link, the user can then easily obtain more information about the solution as is shown in Figure 5-12.

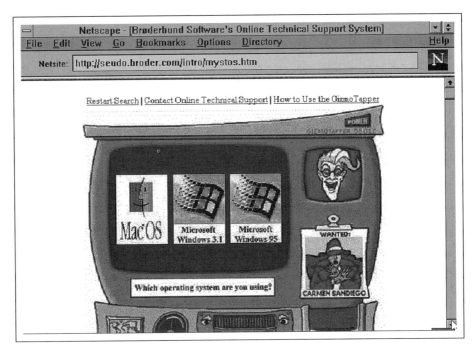

Figure 5-9.   *The GizmoTapper*

The beauty of this implementation is that the case-bases the Gizmo-Tapper uses are exactly the same as those used by the customer support representatives on the telephone lines. Thus, the service provided is consistent in both mediums. Moreover, any changes to the case-bases are immediately available to the GizmoTapper and to the telephone operator.

5.3.4   *Impact*

Before, during, and after business hours, customers can now dial into the Web, access Broderbund's case-base, type in their problem or question, respond to the automatically generated questions, and obtain the same proven resolutions recommended by the Broderbund support staff. In the first week of operation after Christmas 1995, the Web site case-base successfully answered as many after-hours inquiries as two and a half support representatives could have done.

Figure 5-10.
Entering a problem description

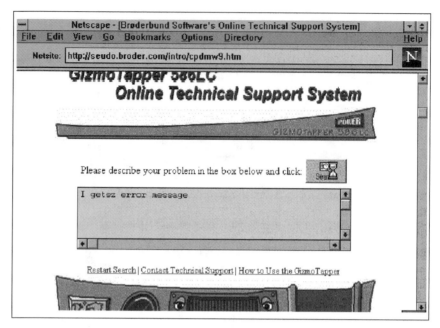

Figure 5-11.
A solution is found

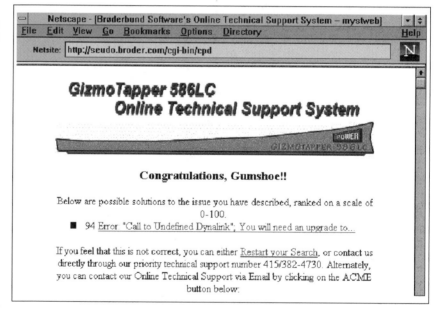

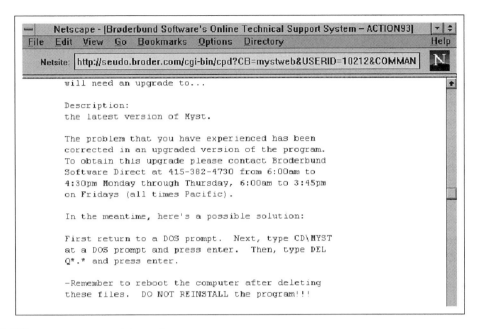

Figure 5-12. *Expanded problem solution*

Broderbund now provides a high level of customer service on demand at whatever time the customer needs it, but without the expense of extended support hours or additional personnel. Broderbund plans to make Web-based support available for each of its products. Over a year after its implementation, Broderbund estimates that the service deals with a workload approaching that of seven full-time support representatives. Consequently, the financial savings are considerable. Moreover, customers also report that they like the service and feel "in control." Doug Carlston, the chair and CEO of Broderbund, says:

> the system will empower our customers and expand their reach. . . . Resolution times are measurably faster, productivity has approximately doubled, and both the solutions and the case-base development guidelines are consistent. Inference's CasePoint WebServer will change the way companies provide customer support by using the Web to give customers direct access to information they need.

More than 20 companies now use this technology to automate their customer support via the Web, including Compaq, the pioneer of case-based customer support; LucasArts Entertainment Co.; Cisco; and 3Com. A demonstration of the CasePoint WebServer can be seen at Inference's Web site (www.inference.com).

Finally, Broderbund's innovative application of a customer support center on the Web received a "Highly Commended" award at the Voice+ Awards at the Voice Europe 1996 Exhibition in London, England, in October 1996. There is no doubt that implementing case-based support centers on the Web will become much more common in the future.

5.4 Legal & General—SWIFT

This case study focuses more on *how* the CBR system was implemented as well as *what* it does. It is intended to give you an understanding of the issues involved in successfully fielding a CBR application for customer support.

5.4.1 *The Problem*

Legal & General (L&G) is a major U.K. provider of financial services. Its IT department has an annual budget of around £60 million ($90 million). In 1993, the company was in the process of downsizing from dumb terminals attached to mainframes, to PC-based LANs. As part of a business process reengineering project, it wanted to provide a streamlined service to employees purchasing PCs, peripherals, software, or upgrades.

In 1993, buying a PC or other computer product was a complex and time-wasting process. Employees had to:

1. Ask a technical support officer to recommend a product to meet their needs

2. Obtain a price from a central register of products

3. Get their line manager to authorize the purchase

4. Place the order with the IT department

5. Wait while the IT department checked whether the product was suitable, made sure the purchase was properly authorized,

ordered the product from external suppliers, and received and configured the product

6. Finally, receive the product on their desk

This process was complicated by the fact that different technical support officers would recommend different solutions for the same requirement, and that the IT department might override the recommendation and recommend an entirely different product. Consequently, the employee might have to go back to the manager and obtain authorization for the new order and then resubmit the order. Or, in some circumstances, an employee might be expecting one product and actually receive another. Moreover, the process was too slow. Employees waited weeks for their orders. Consequently, some more impatient (or proactive) employees were obtaining equipment directly, by mail order from PC magazines or from local retail outlets. This was frustrating the company in its objective of standardizing on a hardware and software platform.

5.4.2 *The Solution*

A week was spent in April 1993 analyzing the existing process and reengineering it. This resulted in a very much simplified design, whereby all L&G's employees would have access to a single point of contact for ordering PC products and upgrades. An essential component of the reengineered process was an expert system that would contain knowledge about L&G's IT strategy, its approved product range, and the hardware/software options that different business units used.

Because of the volatile nature of the PC market, it was decided that it was essential to make the maintenance of the system as easy as possible. It was decided that the managers of the service should be able to maintain the knowledge-base themselves. Consequently, CBR was chosen as the knowledge representation that would best meet these constraints.

Inference's CBR Express and CasePoint combination, Asymetrix ToolBook, and Microsoft's Access database were chosen to develop the demonstration system. After approximately one month of prototyping, a demonstration system called SWIFT was shown at several seminars to stakeholders from business units within L&G.

These presentations were carefully organized as part of a comprehensive communications plan. They were professionally conducted

and involved describing *why* the existing process had to be reengineered and *what* benefits the new process would deliver; they concluded with a demonstration of *how* the CBR software supported the
reengineered process. These sessions were essential in obtaining the
support of the whole company for the project.

The solution was very simple. A customer service center was to be
established. L&G employees could phone the service center, state
their requirements, and obtain a recommendation and quote. The
quote would satisfy L&G's IT strategy and would be faxed back to the
employee. The employee would then obtain an authorizing signature
from a manager and fax it back to the service center, who would then
place the order with suppliers. Delivery of the order to the employee
was to be within five working days of the service center receiving the
authorized order.

5.4.3 *Implementation*

SWIFT was developed very rapidly using an expert system–development
methodology called the *Client-Centered Approach* (CCA). The CCA
combines the linear stages of the conventional *waterfall* approach to
software development with the iterative prototyping methods popular with expert system developers. The CCA explicitly encourages the
involvement of all stakeholders in a project and emphasizes the need
to consider system maintenance from the outset. The CCA has seven
deliverables:

1. A feasibility study that identifies stakeholders, benefits, costs,
   and resources

2. A concept system that illustrates the high-level functionality of
   the system—useful for obtaining resource commitment

3. A demonstrator that proves the system is technically achievable

4. A reliable system where the case-base is sufficiently complete to
   be useful

5. A usable system that addresses interface and integration issues

6. A saleable system that can be *sold* to end users or other organizational units

7. A system embedded-in-use with a managed maintenance plan

After the initial analysis phase, in April 1993, and the development
of the concept system in May 1993, an intensive system-development
stage took place. This involved establishing the required databases

and obtaining cases from different business units. As with the Compaq SMART system, the case-base was partitioned into subsections. This time the case-bases were divided into hardware and software cases.

There was no suitable database of past cases, so cases were obtained by asking representatives (usually IT specialists) from each business unit what hardware or software would be recommended to an employee of a certain grade performing a particular function in a certain office. Thus, an insurance sales representative should be offered a Toshiba T4400SX portable, with L&G's point-of-sale application preloaded, while a finance manager would require an IBM PS/2 with terminal emulation software. Each of these scenarios became a prototypical case.

If an employee had a requirement that could not be dealt with by the case-base, for example, a mathematician requiring a statistical modelling package, an unresolved case would be logged. The software would be sourced manually, and, if successful, a new case for "statistical modelling packages for mathematicians" would be added to the software case-base.

As with the Compaq SMART system, the CBR component had to integrate with existing systems and applications. Consequently, systems integration became a major part of SWIFTs installation. SWIFT had to communicate with many databases, including

- An Employee database, from which a caller's correct name, department, and location could be obtained

- A PC Audit database, so that once the employee had been identified, the equipment they currently used could be obtained to ensure compatibility with their order

- A Connectivity database, which detailed how the employee was or could be connected to the corporate LAN

- A LAN server database, which detailed which servers the employee could connect to

- A Training database, which could be used to recommend training courses if the employee was ordering unfamiliar hardware or software

- The PC Buyers Guide, a database of recommended hardware and software with current prices

- An Orders database, which recorded live orders

- A Disbursements database, which recorded payments to suppliers

In addition, the system had to link to L&G's mainframe system and its NetMan Fixed Asset Register, so that this could be automatically updated once equipment was paid for. Dynamic Data Exchange (DDE) links were also made to Delrina's WinFax software, so quotes could be automatically faxed to employees and so orders could be faxed to suppliers. The resulting architecture is shown in Figure 5-13.

At the beginning of September 1993, less than five months after the project started, the system went live. L&G rolled the system out incrementally:

1. First, it was used by selected people on selected projects and was carefully monitored, enabling bugs, technical difficulties, organizational and communication problems, and simple oversights to be solved.

2. Then, two weeks later, it was rolled out to serve the whole IT department.

3. Finally, it was rolled out, business unit by business unit, over nine months.

This phased rollout was crucial, since it allowed problems to be trapped early and avoided many of the problems associated with a big-bang approach to delivering a new system. By Christmas of 1993, SWIFT was operational across over two-thirds of L&G's business units and was judged a success.

SWIFT works by

1. Obtaining a customer's business unit and location from an employee ID number using the Employee database.

2. Obtaining the customer's current hardware and software configuration from the PC Audit database, along with their connectivity and server information from the Connectivity and LAN Server databases, respectively.

3. Asking if the inquiry is about software, hardware, or upgrades, and opening the relevant case-base.

4. Obtaining a free text query such as "I want to buy a fast modem that lets me send faxes."

5. Using that text to retrieve a set of matching cases.

6. Asking several questions to confirm which case matches best.

7. Offering a solution.

Figure 5-13.
SWIFT system architecture

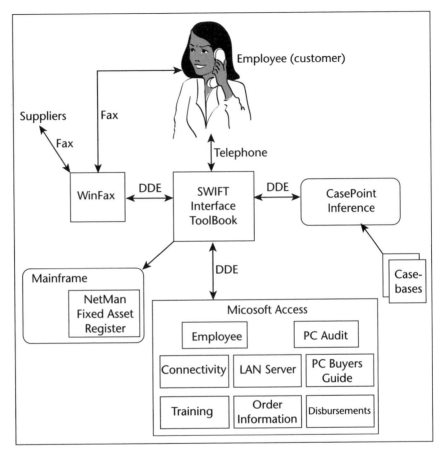

Figure 5-14 shows the interface of SWIFT, illustrating how Inference's CBR technology can be embedded. The interface is largely similar to that of CasePoint (described in the next chapter), but it has been augmented with additional features specific to the task at hand. The interface was created using ToolBook, while the CBR component is accessed via dynamic data exchange.

If the customer accepts the solution, SWIFT enters the product-ordering process and a quote is prepared and automatically faxed back to them. However, if the customer rejects the solution or if SWIFT cannot suggest a solution, a full transcript of the consultation is stored as an *unresolved case*. At a monthly meeting, managers of the service study unresolved cases to determine if existing cases need changing or if new cases are required. Recognizing that knowledge changes is particularly important in personal computing, where new products are brought out almost daily.

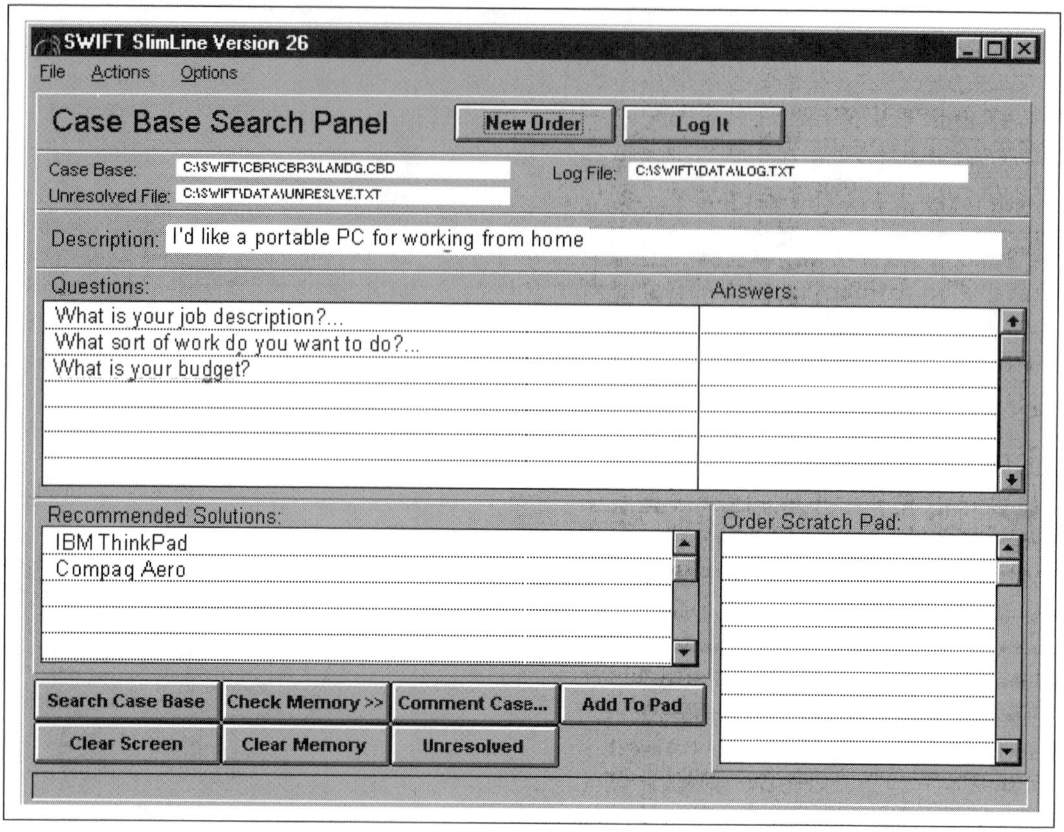

Figure 5-14. *SWIFT interface*

5.4.4 *Impact*

The SWIFT system reduced the average time to order and receive a new PC from 14 working days to 5 and was therefore judged a success. The SWIFT service desk was staffed by four full-time employees who had little or no knowledge of PC products. However, because L&G's IT strategy was encapsulated in the case-bases, they were able to offer consistent advice. Moreover, SWIFT provided L&G with a structured way of reviewing and amending their IT strategy at the monthly case-base maintenance meetings.

The L&G SWIFT system demonstrates that

- CBR systems can be developed quickly.
- CBR systems can be effectively integrated within a wider information system.
- Once established, a CBR system can be maintained by people who are not programmers.

The CCA development methodology, which was developed to assist prototyping expert systems, proved valuable in guiding the development of SWIFT. In particular, the emphasis that the CCA places on involving stakeholders in the development process and the explicit attention to system maintenance from the outset fitted the CBR paradigm well. Moreover, the ability to rapidly prototype the system within the constraints of linear milestones gave developers flexibility and project managers control.

5.5 Summary

Help-desks and customer support are definitely the most successful commercial applications of CBR and will continue to be a growth area for the foreseeable future. There are several reasons for this. CBR is ideally suited to relatively shallow, but broad, diagnostic problem solving. As was explained in Chapter 3, diagnosis is a classification problem, and CBR is suited to classification problems. Diagnostic help-desks classify a customer's problem into one of many known problems to find a solution. However, the problems they are dealing with are not usually complex and can often be successfully classified after only a few questions.

CBR also provides a methodology for capturing new problem-solving experiences, and it is the ease with which new cases can be acquired that ensures the success of the systems once they are operational. Most of the case-bases used in customer support are maintained by end users, which does not require expensive knowledge engineering. There is also another important reason for the success of CBR in help-desks; namely, the functionality and maturity of Inference's CBR software tools. These and the competition are described in the next chapter.

5.6 Further Reading

These papers describe the use of CBR by Compaq:

Acorn, T.L., and Walden, S.H. (1992). SMART: Support Management Cultivated Reasoning Technology for Compaq Customer Service. In *Innovative Applications of Artificial Intelligence 4, Proceedings of AAAI-92*, edited by Scott and Klahr. Cambridge, MA: AAAI Press / MIT Press.

Nguyen, T., Czerwinski, M., and Lee, D. (1993). Compaq QuickSource: Providing the Consumer with the Power of Artificial Intelligence. In *Innovative Applications of Artificial Intelligence 5, Proceedings of AAAI-93*, edited by Klahr and Byrnes. Cambridge, MA: AAAI Press / MIT Press.

The following papers all refer to the use of CBR in help-desks:

Allen, B. (1994). Case-Based Reasoning: Business Applications. *Communications of the ACM*, 37(3), 40–42.

Borron, J., Morales, D., and Klahr, P. (1996). Developing and Deploying Knowledge on a Global Scale. In *Innovative Applications of Artificial Intelligence 8, Proceedings of AAAI-96*. Cambridge, MA: AAAI Press / MIT Press.

Dearden, A.M. and Bridge, D.G. (1993). Choosing a Reasoning Style for a Knowledge-Based System: Lessons from Supporting a Help Desk. *The Knowledge Engineering Review*, 8(3): 210–222.

Klahr, P. (1996). Global Case-Based Development and Deployment. In *Advances in Case-Based Reasoning*, 519–530, edited by I. Smith and B. Faltings. Lecture Notes in Artificial Intelligence 1168. Berlin: Springer-Verlag.

McCarthy, D. (1994). Automation of Help Desks Using Case-Based Reasoning. In *Proc. IEE Colloquium on Case-Based Reasoning: Prospects for Applications*, Digest No: 1994/057, 9/1–9/3.

Simoudis, E. (1992). Using case-based Reasoning for Customer Technical Support. *IEEE Expert 7(5)*, 7–13.

Simoudis, E., and Miller, J.S. (1991). The Application of CBR to Help Desk Applications. In *Proceedings of the DARPA Workshop on Case-Based Reasoning*, edited by R. Bareiss. San Francisco: Morgan Kaufmann Publishers.

Two papers describing the Client-Centered Approach development methodology, used by Legal & General to develop SWIFT:

Watson, I., Basden, A., and Brandon, P.S. (1992). A Client Centred Approach to the Development of Expert Systems. *Expert Systems*, 9(4), 181–188.

Watson, I., Basden, A., and Brandon, P.S. (1992). A Client Centred Approach to the Maintenance of Expert Systems. *Expert Systems*, 9(4), 189–196.

Another paper describing a methodology used to develop a CBR system:

Kitano, H., and Shimazu, H. (1996). The Experience Sharing Architecture: A Case Study in Corporate-Wide Case-Based Software Quality Control. In *Case-Based Reasoning: Experiences, Lessons, & Future Directions*, edited by D.B. Leake. Cambridge, MA: AAAI Press / MIT Press.

6

CBR Software Tools

Cognitive scientists might argue that the current surge in interest in CBR is due to the intuitive nature of CBR and because it closely resembles human reasoning. Software vendors might argue that it is because CBR tools have made the theory practically feasible. There is truth in both views, but certainly the tools have made a contribution. This section reviews the main CBR tools currently available. It concludes with a brief description of other CBR tools.

6.1 ART*Enterprise

ART*Enterprise is the latest incarnation of Brightware's flagship development product. Brightware, based in California, was formerly a division of Inference Corporation, one of the oldest established vendors of AI tools and the major player in the CBR tool market. Brightware markets ART*Enterprise as an integrated, object-oriented, applications development tool, designed for MIS developers and offering a variety of representational paradigms, including

- A procedural programming language
- Objects supporting multiple inheritance, encapsulation, and polymorphism

- Rules
- Cases

This is all packaged with a GUI (Graphical User Interface) builder, sophisticated version control facilities, and an impressive ability to link to data repositories in most proprietary DBMS formats for developing client-server applications. Moreover, ART*Enterprise offers cross-platform support for most operating systems, windowing systems, and hardware platforms (i.e., you can develop on one platform and deliver to others).

The CBR component in ART*Enterprise is essentially the same as that in CBR3, marketed by Inference (this functionality is reviewed below, in Section 6.5). However, because developers have direct access to the CBR functionality, ART*Enterprise is much more controllable than CBR3. With ART*Enterprise, it is possible to create complex hierarchical case-representations and to finely control case indexing and retrieval strategies (Watson and Perera 1995).

In conclusion, ART*Enterprise is perhaps the ideal tool for embedding CBR functionality within a corporate-wide information system. Although the CBR functionality itself is more limited than some tools (i.e., cases are flat attribute:value pairs and there is no support for inductive indexing), the proven knowledge representational abilities of ART make it an excellent tool for performing complex case adaptation. Although ART*Enterprise is available on the PC platform running Windows NT or Windows 95, it is very demanding on resources. A fast Pentium with a minimum of 32MB of RAM is required.

(*Note:* ART-IM, an older product, has similar CBR and knowledge representational functionality to ART*Enterprise but lacks the data integration, GUI builder, and version control features.)

6.2 Case-1

Case-1 is a CBR tool from Astea International (a beta release of version 1.0 was reviewed). The company has a background in providing integrated sales, support, and service systems. Case-1 was obviously developed with Inference's CBR product in mind, and it shares many of its features. Cases are represented as free-form text describing a problem, a set of weighted questions that can confirm or reject a case, and a set of solutions. As with Inference's tool, cases can be authored by people who have no programming experience (see Figure 6-1).

Figure 6-1.
Case-1 developer interface

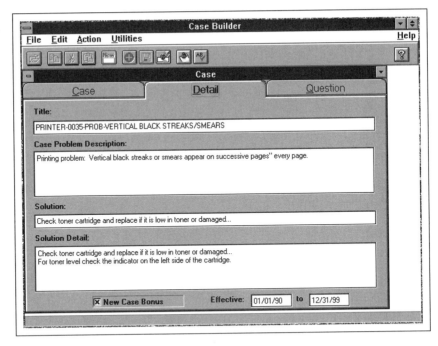

Cases are stored in a relational database, and the interface is developed using Visual Basic (Case-1 runs under MS Windows). The product is not as mature as CBR3 and does not seem to offer any significant functional improvements. However, the tool is well integrated with Astea's PowerHelp customer support tools.

6.3 CaseAdvisor

CaseAdvisor is marketed by Sententia Software at Simon Frazier University in Canada. It is another clone of Inference's CBR product. There are three components to the software: CaseAdvisor Authoring, the case-authoring environment; CaseAdvisor Problem Resolution, the runtime case-retrieval engine; and CaseAdvisor WebServer, a utility to use case-bases on the Web.

CaseAdvisor Authoring (Figure 6-2) is a very simple tool, similar in look to Inference's CBR Express versions 1 and 2. The case author is presented with a syntax-free environment for entering the details of a case's name, description, solution, and confirming questions.

Figure 6-2.
*The CaseAdvisor
authoring
interface*

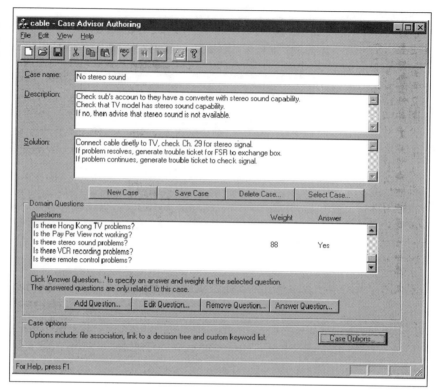

A new case is created by entering its name, description, and solution details and by assigning questions to it to confirm it (note that questions cannot be used to reject a case from consideration as in CBR3). Questions are assigned an importance weighting from Low to High; these qualitative terms are mapped to a 0-to-100 range (see Figure 6-3). Cases can also have attachments that can support text and multimedia files and are viewed through Netscape.

In addition to CBR, CaseAdvisor lets the user create simple diagnostic decision trees. These can be used in conjunction with the CBR system at any point during a diagnosis to lead the user through a series of diagnostic steps. (See Figure 6-4.) The decision trees are created by using a simple textual interface that moves the author through the tree step by step (i.e., answer by answer). It would perhaps be more useful if this feature had been implemented using a graphical representation of the decision tree. (CaseAdvisor Author version 2.1 was reviewed.)

Figure 6-3.
CaseAdvisor question weighting

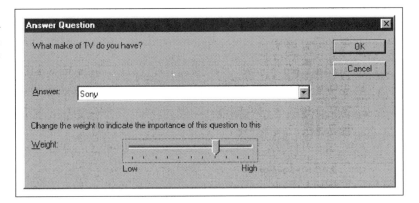

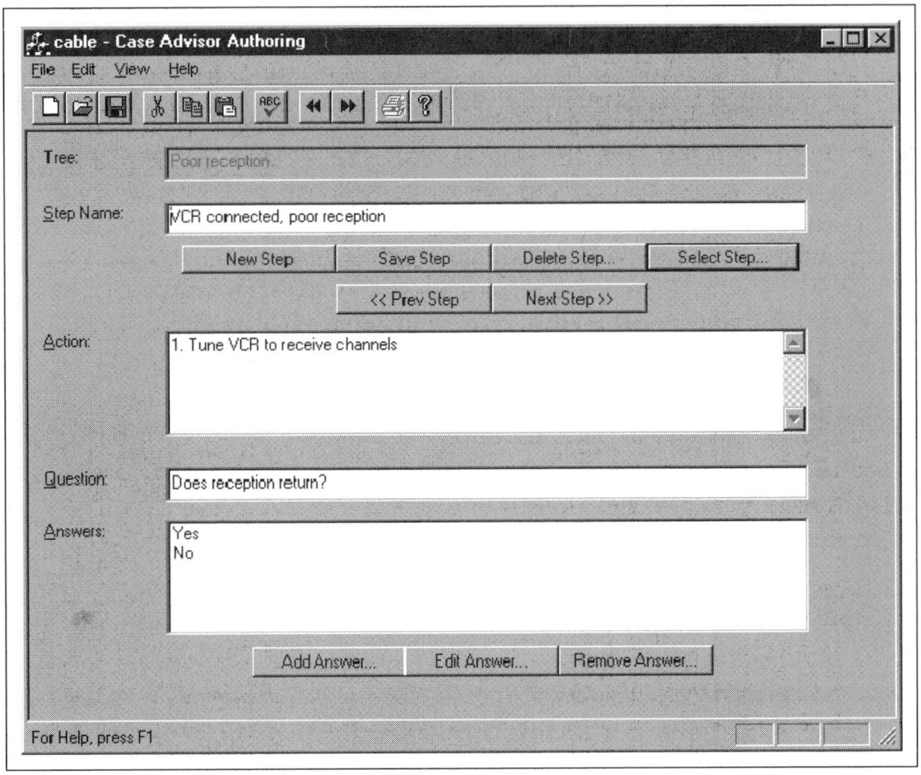

Figure 6-4. *CaseAdvisor decision tree editor*

CaseAdvisor Problem Resolution (Figure 6-5) requires Netscape to operate, since this is used to display solutions (at the time of the review, MS Internet Explorer was not supported). Once again the interface of the retrieval system is similar to that of Inference's Case-Point, with the screen being divided into three sections: problem description, questions, and solution.

Figure 6-5.
CaseAdvisor
Problem
Resolution
interface

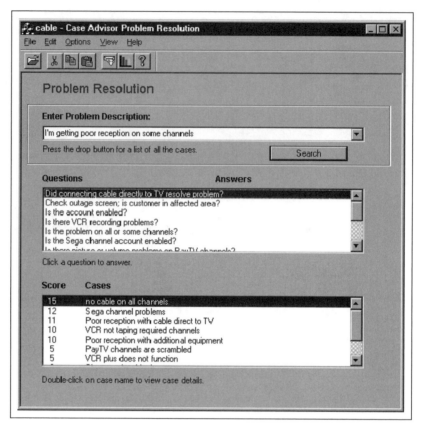

The user types in a description of the problem, and CaseAdvisor matches this against the cases in the case-base. Questions are then displayed to help the user focus on a particular case from the retrieved set of cases. Once a diagnosis is confirmed (by a suitably high case score), clicking on a case in the lower panel will launch Netscape to display the solution details and associated decision trees if required. The diagnostic decision trees are navigated by using the hypertext links of the Web browser (see Figure 6-6). (CaseAdvisor Problem Resolution version 2.1 was reviewed.)

CaseAdvisor WebServer is a CGI or Java interface to case-bases that integrate with standard Web-server software running on Windows NT and UNIX (Sun Solaris). This product was not reviewed, but a demonstration can be used on the Web at Sententia's Web site (www.cs.sfu.ca/cbr/).

Figure 6-6.
Case solution and decision tree

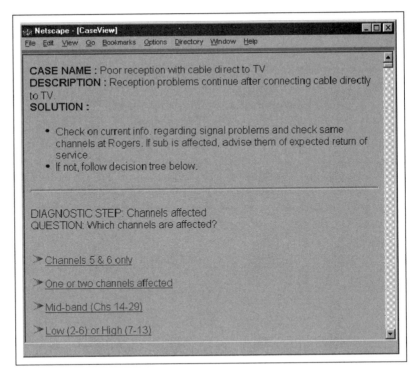

In conclusion, CaseAdvisor is an easy-to-use product that owes a lot in terms of look and feel to Inference's products. It is not as powerful or robust as CBR3 and does not offer as many features. However, it is cheaper than Inference's products and would be suitable for simple case-based diagnostic systems. Version 3.0 promises a C++ programming interface, compatibility with ODBC databases (including Oracle, Sybase, Microsoft SQL Server, Access, etc.), and compatibility with Inference's prepackaged case-bases.

6.4 CasePower

Formerly called Induce-it, Inductive Solutions' CasePower builds its cases within the spreadsheet environment of Microsoft Excel. CasePower is a specialized tool for constructing Excel spreadsheets that can be analyzed using CBR. Within the limited confines of Excel, it provides basic CBR functionality, mainly suitable for numeric applications. Symbolic data can be represented as ordered hierarchies that are mapped to numerical ranges. However, for more complex nonnumerical applications, another CBR tool would be preferable.

CasePower uses nearest-neighbor retrieval and it reduces search time by calculating an index for each case off-line. This can be a lengthy process for a large case-base, but it does reduce retrieval times considerably. The system simply calculates the index for the new case and compares it against the precalculated case-base index. If a new case is to be retained, the entire index must be recalculated. Adaptation can be performed using Excel formulas and macros. Similarly, all the other features of Excel are available, such as graphing, reporting, and dynamic data exchange to other applications.

6.5 CBR3 (CBR Express, CasePoint, Generator, Tester, and CasePoint WebServer)

Produced by Inference Corp., the CBR3 family of products are certainly the most successful and mature CBR products to date, with more than 500,000 end users in 22 countries. CBR3 is specifically tailored to the vertical market of customer support help-desks. The customer support help-desk is becoming an increasingly common feature in the 1990s, and managers of such services face similar problems:

- For a help-desk to be useful, staff require training.
- Training takes time and money.
- Manning a help-desk is not the best job in the world, so staff turnover is high.

Where expertise is scarce, conventional wisdom tells us an expert system is useful. However, as was pointed out in the previous chapter, there is an additional problem. Customer help-desks often deal with technical faults. To implement a rule-based expert system, you need to know the faults and their solutions. But if the manufacturer knew there was a fault, it probably wouldn't release the product. Thus, help-desks often must deal with faults that designers and engineers have not envisaged, and consequently the solutions could not be in the rule-base.

This is where CBR systems offer a solution. Through the application of the CBR-cycle, including case retention (i.e., learning), newly identified faults and their solutions can be added as new cases as they arise (this is simpler than adding new rules). CBR3 applies the CBR-cycle very successfully to the help-desk scenario and is currently the market leader for knowledge-based help-desk software.

The CBR3 family of tools have the following roles:

- CBR Express is the development or authoring environment for case-bases.

- CasePoint is a memory-efficient search engine for case-bases developed using CBR Express.

- Generator is a tool that automates the creation of cases-bases from existing collections of text files, such as technical support literature.

- Tester is a tool that provides a variety of metrics for case-base developers using CBR3.

- CasePoint WebServer is a tool that supports the functionality of CasePoint on the Internet, enabling call centers to be set up on the World Wide Web.

A beta release of CBR3 was reviewed (R3 Beta A5), and the final release is due in 1997. CBR3 represents a complete rewrite of the previous product suite, CBR2. In particular, the development environment, CBR Express, has undergone a total transformation. Additional functionality for case retrieval and feedback have also been included.

CBR3 uses a simple case structure of records that are stored in a relational database (Raima by default, but Microsoft SQL Server, Sybase SQL Server, Oracle, and Informix are also supported). Cases comprise a title, a description, a set of weighted questions (effectively attribute:value pairs), and a set of actions. CBR3 is network-ready, and case-bases can be shared across an organization's network.

A report on a sample case from CBR3 that diagnoses faults in laser printers is shown in Figure 6-7. However, developers using CBR3 do not interact with it programmatically, but rather through the excellent interface of CBR Express (Figure 6-8). CBR Express deals with all programming elements in case creation or editing, resulting in a syntax-free environment that lets people without programming experience quickly develop case-bases.

Figure 6-7.
*CBR3 case
exported as
a report*

```
BEGIN CASE CASE11
   TITLE
      Ink cartridge is damaged, causing black stains.
   DESCRIPTION
      Stains appear as small, round, black dots that
      occur on front or back of page.
      Sometimes wide inconsistent stains appear.
   QUESTIONS
      Are you having print quality problems?
         ANSWER  : Yes
         SCORING : (-)
      What does the print quality look like?...
         ANSWER  : Black Stains
         SCORING : (default)
      Does cleaning the printer with cleaning paper
      remove problem?
         ANSWER  : No
         SCORING : (default)
   ACTIONS
      Check toner cartridge and replace if it is low in
      toner or damaged...
   BROWSE TEXT
   CREATION     29/7/91 14:19:22
   LAST_UPDATE 29/7/91 14:19:22
   LAST_USED   29/7/91 14:19:22
   STATUS ACTIVE
END CASE
```

CBR3 uses nearest-neighbor matching to retrieve cases by matching a user's free text query against the title and descriptions of cases in the case-base. A key feature of CBR3 is its ability to handle free-form text. This was felt to be vital to the help-desk market since it lets customers describe their problems in their own words rather than being taken through a decision tree–style question-and-answer session.

CBR3 ignores such words as "and", "or", "I", "there", and so on. It can use synonyms, and represents words as a set of trigrams. For example, the trigram for *cartridge* is: CAR, ART, RTR, TRI, RID, IDG, DGE. The use of trigrams means that CBR3 is very tolerant of spelling mistakes and typing errors such as letter transpositions. The trigrams for *ca*r*tridge* and *cat*r*ridge* will still match closely. Although there are obvious problems with this lexical approach (such as not recognizing negative statements), it is nonetheless surprisingly powerful and very useful for CBR3's market.

Figure 6-8.
*CBR Express
developer's
interface*

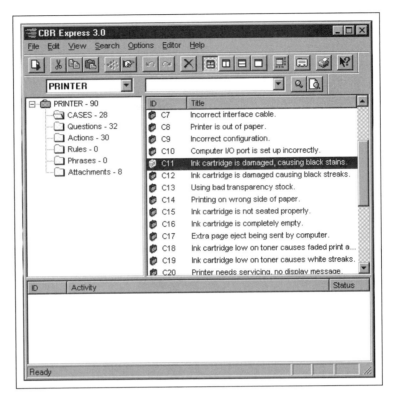

The interface of CBR Express 3.0 has been completely reimplemented from the previous version and now provides an interface that better supports case authoring. A case is now represented using a folder structure, similar to that of the Windows 95 Explorer, that provides easy access to cases and their associated questions, rules, actions, and attachments.

Individual editors are used to edit a case's components (the Case Editor is shown in Figure 6-9). The editors now all support drag-and-drop, and creating a case can be as simple as dragging the appropriate questions and actions onto the Case Editor. The process of editing cases is described in detail in the next chapter. A significant new feature is that cases can now inherit features from other cases. This lets the developer define an important question once and then define a subset of cases that all include that question. The interface also allows the developer to edit more than one case-base at once and to arrange case-bases into hierarchies. In this way, large case-bases can be efficiently structured and navigated.

Figure 6-9.
*CBR Express
Case Editor*

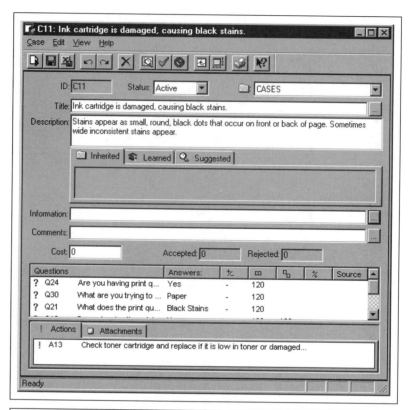

Figure 6-10.
*CasePoint
interface*

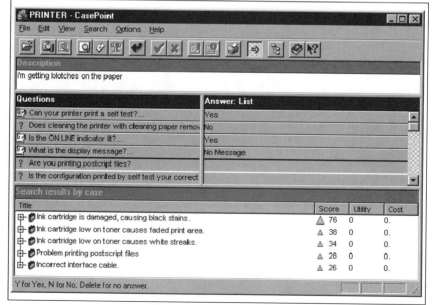

Searching a case-base is done using CasePoint, which examines a user's free-form text entry and matches it against case titles and descriptions (Figure 6-10). This results in the retrieval of a set of cases. A list of ranked solutions with likelihood values is generated from the cases, and the user is offered these along with a set of questions. Answers to these questions help narrow the number of cases that match, leading to a more accurate solution that is then presented to the user. In the event a solution is not reached (CBR3 has a customizable threshold value) or is not satisfactory, the CBR-cycle is closed by using the concept of an *unresolved case* (Case-1 has borrowed this concept from Inference). An unresolved case either saves the entire transcript of the consultation to a file or e-mails the case-base administrator. The administrator can subsequently find out what that case's solution was and modify the unresolved case to create a new case.

If you want to integrate or embed CBR3, it is probably more efficient to use CasePoint as a DDE server application (it is also now available as a DLL and as an API). A criticism of nearest-neighbor matching is that if a case-base is large with many features, it is not an efficient process. However, the algorithm that CasePoint uses is extremely fast, so retrieval time remains almost constant as case-base size increases. CasePoint also supports the use of rules that identify keywords in the query text and automatically answer certain questions. It can also order questions so that they best discriminate between cases under consideration and rank cases either by their utility (i.e., how useful a solution might be) or by their cost (i.e., how costly a solution might be).

Generator (see Figure 6-11) is an application that can parse text files (ASCII, MS Word, RTF, HTML, and Windows Help Files) to deduce their content and create cases that index them. It can be used as a document-retrieval system or as a means of semiautomatically generating a case-base from existing technical documentation.

CBR Express Tester (see Figure 6-12) helps the case-base designer evaluate the quality of cases in a case-base. It is worthwhile noting that Inference is the only company to take the testing of case-bases seriously by providing comprehensive tool support for this vital activity. CBR Express Tester provides both static and dynamic analyses of a case-base. The Tester module can split a case-base into smaller subsets of cases, which can subsequently be imported into new case-bases.

Figure 6-11.
*The Generator
interface*

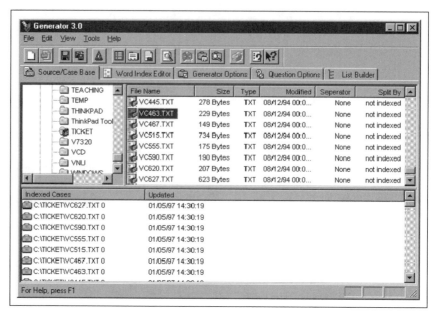

Figure 6-12.
*CBR Express
Tester Module*

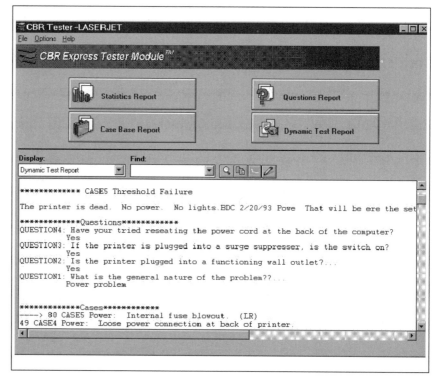

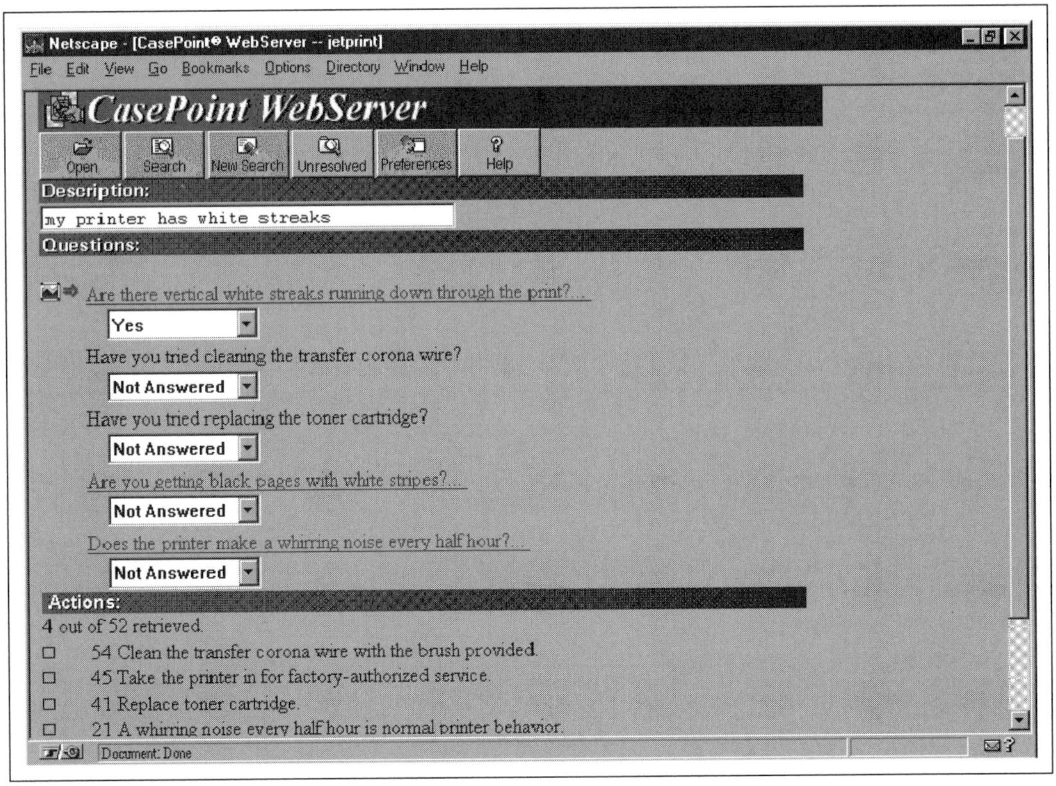

Figure 6-13. *CasePoint WebServer*

CasePoint WebServer (see Figure 6-13) is a CGI interface to CBR3 case-bases. Through an HTML interface, it provides access to the same functionality as CasePoint. This lets an organization make its case-bases available through the World Wide Web to a wider audience of users and extend customer service to 24-hour, 7-day coverage without a significant increase in staffing costs.

CasePoint WebServer uses HTML to provide the interface to the case-base. It allows screen customization to support a corporate Web style (as was shown in the Broderbund case study). It integrates with most standard Web server software (Solaris, NT, HP-UX, and OS/2) and allows centralized content management for global case-bases. The architecture is organized into three main parts: CasePoint Driver, CasePoint Server, and CasePoint Search Engine. Application developers use the usual security features of their HTTP server to prevent unauthorized access to case-bases, while the WebServer software has built-in security to allow the developer to restrict access to a list of users.

Inference has recently formed a Knowledge Publishing Division that retails shrinkwrapped case-bases (Case Solutions, as they term them). These include case-bases for troubleshooting Windows 95, general PC diagnostics, and case-bases for common software applications such as Microsoft Office. These let groups such as internal IT support centers provide case solutions "out of the box." These case-bases can then be customized and extended to reflect local differences.

In conclusion, Inference's CBR products are deservedly market leaders. Their range of products are mature, robust, and well suited to their market. CBR3 is a significant improvement over CBR2 in terms of functionality and ease of use. It is consequently no surprise that other vendors have copied the look and feel of these products (imitation is after all the sincerest form of flattery). The technical excellence of these products, combined with Inference's experience of developing and delivering business solutions and their strong global presence, makes CBR3 the product of choice for any serious organization wanting to develop a case-based customer support service. The next chapter describes in detail how CBR3 can be used to develop a simple diagnostic system.

6.6 Eclipse—The Easy Reasoner

Eclipse from Haley Enterprises is a close relative of ART. The forward-chaining functionality of ART, written in Lisp, was reimplemented in C by NASA, entering the public domain as the language CLIPS. In the late 1980s, Paul Haley, the former chief scientist of Inference Corp., developed a new ART-like language compatible with CLIPS. This became Eclipse.

Like ART, Eclipse offers objects, only this time fully compatible C++ objects, and optimized forward chaining using the Rete algorithm. Eclipse is available for the DOS operating system, MS Windows, UNIX platforms, and certain mainframe environments.

The Easy Reasoner is a C library supplied with Eclipse that provides CBR functionality. The Easy Reasoner provides nearest-neighbor and inductive retrieval of records in a database. Once records have been retrieved, they can be asserted as Eclipse objects for adaptation by its rule-base. Eclipse supports the usual range of variable types and offers similar text-handling facilities to ART (i.e., ignoring noise words and using trigrams to cope with spelling mistakes). Interestingly, Eclipse also uses *stems* to identify, for example, that "magnetically" and "magnetic" all stem from "magnet."

Eclipse does not provide a development environment like ART*Enterprise, but it can integrate data from disparate, heterogeneous databases. But, for an experienced C++ programmer, Eclipse may offer some advantages—it is extremely fast, and it can be embedded within a C++ application. (The product reviewed was Eclipse version 1.1.)

In addition to the Easy Reasoner, Haley Enterprises offers two other products with CBR functionality:

- *CPR C++ Class Library*. Provides case-based problem resolution in an embeddable C++ class library. CPR is designed for stand-alone and multiuser application and is targeted for custom help-desk applications, embedded-problem resolution (within call-tracking systems), diagnostic knowledge authoring and publishing, end user problem resolution, and information retrieval. CPR provides C++ classes for problems (including symptoms and faults), questions, answers, and other objects that comprise solved problems. In addition, CPR provides a "session" object in which symptoms are entered, cases (including problems, questions, and actions) are retrieved and ranked, and diagnosis proceeds by answering questions and adjusting the rank of cases based on the accumulating evidence.

- *Help!CPR*. A Windows application that uses the CPR C++ library to import third-party case-bases from ServiceWare and KnowledgeBrokers, to import case-bases authored using CBR Express from Inference Corporation, to author or customize diagnostic case-bases, and to perform case-based problem resolution.

6.7 ESTEEM

ESTEEM, from Esteem Software, is written in Intellicorp's Kappa-PC and is now in version 1.4. ESTEEM uses Kappa's inference engine, thus enabling developers to create adaptation rules. It supports applications that access multiple case-bases and nested cases. This means that one can reference another case-base through an attribute slot in a case. ESTEEM supports various similarity-assessment methods, including *feature counting, weighted feature computation,* and *inferred feature computation.* It also can automatically generate feature weights, either using an *ID3 weight-generation method*, or a *gradient descent weight-generation method*. Moreover, users can incorporate their own similarity functions into ESTEEM if they wish.

The tool shown in Figure 6-14 has a simple GUI that can enable nonprogrammers to develop a case-base and simple user interface. The development interface comprises five editors that define cases, customize similarity assessment and retrieval, define adaptation rules, import data from ASCII files of databases, and create simple user interfaces. Version 1.4 now supports multimedia as a feature type and ESTEEM can be used as a DDE server for application embedding. ESTEEM is also available as native Kappa-PC KAL code and can, therefore, be integrated within Kappa applications. ESTEEM runs on MS Windows and, since it combines a range of CBR techniques within an environment that can be easily extended, it represents an exceptionally good value for the money and is a good tool for people interested in exploring the potential of CBR within their organizations. However, its slowness and inflexible interface would make it inappropriate for developing serious applications for delivery.

Figure 6-14.
ESTEEM showing the Case Definition Editor

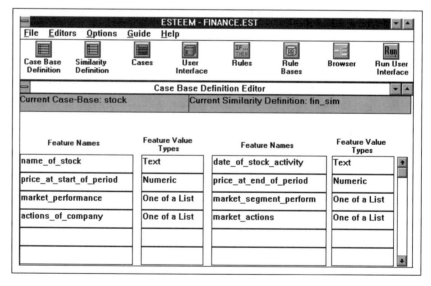

6.8 KATE

KATE, produced by AcknoSoft in Paris, is made up of a set of tools sometimes referred to as CASECRAFT: KATE-INDUCTION, KATE-CBR, KATE-EDITOR, and KATE-RUNTIME. Development should be on MS Windows (as the interface components are made with ToolBook), but deployment can be on MS Windows, Mac, or SUN.

- KATE-INDUCTION is an ID3-based induction system that supports an object-oriented representation for cases. Cases can be imported from many database and spreadsheet formats. The induction algorithm is tolerant of missing data and can make use of background knowledge. Retrieval using trees generated by the induction algorithm is extremely fast.

- KATE-CBR is the nearest-neighbor component of the suite. Users can customize similarity assessments and, since it supports the same object hierarchies as KATE-INDUCTION, the two techniques can be combined in a single application.

- KATE-EDITOR is a set of C DLLs that are integrated with Tool-Book to form a customizable developer's interface. In particular, forms can be developed to assist case entry.

- KATE-RUNTIME is another set of interface utilities that can be customized with ToolBook to deliver an application. KATE can also be delivered as embedded C code.

The KATE tools are a powerful set of well-integrated CBR tools. Retrieval is extremely fast (even with large case-bases) and can be customized by experienced developers. KATE is one of the few tools to include some testing routines. KATE has been used successfully for several very complex diagnostic tasks in Europe (e.g., the diagnosis of faults in CFM 56-3 aircraft engines) but it is not really available as a shrinkwrapped product. AcknoSoft prefers to sell it along with its own consultancy services.

6.9 ReCall

ReCall is a CBR trademark of the Paris-based AI company ISoft. This tool also offers a combination of nearest-neighbor and inductive case retrieval. ReCall is coded in C++ and is available on the PC under

Windows and on UNIX workstations under Motif for SUN, IBM RS6000, BULL DPX20, HP series 700, and DEC Alpha. It is designed on an open architecture, allowing users to add CBR functionality to their own applications.

ReCall uses an object-oriented representation with taxonomies, inheritance mechanisms, typed descriptors, facets, demons, and relationships between objects (individual cases in a case-base are represented as instances; see Figure 6-11). This allows users to specify complex domain knowledge in a structured but modular way as in Figures 6-15 and 6-16, and to describe cases having noisy, incomplete, and uncertain descriptions, since feature values can be inherited. ReCall provides multiple hierarchical indexes, which are used for organization purposes and for efficient case retrieval.

ReCall provides different methods for automatically analyzing the case-base and providing for selection of indexes as well as their organization. However, experienced developers can impose their own organization upon a case-base. Automatic procedures are based on inductive techniques. The automatic procedures take into account the domain knowledge defined in the cases, helping users to develop applications interactively. Similarity functions take into account both the properties and values of descriptors, as well as structural differences between cases. ReCall uses a variant of a nearest-neighbor algorithm that improves similarity computations.

ReCall supports two different adaptation mechanisms: a default adaptation mechanism based on a voting principle, and user-defined adaptation rules. As ReCall is based on C++, external function calls can provide more complex adaptation. ReCall can be interfaced to external applications, in particular with databases, and since ReCall is available as a C++ library, CBR functionality can be integrated with other applications.

Through the use of specialized graphical editors, the developer can define objects, relationships between objects, taxonomies, demons, and adaptation rules. A tree editor allows the user to interact directly with the case classification created by the induction algorithm to control and modify the index tree (see Figure 6-17).

Figure 6-15.
Object hierarchies in ReCall

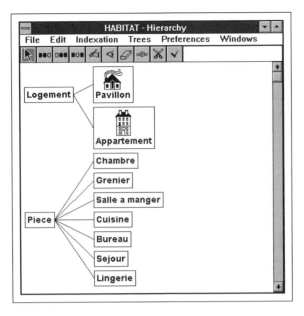

Figure 6-16.
Attributes of an object in ReCall

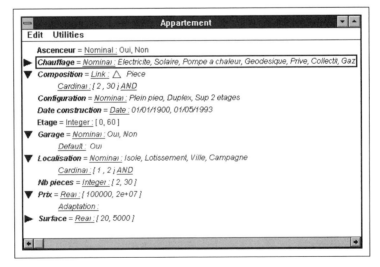

Figure 6-17.
Cases as
instances in
ReCall

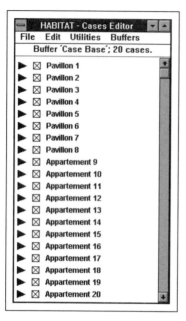

6.10 ReMind

ReMind, produced by Cognitive Systems, was developed with support from the U.S. DARPA program. It was originally developed for the Macintosh and has since been ported to MS Windows and UNIX platforms. It is available as a C library for embedding in other applications, and as an interactive development environment. (The product reviewed was the MS Windows version 1.1.) Unfortunately, Cognitive Systems went out of business in 1996. However, ReMind version 2.0 is under development at the Navy Center for Applied Research in Artificial Intelligence at the Naval Research Laboratory in Washington, D.C. It is not clear, though, when the new version will be released or who may retail it. The review of ReMind 1.1 has been included because it is still widely used and is available and supported by some distributors. Moreover, ReMind has been a very influential tool and will continue to influence the functionality and look and feel of CBR tools. ReMind's cases are represented as attribute:value pairs (see Figure 6-18).

Figure 6-18.
ReMind developer's interface

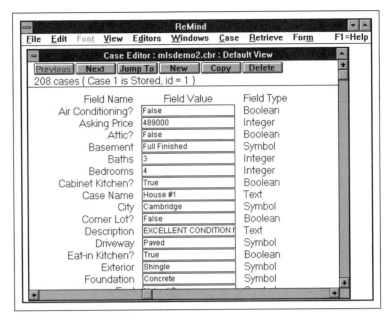

ReMind offers template, nearest-neighbor, inductive, and knowledge-guided inductive retrieval. The template retrieval supports simple SQL-like queries, returning all cases that fall within set parameters. The nearest-neighbor retrieval is informed by user-defined importance weightings that can be placed on case features. Inductive retrieval involves building a decision tree that indexes the cases. This can be done automatically by ReMind with no user involvement, or the user can create a *qualitative model* to guide the induction algorithm with background knowledge.

Qualitative models (Q-models) are created graphically to indicate which concepts (case features) are dependent on other concepts. Qualitative weightings can be placed on these dependencies, and ReMind then uses the qualitative model to guide the induction algorithm (hence *knowledge-guided induction*), resulting in decision trees that more closely reflect the causal relationship of concepts in the cases. Interestingly, different qualitative models can be created to explore different theories about the domain and to allow *what-if* questions to be asked. (See Figure 6-19.)

Figure 6-19.
A Q-model
from ReMind

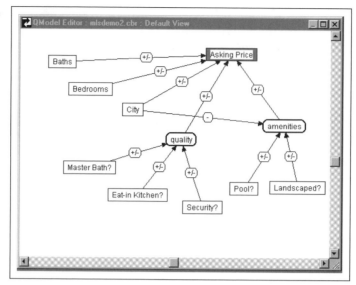

When cases have been retrieved inductively, ReMind is able to explain why the cases were retrieved. This explanation, shown in Figure 6-20, describes the path through the induced tree of cases that ReMind took to retrieve similar cases. The explanation also indicates how the retrieved cases may be adapted. The example shown is from a demo case-base of properties for sale in the Boston region of the United States (called the MLS Library). The explanation indicates that the asking price of the retrieved case is lower than the input case. This is because the input case has three bathrooms, is made of brick, and is in Cambridge, presumably a more upmarket suburb.

Figure 6-20.
An inductive
explanation
from ReMind

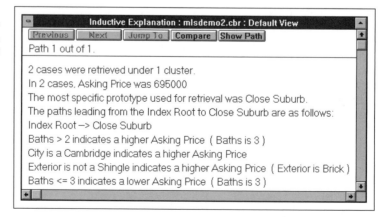

Figure 6-21.
Comparing cases

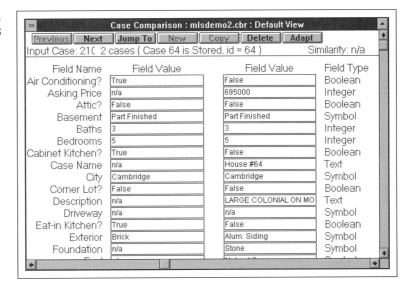

The "Show Path" button on the toolbar in Figure 6-20 will display a graphical representation of the path through the induced tree of cases, while the "Compare" button will display the target case (or hypothetical case in ReMind's jargon) and retrieved source cases side by side, as in Figure 6-21. The input target case is on the left, and a retrieved source case is on the right. It is possible to move through retrieved source cases using the "Previous" and "Next" buttons. Finally, the solution of the retrieved source case, in this example the asking price, may be adapted using adaptation formulas.

Case adaptation is provided by creating adaptation formulas that adjust values based on the difference between the retrieved and the new case. These are also created graphically using a visual programming technique. Although this takes a little getting used to, the extremely close typing of case features combined with the close typing of the operators does reduce syntax errors. Finally, ReMind can import case-bases from existing databases, making case entry easier.

ReMind is a very flexible CBR tool, offering a wide range of case-retrieval methods, along with interesting concepts such as qualitative models and visual adaptation formulas. It does not have the powerful text-handling features of Inference's products or Eclipse, though it does provide an elementary natural-language capability via a lexicon of terms that can be mapped to an ordered symbol hierarchy. However, in general, users are forced to select rather than describe a situation.

Perhaps ReMind's greatest limitation is its retrieval speed. Nearest-neighbor retrieval is quite slow even on a relatively small case-base. Inductive retrieval on the other hand is fast, but creating the inductive index is slow. Version 2.0, when it is released, promises a complete rewrite for Windows 95 and NT. It will support OLE (Object Linking and Embedding) and be able to access data in ODBC-compliant databases.

6.11 Other CBR Tools

AI software companies tend to come and go, but at the time of writing, the following tools with a CBR component have been reported. This is not necessarily a complete list, and I do not necessarily have firsthand experience of all of these products.

6.11.1 CASUEL

CASUEL, the Common Case Representation language developed by the European INRECA project (INtegrated REasoning from CAses), is the interface language between all the INRECA component systems. It is also intended to serve as the interface language between the INRECA integrated system and the external world, and as a standard for exchanging information between classification and diagnostic systems that use cases. CASUEL is a flexible, object-oriented, framelike language for storing and exchanging descriptive models and case-libraries as ASCII files. It is designed to model naturally the complexities of real cases. CASUEL represents domain objects in a class hierarchy using inheritance, slots being used to describe the objects, with typing constraints on slot values, as well as different kinds of relationships between objects.

CASUEL also supports a rule formalism for exchanging case completion rules and case adaptation rules, as well as a mechanism for defining similarity measures. CASUEL is more concise than flat feature-value vectors for the representation of objects with a large number of potentially relevant attributes of different types, only a few of which are applicable to any given case. Its use reduces the number of information-gain calculations needed for induction systems or similarity computations required for case-based reasoning.

Although CASUEL provides a lot of features, it does not require applications to use all of them. CASUEL is a keyword-driven language that allows different system components to ignore irrelevant definitions. CASUEL is also open in the sense that new features can be defined, if necessary, for a particular kind of application or component.

CASUEL is intended to become the European standard for exchanging case-bases. It is planned to use CASUEL as a starting point from which a more general (including planning and design tasks) Case Interchange Format can be developed in a joint European CBR project.

CASUEL version 2.0 is available in the public domain from the University of Kaiserslautern. The package includes:

- A document describing the CASUEL version 2.0 syntax
- A set of case-bases in CASUEL version 2.0 format
- A CASUEL version 2.0 parser (written in C)

Further information on CASUEL and details on how to download it can be obtained by e-mail from casuel@informatik.uni-kl.de.

6.11.2 *CASPIAN*

CASPIAN is a CBR tool in the public domain developed at the University of Aberystwyth in Wales (see Figure 6-22). It was used as the CBR component of the Wayland system described in Chapter 4. CASPIAN is written in C and can run on MS-DOS or the Macintosh. It has a simple command line interface, but can be integrated with a GUI front end if required. CASPIAN performs simple nearest-neighbor matching and uses rules for case adaptation. It stores a case-base, including adaptation rules, in an ASCII file. An individual case comprises a series of attributes and a solution, as shown in Figure 6-23. CASPIAN can be downloaded from the Web (www.aber.ac.uk/~cjp/getting-caspian.html), and details can be obtained from Dr. Chris Price (cjp@cs.aber.ac.uk).

6.11.3 *Recon*

Recon is a tool developed at the Lockheed AI Center for data mining to support its financial activities. Recon can interface with a wide variety of data sources (e.g., Oracle, DB2, Paradox) and combines CBR and rule-based technologies.

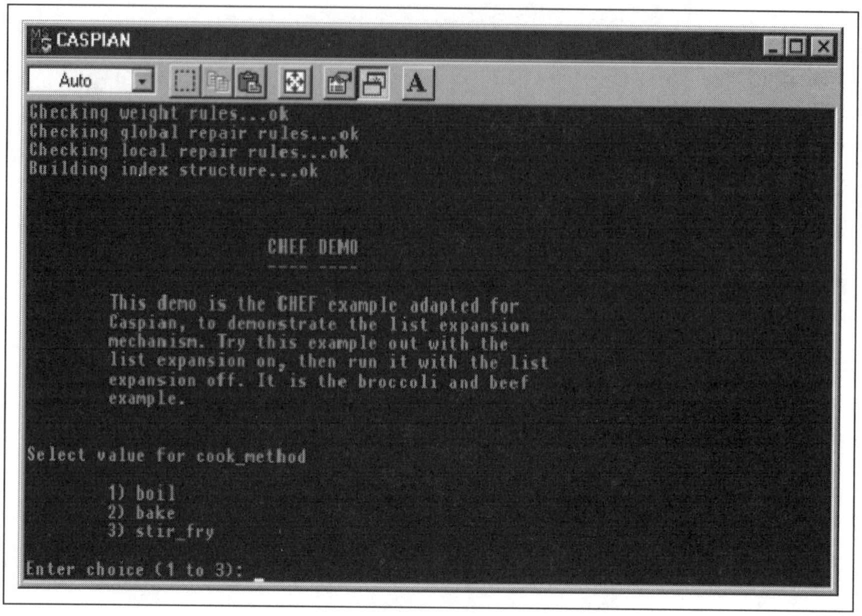

Figure 6-22.
*CASPIAN
running the
CHEF demo*

Figure 6-23.
*A case in
CASPIAN*

```
case instance mange_tout is

        vegetable = green_beans;
        cook_method = stir_fry;

local field definition is

        field vegetable type is (snow_peas, broccoli, green_beans);

solution is

        recipe = [ cook_method the vegetable ];

end;
```

6.11.4 CBRWorks

CBRWorks is the latest incarnation of S_3-Case, from the German company techInno, running on MS Windows, Mac, OS/2, and various UNIX platforms. Written in SMALLTALK, it supports an object-oriented model and flexible retrieval methods. The case editor is shown in Figure 6-24.

Figure 6-24.
CBRWorks case editor

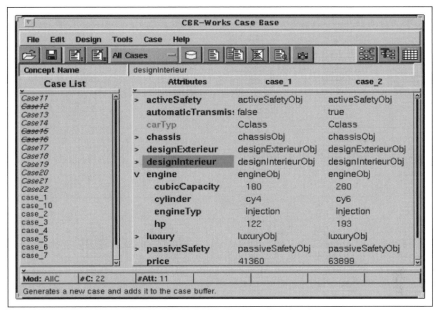

It supports the definition of concept and type hierarchies (shown in Figure 6-25) to help define similarity of symbolic concepts. Experienced SMALLTALK developers can embed or extend the functionality of CBRWorks. CBRWorks can import case-bases from Microsoft Excel and in the CASUEL case format. The tool is still very much a development prototype.

6.11.5 *Public Domain CBR Software*

In addition to CASPIAN and CBRWorks, the following CBR software is in the public domain.

Programs referred to in Riesbeck and Schank 1989, *Inside Case-Based Reasoning,* can be obtained via anonymous ftp (file transfer protocol) from cs.umd.edu in the directory /pub/schank/icbr. This source contains Common Lisp implementations of the programs from *Inside Case-Based Reasoning.* These programs have been written to run in any standard Common Lisp environment and should work without modification. See the last section in the book on support if they do not work in your Lisp environment. The programs are identical in functionality to those in the book, with the exception that some of the functions have been optimized to achieve more reasonable performance.

Figure 6-25.
CBRWorks
concept hierarchy

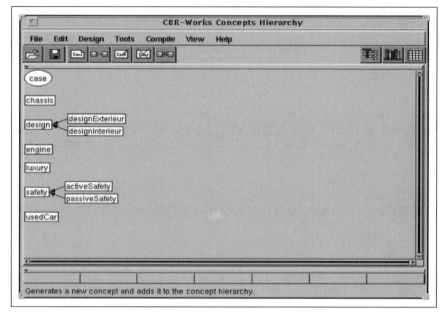

In order to use these programs effectively, you will need a copy of the text, since a lot of critical documentation is not repeated in the source code, nor are the exercises for extending the programs.

CL-Protos referred to in Bareiss 1989, *Exemplar-Based Knowledge Acquisition,* can be obtained via anonymous ftp from cs.utexas.edu in the directory /pub/porter.

CL-Protos is a Common Lisp reconstruction of the research version of the PROTOS exemplar-based learning system written by Bareiss and Porter, of the Artificial Intelligence Laboratory at the University of Texas at Austin. PROTOS was originally developed as an experiment in knowledge acquisition for heuristic classification tasks. The original research version of PROTOS was written in Prolog. This Common Lisp implementation is a reconstruction, not a Prolog-to-Lisp rewrite. Thus, CL-Protos differs from the original version in several places, but mostly by intention. Ray Bareiss had a consulting role in this reconstruction and suggested many of the changes.

CL-Protos is a research tool, not a product, so no warranties are given about the absence of bugs. CL-Protos is distributed as a courtesy among researchers and all commercial rights are reserved.

Table 6-1. Summary of CBR tools

Product Vendor	Platforms	Representation	Retrieval	Adaptation	Interface	Other comments	Price (approx.)
ART*Enterprise *Inference Corp.*	a wide variety of PC, workstation, DEC, IBM, HP, and mainframe environments	flat attribute:value pairs supporting a full range of variable types	nearest-neighbor but can be augmented using ART's programming environment	functions, rules, and other knowledge-based techniques	fully featured GUI builder	excellent data integration with most DBMS formats and version control	PC version $12,000
Case-1 *Astea International*	PC Windows	flat records supporting text and weighted questions	nearest-neighbor and knowledge-guided	no adaptation features	interface cannot be customized	designed for help-desks; version 1.0 is now shipping	price on request
CaseAdvisor *Sententia Software*	PC Windows	flat records supporting text and weighted questions	nearest-neighbor and knowledge-guided	no adaptation features	uses Netscape	uses decision trees as well; WebServer module available	less than $1,000
CasePower *Inductive Solutions*	PC Windows, Mac, OS/2	MS Excel spreadsheet, ordered-symbol hierarchies, and nested cases	nearest-neighbor	via Excel functions and macros	Excel interface	Excel must be bought to use this product	less than $1,000
CBR3 *Inference Corp.*	PC Windows and MVS version	flat records supporting text and weighted questions	nearest-neighbor and knowledge-guided	no adaptation features	CasePoint available as a DLL or API and CGI scripts	runtime, tester, generator, and WebServer modules available	PC version CBR Express $10,000
Eclipse *The Haley Enterprise*	any ANSI C environment	flat attribute:value pairs, full range of variable types	nearest-neighbor	functions, rules, and other knowledge-based techniques	no interface, only supplied as a C library	fast ART-like product also with CPR and Help!CPR	???
ESTEEM *Esteem Software*	PC Windows	cases can be nested	nearest-neighbor with inductive weight generation	functions and rules	simple form-based GUI builder	now supports DDE access and multi-media	$495
KATE *AcknoSoft*	PC Windows and UNIX	hierarchical cases	nearest-neighbor and induction		ToolBook interface can be customized	available as a C library for embedding	negotiable
ReCall *ISoft*	PC Windows and UNIX	hierarchical cases with relationships	nearest-neighbor and induction	demons	graphical development environment	available as a C++ library for embedding	$9,000
ReMind *Cognitive Systems*	PC Windows, Mac, and UNIX	nested flat cases and ordered-symbol hierarchies	nearest-neighbor, induction, and template	formulas	development interface can be customized	available as a C library for embedding	$6,000

6.12 **Summary**

This chapter introduces readers to all the major CBR tools currently on the market (Table 6-1 presents a summary of their key features). Whatever your budget and requirements, there is a CBR tool that will best suit you. This market is developing very rapidly at the moment, so expect changes. There will probably be more imitators of Inference's successful CBR3 along the lines of Case-1 and CaseAdvisor. Certainly more companies will be producing WebServer CGI or Java implementations of their products to enable them to function over the Web. There will also be further developments in integrating CBR with other AI technologies. I would expect to see some expert system shells or development environments including CBR functionality within their tools over the next few years. Finally, perhaps the most interesting developments will be the addition of case-based retrieval to conventional database-management systems.

6.13 **Vendor Information**

This section provides contact information for vendors of the tools described in this chapter.

AknoSoft, *KATE*
58a, Rue du Dessous des Berger
75013 Paris, France
Tel: (33-1) 44 24 88 00
Fax: (33-1) 44 24 88 66
http://www.acknosoft.com/

Astea International, *Case-1*
55 Middlesex Turnpike
Dedford, MA 01730, USA
Tel: (617) 275-5440
Fax: (617) 275-1910
http://www.astea.com

Brightware Inc., *ART*Enterprise*
350 Ignacio Boulevard
Novato, CA 94949, USA
Tel: (800) 532-2890
Fax: (415) 884-4740
info@brightware.com
http://www.brightware.com/

Cognitive Systems, *ReMind*
220-230 Commercial Street
Boston, MA 02109, USA
Tel: (617) 742-7227
Fax: (617) 742-1139
Note: This is the last known address of Cognitive Systems who are currently not in business. In Europe, ReMind can still be purchased from Intelligent Applications Ltd. (see below).

Esteem Software, *ESTEEM*
302 E. Main Street
Cambridge City, IN 47327, USA
Tel: (317) 478-3955
Fax: (317) 478-3550

The Haley Enterprise, *Eclipse*
413 Orchard Street
Sewickley, PA 15143, USA
Tel: (412) 741-6420
Fax: (412) 741-6457
http://www.haley.com/

Inductive Solutions, *CasePower*
380 Rector Place, Suite 4A
New York, NY 10280, USA
Tel: (212) 945-0630
Fax: (212) 945-0367

Inference Corporation (US), *CBR3*
100 Rowland Way
Novato, CA 94947, USA
Tel: (415) 893-7200
Fax: (415) 899-9080
info@inference.com
http://www.inference.com/

Inference Ltd. (UK), *CBR3*
258 Bath Road
Slough, Berks, England SL1 4DX
Tel: 44 (0)1753 771100
Fax: 44 (0)1753 771101
srauf@inference.co.uk
http://www.inference.com/

Intelligent Applications Ltd., *ReMind*
1 Michaelson Square, Livingstone
West Lothian, Scotland EH54 7DP
Tel: 44 (0)1506-472047
Fax: 44 (0)1506-472282

Isoft, *ReCall*
Chemin de Moulon
F-91190 Gif sur Yvette, France
Tel: (33-1) 69 41 27 77
Fax: (33-1) 69 41 25 32
http://www.alice.fr

Sententia Software, *CaseAdvisor*
Simon Frazier University, ASB 9971
Burnaby, BC, Canada V5A 1S6
Tel: (604) 291-5415
Fax: (604) 291-3045
cbr@cs.sfu.ca
http://www.cs.sfu.ca/cbr/

techInno GmbH, *CBRWorks*
Sauerwiesen 2
67661 Kaiserslautern, Germany
Tel: (49) 6301-60-60
Fax: (49) 6301-60-666
http://wwwagr.informatik.uni-kl.de/~trappi/

6.14 Further Reading

An early review of U.S. CBR tools was written by P. Harmon:

Harmon, P. (1992). Case-based reasoning III. *Intelligent Software Strategies*, 8(i).

A detailed comparison of the performance of CBR Express (version 2.0), ESTEEM, ReMind, and KATE using standardized experiments along with details of the functionality of some other CBR tools is given in the following report:

Althoff, K-D, Auriol, E., Barletta, R., and Manago, M. (1995). *A Review of Industrial Case-Based Reasoning Tools*. Oxford: AI Intelligence.

A review covering all the tools mentioned in this book (with the exception of CaseAdvisor):

Watson, I. (1996). Case-Based Reasoning Tools: An Overview. In *Progress in Case-Based Reasoning, Proceeding of the Second U.K. Workshop on Case-Based Reasoning,* 71–88, edited by I. Watson. Salford, UK: Salford University.

A paper describing the use of ART*Enterprise* to create a hierarchical case representation:

Watson, I.D., and Perera, R.S. (1995). NIRMANI: A Case-Based Expert System for Integrated Design & Estimating, edited by A. Macintosh and C. Cooper. *Applications and Innovations in Expert Systems III,* 335–348, Proceedings of Expert Systems '95, Oxford: SGES Publications.

The CASPIAN tool is described in:

Pegler, I., & Price, C.J. (1996). Caspian: A freeware case-based reasoning shell. In *Proceedings of the Second U.K. Workshop on Case-Based Reasoning,* edited by I. Watson. Salford, UK: Salford University.

A continually updated review of CBR tools along with information and links to vendors can be found at the AI-CBR Web site: http://www.surveying.salford.ac.uk/ai-cbr

7

Building a Diagnostic Case-Base

This chapter will take you through the process of building a diagnostic case-base using Inference's CBR3 product. This is the sort of case-base you might build if you were supporting a product or service through a customer help-desk. This chapter does not assume that you have any programming experience or that you necessarily have Inference's CBR3. It will, however, show you how simple a CBR tool can be to use and further illustrate the functionality of the market-leading CBR tool. If you do not have CBR3, you can use the printer case-base (the example used in this chapter) via the CasePoint WebServer at Inference's Web site (www.inference.com).

7.1 The Problem

Let us assume you've been asked to develop a system that can help the IT department in your company. As in many companies, the IT department offers technical support to its employees. Experienced technicians find that they spend hours every day dealing with trivial problems, which could be solved easily by less-experienced people or even by employees themselves.

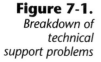

Figure 7-1.
*Breakdown of
technical
support problems*

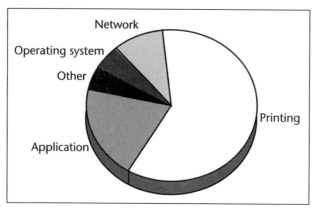

For example, sometimes they have to drive to the neighboring office just to find that a printer is out of toner or a computer monitor hasn't been turned on. The approximate daily breakdown of problem types is shown in Figure 7-1. So, you decide that you will first develop a CBR system to help solve problems with laser printers, since around 60% of recorded daily problems are with printing.

7.1.1 *The Existing Records*

The IT department keeps good records, and there are log books of calls detailing when the call was made, what the problem description was, and what remedial action was taken. Let's look at a few of these logs.

LOG: 29/7/96 14:19:15 - Lower cassette tray was installed improperly. The printer didn't print, and couldn't print a self-test. On inspection the printer's display message was: "14 Lower Tray" and the optional Lower Cassette tray was installed incorrectly. The action taken was to reinstall the Lower Cassette tray.
Call Out Time: 15 mins.

LOG: 29/7/96 14:40:21 Computer I/O port set up incorrectly. The printer couldn't print from this computer, but the printer could print a self-test and the configuration printed by the self-test was correct. The display message on the printer was: "03 I/O Problem." It was also impossible to print any data from the computer or to use any other peripheral devices. The solution was to set up the computer's I/O port correctly. The engineer had to refer to the computer manuals to do this.
Call Out Time: 35 mins.

LOG: 29/7/96 15:20:22 Ink cartridge is damaged, causing black stains. Stains appearing as small, round, black dots were occurring on the front and back of pages. Sometimes wide inconsistent stains appeared. Cleaning the printer with cleaning paper had not helped the problem. The engineer found that the toner cartridge was damaged and replaced it.
Call Out Time: 15 mins.

LOG: 29/7/95 16:10:32 Ink cartridge low on toner causes faded print area. Faded areas and faded blocks of vertical white streaks were reported on the printing. The employee was asked to check the toner cartridge to see if it was low. It was, and they replaced it.
Call Out Time: telephone only.

7.1.2 *Analyzing the Cases*

The four cases shown above range from very simple, such as an incorrectly seated paper tray, to a complex problem involving a computer's I/O (input/output) settings. However, even in simple cases an engineer was sometimes called out. How do we start putting this information into a case-base? CBR Express represents cases in two parts: the problem description and its solution (called an *action* by CBR Express).

The description is broken down into three sections:

1. A title for the case

2. Some text describing the problem

3. A set of questions that help confirm or reject the case

To author a case, we must decide how the logs can be divided sensibly into these sections.

7.1.3 *Authoring the First Case*

Building a case is as simple as deciding what information from the records should be put in each part of a case. Let's look at the first case again.

LOG: 29/7/96 14:19:15 - Lower cassette tray is installed improperly. The printer didn't print, and couldn't print a self-test. On inspection the printer's display message was: "14 Lower Tray" and the optional Lower Cassette tray was installed incorrectly. The action taken was to reinstall the Lower Cassette tray.
Call Out Time: 15 mins.

Well, the case's title might as well be: "Lower cassette tray is installed improperly"

In CBR Express, a case description should reflect how a person would describe the problem or the symptoms they see or are experiencing. You should also consider alternative ways they might describe their problem, since CBR Express can handle natural-language queries. So the description could be:

"Printer doesn't print, and won't print a self-test. Nothing happens. It doesn't work."

What questions would confirm this case? You can think of these as tests a user could perform on the printer or simple observations they could make. Well, being able to print a self-test is one test they could perform, and the display message reading "14 Lower Tray" is an observation they could make. Checking to see if the lower tray is correctly fitted is another test they could perform.

Finally, the solution to the problem (or action, in CBR Express terminology) is:

"reinstall the Lower Cassette tray"

Let's structure all that information better.

Case Title:	Lower cassette tray is installed improperly.
Case Description:	Printer doesn't print, and won't print a self-test. Nothing happens. It doesn't work.
Questions:	Answers:
Can your printer print a self-test?	NO
What is the display message?	14 Lower Tray
Is optional Lower Cassette tray installed correctly?	NO
Action:	Reinstall the Lower Cassette tray

So we are now ready to enter this into CBR Express. We first have to open a new case-base, which we'll call "printer." At this point, CBR Express asks what database format you wish to use. The default is the Raima database supplied with CBR3. At the Case Panel, we can enter the details of our first case, as in Figure 7-2.

Figure 7-2.
CBR Express
Case Editor

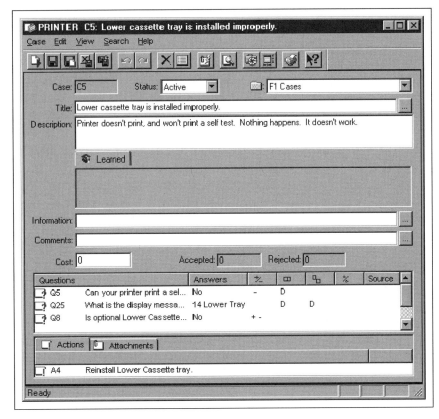

As you can see from Figure 7-2, CBR Express makes this task easy, since its interface is clearly divided into Title, Description, Question, and Action sections. Also, there are none of the usual problems you might expect in programming, such as complex syntax, keywords, brackets, semicolons, or commas. Using CBR Express is almost as easy as entering data into a database. We just have to type in the case's title and description, create three new questions, and create one new action, using the Question and Action editors of CBR Express.

7.1.4 *Scoring Questions*

There is one part of authoring a case that needs more explanation. We can inform CBR Express what to do with the answers it receives to questions. CBR Express uses the text that a user enters for the initial search to retrieve several cases from the case-base. The search is subsequently focused by the user answering questions (Figure 7-3).

Figure 7-3.
Case questions

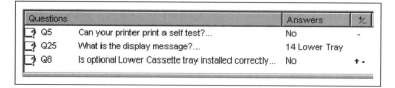

In Figure 7-3, after the answer "No" to "Can your printer print a self test?" there is a minus sign. After the second "No" answer, there is a plus and a minus sign. What can these mean? Well, when a user answers a question, there are several ways CBR Express will handle the answer. The minus sign after the first question indicates that if the user doesn't answer "No" to that question, then CBR Express will disqualify the case from further consideration.

These options are chosen by selecting a question and opening a menu by using a mouse to click over the question. The default action is to increment a case's score for a correct answer and decrement it for an incorrect one (as with the second question). Minus indicates that a case will be excluded for an incorrect answer (as in the first question). Plus indicates that a correct answer will confirm the case, and plus and minus together means a case will be excluded if the answer is wrong or confirmed if the answer is correct.

Thus, the third question in our case will either disqualify or confirm the case. It is important here to remember that in CBR3 the user is free to answer questions in any order. However, CBR3 will place questions on the search panel in an order that best discriminates between cases under consideration. Consequently, questions may not be presented to the user in the order in which we author them for any individual case.

7.1.5 Creating Actions

A case is usually made up of two components: the problem description and the solutions. In CBR3, the solution is called an *action*. That is, the action that a person should take to fix the problem. Actions are created using the Action Editor, as shown in Figure 7-4.

Figure 7-4.
*CBR Express
Action Editor*

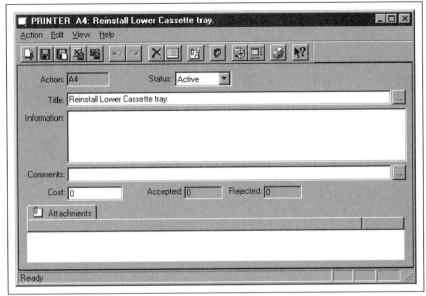

Once again, the text of the action can simply be typed into the Title field along with supporting information and other file attachments if required. It is also possible to add a cost to the action. You may interpret Cost in any way you wish. The number in this field is used by CasePoint simply as an index for sorting search results from *most expensive* to *least expensive* or vice versa. There are no calculations performed on this field. The default for this field is 0. This concept is a functional improvement over previous versions and reflects a common practice in diagnosis: namely, perform low-cost remedies, even if they may be less likely to cure the problem, before trying more expensive solutions.

There are two other fields on this editor: 1) the Accepted Field, which records how many times this action been selected as being the *right* answer by CasePoint users, and 2) the Rejected Field, which records how many times this action been rejected by CasePoint users. These two metrics let developers monitor how often an action is successful.

7.1.6 *Adding More Cases*

Authoring more cases is just as simple as with the first one. First we should structure the cases as we did before.

Case Title:	Computer I/O port is set up incorrectly.
Case Description:	Printer doesn't print from computer, self-test is OK.
Questions:	Answers:
Can your printer print a self-test?	YES
What is the display message?	03 IO Problem
Can you print data from your computer?	NO
Is the configuration printed by self-test the correct configuration?	YES
Does the computer's I/O port work with other devices?	NO
Action:	See software application notes or computer manuals to set up I/O port correctly.

CBR Express treats questions and actions as *resources* that can be used by more than one case. Thus, in any case-base one would expect several cases to use the same question. For example, with only two cases entered, they both use the *self-test* question; moreover, they also use the *display message* question. This is not a simple yes/no question but should be a list-type question. You will find this type of question to be the most useful in CBR Express, since it gives the user a range of precise answers from which to choose.

Figure 7-5 shows the editor in which questions are created. Questions may have simple yes/no answers, be a number within a min-max range, be text, or, as in this example, be a selection list. This screen shows some of the answers that correspond to the display message of the printer. Also of interest is the Attachments pane at the bottom of the screen. This facility lets CBR Express integrate multimedia into your case-base. In this example, a file called *printer.tbk* (an Asymetrix ToolBook file) can be accessed to provide information to support the question. Any MS Windows application file can be launched using this facility—such as a movie, a spreadsheet, an animation, or a document—to help the user answer the question.

Figure 7-5.
CBR3
Question
Editor

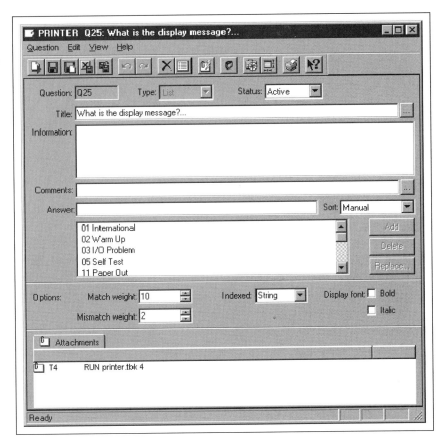

It is quite common to find, as one authors a case-base, that some individual yes/no questions are better aggregated into single list questions. However, this may mean you will have to change the question's answer in many cases. Consequently, to save yourself work, it is better to do some preparation on paper before starting to enter cases into CBR Express. Planning and preparation are, after all, required for any software engineering activity. It is inevitable that eventually you will want to change a question as the case-base evolves. CBR Express helps by identifying all the cases that use a specific question, action, or attachment.

Our completed second case is shown in Figure 7-6. The third and subsequent cases can now be added in a similar fashion.

Figure 7-6.
The second case

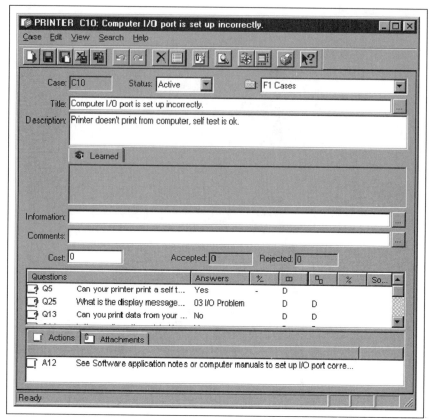

7.2 Preparing the Case-Base for Use

Once you have finished authoring a sufficient number of cases, you will want to prepare the case-base for operational use and test it before you use it. Before the case-base can be used, it must be indexed. Remember that nearest-neighbor can be slow unless the case-base is indexed; consequently, CBR Express indexes cases to make retrieval efficient. From the toolbar, you must select the *Reindex Case Base* button (Figure 7-7). Depending on the size of your case-base, this may take a few seconds or a few minutes. The case-base is now ready for use.

Figure 7-7.
The Reindex Case Base button

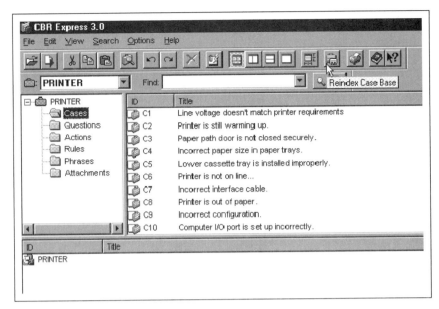

7.3 Using the Printer Case-Base

To search the case-base, you need to start CasePoint. Let us assume we have the problem with the lower paper tray we defined in the first case. Type "no paper is coming out" in the Description field and press the *Search Case Base* button (or just press Enter). After a second, the window will look like Figure 7-8. If you do not have CBR3, you can use the printer case-base described here via the CasePoint WebServer on Inference's Web site (www.inference.com).

In the middle of the window are questions CasePoint thinks should be answered, and at the bottom is a list of cases under consideration. The numbers in the Score column after the case titles (e.g., 24 and 20) indicate how confident CasePoint is in a case. Thus, at the moment, it is 24% sure that the problem is that the paper path door is not closed securely. It is also considering whether the paper has run out and if the computer is configured properly. In fact, at the moment, it's not very confident at all, so let's answer a question.

Figure 7-8.
The CasePoint
interface

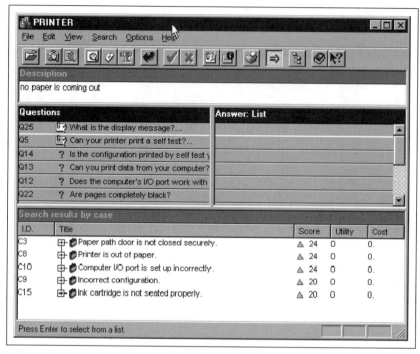

CasePoint orders the question so that the one it thinks is most relevant (i.e., most likely to discriminate between the cases under consideration) is at the top of the list. You can, however, answer the questions in any order. We'll answer the first one. This is a list question (Figure 7-9), and we have to select one answer from the list.

We will assume that the printer's display panel is showing "14 Lower Tray." After answering the question, CasePoint will update the search panel, which will now look like Figure 7-10.

Notice that the score of the topmost case has increased to 100 and an icon of a trophy has appeared beside the score. CasePoint is now certain that the problem is that the lower tray is not seated properly. You may look at the action or solution associated with the topmost case by clicking on the case as in Figure 7-11.

Figure 7-9.
*A list question
dialog box*

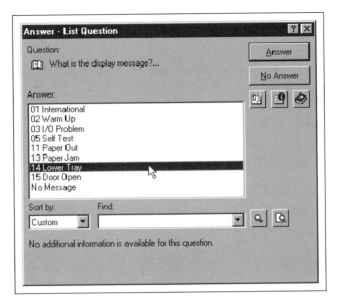

Figure 7-10.
*The updated
search panel*

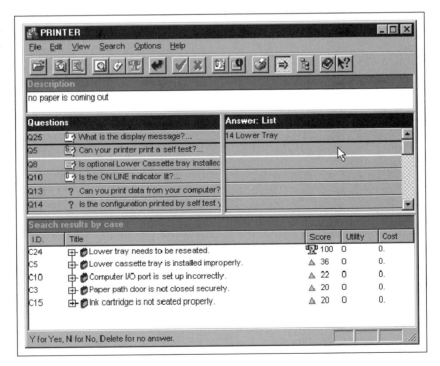

Figure 7-11.
An action
associated with
a case

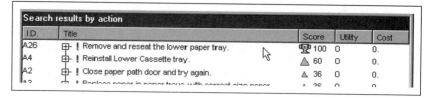

7.4 Acquiring New Experiences as Cases

In the previous search, we gave CasePoint a problem that we knew we had a case for. However, during the use of a case-base it is highly probable that problems will occur for which we do not yet have solutions. First, we have to tell CasePoint where feedback from the case-base should be sent.

Using the Case Base Properties option (Figure 7-12), we will send feedback to a file called *feedback.txt*. Notice that feedback can also be sent via e-mail to anyone in the world. This can be very useful if case-bases are fielded globally but developed and maintained in one location.

Let us assume that someone has a faulty toner cartridge and that some liquid is leaking out of the cartridge onto the page. If you type "wet areas on pages" into the Description field and press the *Search Case Base* button, you should see a screen like Figure 7-13.

If you then answer "Yes" to the "Are you having print quality problems?" you will see that the confidence in "Ink cartridge is damaged..." (the second case) remains at 24%. However, you can't answer the "What does the print quality look like?" question, because there isn't an answer for "wet areas." However, you are using the correct side of the paper and you are printing on paper, so answer those questions. Cleaning the printer doesn't help, either. CasePoint's confidence in the problem will increase to 65% but will go no higher, indicating that it is not able to confirm a solution. In a help-desk environment, the operator should now escalate the problem to an experienced engineer. They should also select the *Feedback* button.

Figure 7-12.
*The feedback
dialog box*

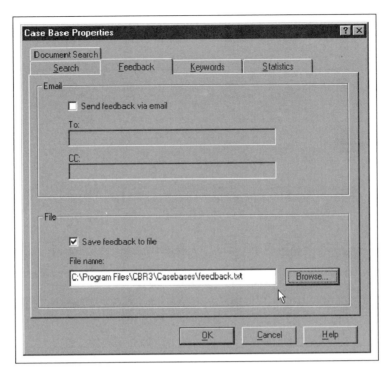

Figure 7-13.
A problem case

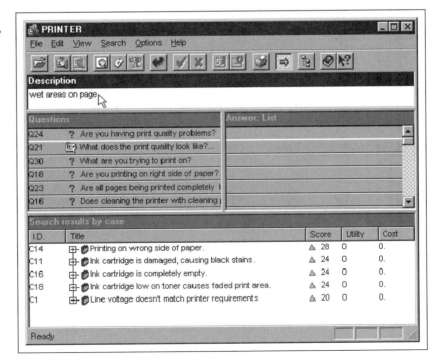

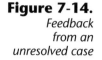

Figure 7-14.
*Feedback
from an
unresolved case*

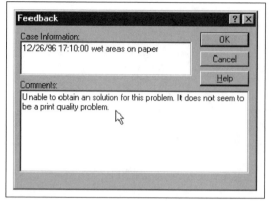

When the *Feedback* button is pressed, the details of the case are time and date stamped and logged so they can be retrieved later (Figure 7-14). All of the details, including the answers to questions, are recorded, and the operator can add their own comments to the feedback. The maintainer can now find out what happened in this case, perhaps by contacting the call-out engineer and authoring a new case using the details of the unresolved case. In this manner, CBR3 provides a method for acquiring new cases.

7.5 Using Rules

You may have noticed that CBR3 often asks questions to confirm what a user may have already stated in the problem description. For example, if a user stated their problem as "I am getting black stains on the paper," a symptom of a damaged toner cartridge, CasePoint would want to ask the questions "Are you having print quality problems?" and "What does the print quality look like?" This is shown in Figure 7-15.

While it is important for CasePoint to confirm a user's description of their problem, it can be irritating and time consuming. Moreover, it doesn't look very intelligent. CBR3 overcomes this problem by letting you define pattern-matching rules that look for keywords in the problem description. These are very useful if users make statements like "I'm using Microsoft Excel and I can't print graphs." Rules can be defined that look for words like "Excel" and automatically answer questions like "What application are you using?"

Figure 7-15.
*"Black stains on
the paper"*

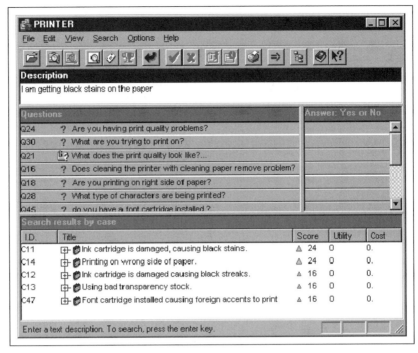

Figure 7-16 shows the CBR Express Rule Editor with a rule created that will look for the phrase "black stains" in a problem description. If it finds the phrase, CasePoint will automatically answer question 21 ("What does the print quality look like?") with the answer "black stains." This will improve the score of the damaged toner cartridge case and has the benefit that the user doesn't have to answer question 21. You will also notice in Figure 7-16 that there are a variety of different ways rules can be defined, providing a powerful inferencing capability within CasePoint.

CasePoint does not use pattern-matching rules by default; this feature can be turned on by using the *Run Rules* button on the CasePoint toolbar, as shown in Figure 7-17. With this option on, CasePoint will automatically answer the print quality question if the phrase "black stains" is in the problem description. This is shown in Figure 7-18. Notice that Case 11 now has a score of 43, whereas before the rule was defined, in Figure 7-15, with exactly the same problem description, Case 11 only had a score of 24.

Figure 7-16.
*CBR Express
Rule Editor*

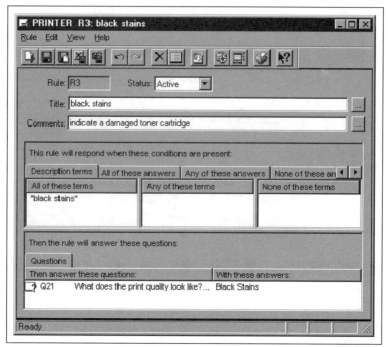

Figure 7-17.
*The Run Rules
button*

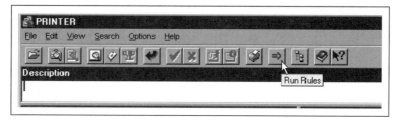

CBR3 lets rules be chained together, using forward chaining. For example, "black stains" indicates a type of print quality problem, so it would make sense to also answer yes to question 24, "Are you having print quality problems?" We can do this by defining a new rule, as shown in Figure 7-19. This rule differs from the first rule because it doesn't look for a phrase in the problem description. Instead it *fires* when question 21 is answered.

If CasePoint is now run with both rules active and exactly the same problem description as before (see Figure 7-20), you will see that two questions are now answered automatically and the score of Case 11 increases to 63%. This is a fairly confident score, and the user would be offered a solution more quickly.

Figure 7-18.
A rule has answered a question

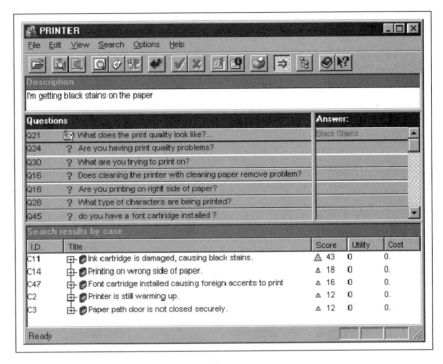

Figure 7-19.
A second rule fires

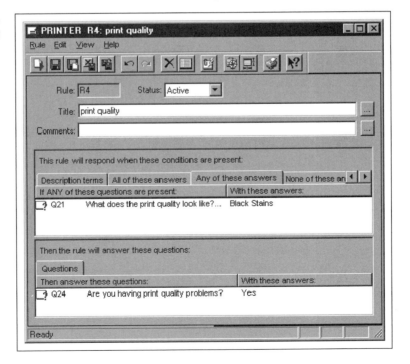

Figure 7-20.
*Rules answer
two questions*

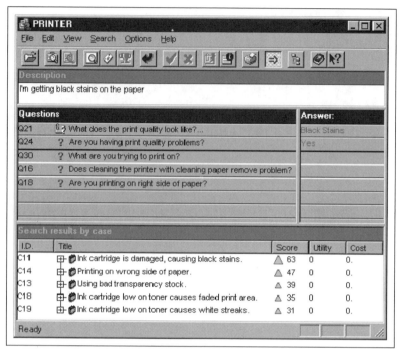

The rules are a powerful adjunct to case-base retrieval in CBR3. They answer questions automatically, based on information contained in the CasePoint problem description and on the answers to other questions. Through the rules, the developer can augment the simple matching behavior of the case-base with information about how various concepts in the case-base relate to each other. As I have shown, rules can chain, meaning that one rule can react to the actions of another. As a result, a very small piece of information provided in CasePoint can cause a chain reaction of rule firings that will answer many questions and narrow the search quite rapidly. The whole point of automatically answering questions is to speed up the search and to help the CasePoint user find the right answer as quickly as possible.

However, rules should be used with caution. While they can speed up the search, they are not *case-based*. It is easy to create dozens of rules that interact in complicated ways and find that retrieval starts becoming very deterministic. One of the advantages of cases is that they are not linked or related to one another. This lets the retrieval algorithm direct the search for a nearest neighbor, rather than using explicitly created rules dependent on knowledge about the problem situation to direct the search.

7.6 Summary

In this chapter you have seen how easy it is to create a case-based help-desk using CBR3. There are many companies where case-bases are authored and maintained by end users of the help system after only a few hours' training. This has the following advantages for a company:

- By involving users in the development and maintenance of the system, they have a sense of ownership and are more supportive of its use.
- Users are best placed to maintain a system since they understand its daily operational problems.
- By using in-house staff to develop and maintain the case-base, expensive consultancy is kept to a minimum.

This last point will obviously be of interest to financial directors; however, consultancy is essential when a case-base is first established. Using experienced CBR consultants will result in a better initial case-base design and is essential to train an organization's own personnel. You should also not assume from this simple walk-through that case-bases are always easy to implement. Very often, adequate records do not exist and a considerable amount of knowledge engineering will be required. This will still usually be easier than implementing a rule-based system. You must also remember that the CBR system will need to be integrated with other computer systems. This always takes considerable planning, skill, and effort and cannot be overlooked.

If you do not own a copy of CBR3, you can still see a working version of the printer case-base developed in this chapter on the Internet, using the CasePoint WebServer, at Inference's Web site (www. inference.com).

The next chapter deals with issues relating to creating, testing, and maintaining case-bases.

7.7 **Further Reading**

There are no books, reports, or papers that describe using CBR3 to develop a case-base. The following report describes using CBR2:

Althoff, K-D, Auriol, E., Barletta, R., and Manago, M. (1995). *A Review of Industrial Case-Based Reasoning Tools*. Oxford: AI Intelligence.

Further information can be obtained from Inference Corporation (www.inference.com).

Building, Testing, and Maintaining Case-Bases

It is a sign of maturity in a technology when people stop asking "can it be done?" and start asking "how can it be done well?" If you have just purchased a CBR tool, you will require practical advice on how to build, test, and maintain your CBR applications. This chapter, therefore, offers practical advice and guidelines for building, testing, and maintaining reliable and robust case-bases. The CBR tool used in the previous chapter, Inference's CBR3, is used again to illustrate these points. The first section of this chapter considers what characterizes a good case-base. The second outlines the features supported by CBR3 that can be used to improve case-base quality. The final sections offer practical step-by-step advice to developers on how to test and maintain their case-bases.

8.1 Characterizing a Good Case-Base

Applications using CBR will very rarely be built by simply taking an existing database of records and importing them into a CBR tool. Obtaining cases and defining their relevant features is a task akin to conventional knowledge engineering. The task may be simpler than eliciting knowledge in the form of rules, but it does require care and planning.

> [A] robust case library, containing a representative and well-distributed set of cases, is the foundation for a good CBR system.
>
> —Kriegasman and Barletta 1993

The quotation above very neatly describes the features a good case-base should have. However, as with many seemingly simple statements, it hides complexity. The following sections deal with issues raised by the quotation.

8.1.1 *Representative Cases*

When acquiring cases, it is important that they are representative of the problem domain. This presents developers of a CBR system with two problems:

1. What features the cases should have
2. Which cases should be acquired

8.1.1.1 Acquiring Case Features

Case-bases in general divide into two categories:

1. *Homogenous case-bases,* where all cases share the same record structure—that is, cases have the same attributes but varying values
2. *Heterogeneous case-bases*, where cases have varied record structures—that is, cases may have different attributes *and* varying values

A good example of a *homogenous* CBR system is the MLS Library shipped with the tool ReMind. This case-base is of houses for sale in suburbs of Boston. Every house (case) in the case-base has exactly the same case structure; that is, the same fields are recorded for every property.

A good example of a *heterogeneous* case-base would be the printer diagnostic case-base shipped with CBR3 and used as an example in Chapter 7. This case-base has 26 possible attributes, which are represented as questions in CBR3. Any individual case has 2 textual attributes (e.g., title and description) plus, on average, 3 question features ranging from "Is the printer out of paper?" to "Does printer power come on?"

For a realtor case-base, there may be around 50 features that adequately describe houses (e.g., sale price, lot size, number of garages, etc.), and it would be relatively straightforward to identify a complete set of features, since all realtors keep records of properties. Thus, it would be reasonable to assume that they will have recorded necessary and sufficient information.

However, where good historical records do not exist, developers must elicit case features. This is a knowledge-engineering task where the developer is seeking *feature stabilization*. This occurs when no new relevant case features can be identified either by challenging domain experts or by acquiring new cases. This is likely to be easier for a homogenous case-base.

For example, in the realtor case-base, you only have to think of the set of all features that could possibly describe a residential house. This set can be reduced by only considering features that affect property values (remember, case features should be predictive). Thus, the number of bedrooms and bathrooms are good features, while the color of the carpets is probably not.

When developing a heterogeneous case-base, developers may never be sure they have a complete feature set. For example, in the printer diagnostic case-base in Chapter 7, developers could list all possible features of a laser printer, plus all possible states that the printer could be in. This might result in several hundred possible features. However, it is certain that some would not have been imagined; for example, we probably would not have thought of, "Have cockroaches infested the printer?" But potentially this could be a problem somebody has experienced or will experience in the future.

Thus, when developing a heterogeneous case-base, it may be fruitless to imagine *all* possible features. Instead, developers must rely on historical records. If these are not available, developing a reliable case-base will be difficult and will require extensive knowledge elicitation.

8.1.1.2 Acquiring Representative Cases

This relates to the *completeness problem* in conventional knowledge engineering. It has been reported that CBR systems have a significant advantage over rule-based systems in that they can be delivered with incomplete case-bases. For example, CLAVIER went live with only 20 cases. However, developers with Inference have reported at their user group meetings that if a case-base is underpopulated when the application goes live, users may reject the system because it fails to deal adequately with a majority of problems. They advise that case-bases should be 80% complete before delivery.

Thus, it is important to consider when a representative set of cases has been acquired. This becomes more important if the system uses adaptation, since the greater the number of cases (i.e., the greater the coverage of the problem space) the less adaptation will be required. To help with this, developers should try to obtain information about the frequency of case occurrence. For example, in a diagnostic problem such as those often encountered in help-desks, a log should be kept over a period of time.

For example, this might categorize cases into six problem types (e.g., *p1 to p6*). Their frequency of occurrence over a week might be recorded as shown in Figure 8-1. Case-based developers should therefore ensure that initially the majority of their cases deal with problem types *p3, p4,* and *p5,* since these account for 80% of problems encountered.

8.1.2 *Case Distribution*

Acquiring representative cases and case distribution are very closely linked. Case distribution refers to the coverage of cases across features. This section will consider two aspects of case distribution: feature shift and feature range.

8.1.2.1 **Feature Shift**

Let us consider a simple hypothetical medical problem: determining a correct dosage for a new drug. For the purpose of this explanation, assume that clinical trials suggest that the correct dosage corresponds to one-hundredth of a milligram per pound of body weight. Thus, in clinical trials, successful results were found when a person who weighed 120 pounds received a dosage of 1.2 mg. If the case-base had 10 cases representing this problem, ideally they should be evenly distributed (in Figure 8-2 cases are represented by squares).

Thus, if a man weighing 190 pounds presented himself, the nearest matching case would be the 200-pound case, recommending a dosage of 2 mg. Even without adaptation, this may result in a successful treatment. However, a simple linear adaptation function could easily adapt the retrieved dosage to the correct dosage of 1.9 mg.

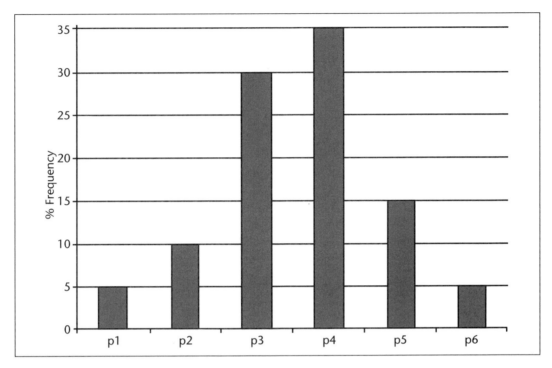

Figure 8-1. *Frequency of problems (%)*

Figure 8-2.
*An even case
distribution*

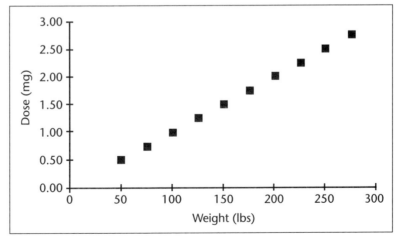

Assume that clinical trials are extended to cover very young children and babies. These new trials indicate some problems with the drug, showing that it can have very serious side effects on patients who weigh less than 50 pounds, regardless of dose (let us assume that a baby weighing 30 pounds nearly died from a dose of 0.3 mg).

With the case distribution indicated in Figure 8-3, if a patient was presented who weighed 45 pounds, the nearest neighboring case (i.e., 50 pounds) would recommend a dosage of 0.5 mg. If the simple linear adaptation function (derived from the vast majority of cases) were used, the dose might be adapted to 0.45 mg. However, this does not reflect the sudden change in recommended dosage at low weights. This *feature shift* demands that cases be clustered more closely around the point of feature shift, particularly if relatively simple structural adaptation techniques (such as interpolation) are used.

Thus, case distribution should reflect the features of the solution space, not just the historical precedents of the problem space. It is worth noting that feature shifts can either be identified by analyzing case data or by knowledge-engineering techniques (e.g., questioning experts, "Is there any context in which you would not recommend a dose of approximately one-hundredth of a milligram per pound?"). However, developers should not assume that cases they have obtained will adequately identify the point at which a feature shifts, or that they have asked *all* the right questions.

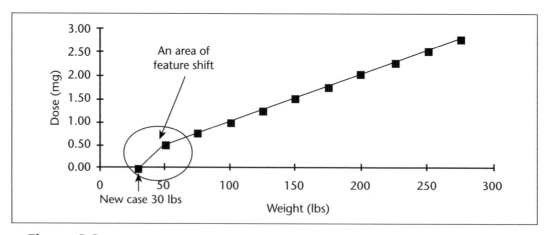

Figure 8-3.   *A feature shift*

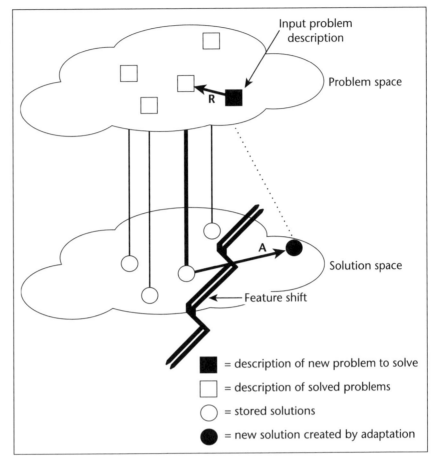

Figure 8-4.
*A feature shift in
the solution space*

Input problem
description

Problem space

R

Solution space

A

Feature shift

■ = description of new problem to solve

☐ = description of solved problems

○ = stored solutions

● = new solution created by adaptation

Figure 8-4 shows, conceptually, a situation where the solution space does not map directly to the problem space. There is a possibly unknown boundary in the solution space, where solution features on one side are in some way very different from those on the other. Consequently, the adaptation distance (the arrow labelled "A") is not conceptually the inverse of the retrieval distance (the arrow labelled "R").

8.1.2.2 Feature Range

Many similarity functions, particularly those for assessing similarity between numerical features, consider the range of the feature. This concept can be simply illustrated: if a feature called *age* (i.e., the age of patients) has a range from 0 to 105 years, then 50 is relatively similar to 60. However, if the range of the feature *age* is reduced from 0 to 12 years (i.e., the age of children), then 2 is not at all similar to 12, even though the difference in age in both examples is still 10 years.

Consequently, it is very important for developers to consider the range of features in the case-base, their mean value, and their standard deviation. If there is one case with an abnormally low or high value (e.g., an age of 110 when most patients are in the range 0 to 70), it can distort the accuracy of the similarity measure. Hence, developers should identify cases that are isolates and consider if they are required in the case-base. If they are required, they should seek to obtain more cases to provide a more even case distribution.

8.1.2.3 Feature Weightings

Many CBR tools allow developers to adjust parameters that will affect the retrieval techniques. ReMind is a good example of a tool that allows users to alter weightings in nearest-neighbor retrieval and alter the way the induction algorithm generates its index tree by using *qualitative models*.

The weighting given a feature will affect the degree that it influences the closeness of a match during retrieval. Consequently, it is important that developers consider how feature weightings are assigned. Very often this seems to be a relatively ad hoc process, with developers, perhaps in conjunction with domain experts or users, judging that one feature is more important than another. Some researchers have suggested a more formal approach by using statistical techniques to analyze the case data. Early results indicate that it is possible to derive feature weightings by determining the correlation between features.

Results also suggest that it is possible to use statistical techniques to identify which features affect the outcome (a single outcome feature is required to construct an inductive index tree) and proportionally what their impact is. This can be used to develop Q-models in ReMind and to assign weights to the relationships between nodes. The use of such statistical techniques when fine-tuning a case-base is to be welcomed, since it should produce more reliable case-bases that are based on sound principles.

8.2 Tool Support

This section primarily looks at the features of CBR3 (principally the Tester module) that support the developer in designing good case-bases. CBR Express provides the developer with a *Test* function where the features of a newly authored case are used to search the existing case-base. This will identify if there is already a case in existence that is very similar (i.e., it closely matches the features of the new case) or indeed if there is no similar case in the case-base.

Other CBR tools offer support for determining case distribution. For example, ReMind has a *Generalize* feature that offers information on the maximum and minimum values of a field, the mean and standard deviation, and the number of cases that share this value (if it is a symbolic variable). Figure 8-5 shows some statistical information from ReMind concerning bedrooms (taken from the MLS Library). It can be seen that the range is small (i.e., 2 to 8 bedrooms per house), the mean is approximately in the middle of the range, and the standard deviation is low. The distribution of this feature is okay.

If, however, a movie star's mansion with 45 bedrooms is added to the case-base, this will distort the case-base.

Figure 8-6 shows that the range of the feature has now increased considerably, the standard deviation is now greater than the mean, and the mean is now at the bottom of the feature range. This will affect how the similarity of this feature is measured, and it would be wise to consider if this abnormal case is required in the case-base.

Figure 8-5.
Statistical information on a numeric feature

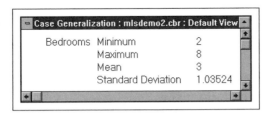

Figure 8-6.
A distorted feature distribution

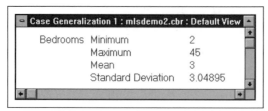

The Tester module developed by Inference is an automated testing tool for the case-base developer to evaluate the quality of cases in the case-base. Tester is a stand-alone module that provides static analysis, case-base subsetting, question-distribution analysis, and dynamic analysis of cases. It is designed to be used in conjunction with CBR Express, the case-base authoring environment of CBR3. This provides a much more comprehensive set of test features than any CBR tool currently on the market.

Tester provides a variety of housekeeping functions such as identifying questions or actions in the case-base that are not used by any case and counting how many cases fall into each of the categories *active, archived, unresolved,* and *draft.* More importantly, it can identify the cases with the longest and shortest case descriptions.

This is important, since CBR Express uses case descriptions to perform its initial match. Inference advises that case descriptions should be similar lengths, since this affects the performance of the similarity measure. Tester can also indicate what percentage of the cases have a greater than 70% overlap between title and description features, as well as the average overlap. This allows the designer to assess case coverage.

The Question Use Summary report (Figure 8-7) provides some basic statistics on question usage: minimum, maximum, and average number of questions per case. This provides some input for a case-base design review. A minimum of 0 identifies potentially unfinished cases.

Tester determines the minimum, maximum, and average number of questions per case. This is of use since cases in a case-base should have similar numbers of questions. Cases with abnormally small numbers of questions may match too easily, while cases with abnormally large numbers of questions may never match sufficiently. Tester also offers a utility that profiles the number of times each question appears in the case-base. This provides the designer with some interesting feedback on the case-base architecture (see Figure 8-8).

Figure 8-7.
Question Use Summary report

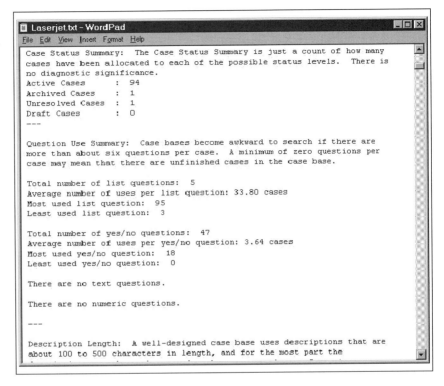

Figure 8-8.
Question distribution

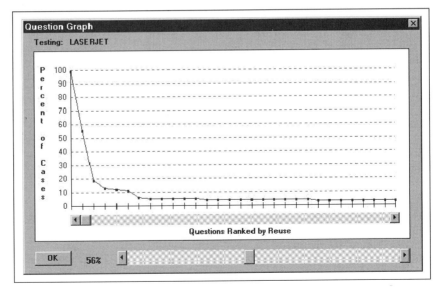

Figure 8-9.

Tester options

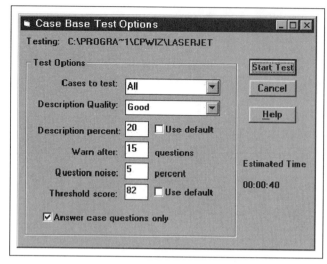

Tester's dynamic testing simulates a variety of users that would access the case-base using CasePoint. Tester uses the CasePoint Search Engine API to test and collect the results of each search, then saves the results in the dynamic analysis report. Common dynamic analyses are finding duplicate cases, identifying cases that cannot reach the success threshold, and validating case-base structure.

To find duplicate cases, Tester performs a series of *perfect* incremental searches for individual cases by initially sending the title and description, and then answering questions from that case. If a different case were to exceed the threshold first, it would imply that it is a duplicate case. Tester can also check that all cases can reach the minimum threshold for success (i.e., they can be confirmed). In this test, shown in Figure 8-9, descriptions can be given that provide initial descriptions from perfect to poor, and questions are answered in an attempt to ensure that the cases are all theoretically accessible.

These features go a considerable way to helping a developer using CBR3 produce a robust and reliable case-base.

8.3 Testing Case-Bases

Testing or evaluating a CBR system involves two separate processes, called *verification* and *validation*:

- *Verification* is concerned with building the system right.
- *Validation* is about building the right system.

In other words, verification is concerned with ensuring that the system gives correct answers, and validation ensures that the system is one the users want. There is no point in developing a perfect system if it solves a problem nobody wants solved. Validation is a complex sociotechnical problem, and it will not be dealt with further in this book.

I will assume that, whatever CBR system you have built, you know that it is the right system for the job. You now have to verify that it correctly solves the problem. To verify a traditional rule-based system, you might

1. Check the logical validity of the rule-base for

    ❑ Duplications (i.e., different rules that perform the same actions)

    ❑ Inconsistencies (i.e., different rules that came to different conclusions given the same inputs)

    ❑ Omissions (i.e., input conditions that never cause any rules to fire)

    ❑ Isolates (i.e., rules that never fire because their inputs cannot occur)

2. Compare its performance on test problems to that of an expert or group of experts. If the rule-based system was 90% as accurate as the experts, you may be satisfied.

In essence, you should perform similar verification checks on a CBR system. However, verification is more difficult for CBR than for rule-based systems. Although CBR provides a more plausible and natural model of human reasoning than rule-based reasoning, CBR technology is still relatively new, and more work is needed to fine-tune evaluation methods. Unlike rule-based systems, CBR systems are dynamic and add cases to the case-base as the system learns, hence the case-base is continually expanding. Consequently, system performance will change over time as verification results will almost always be affected by learning. Given these problems, I will set out a series of actions that are advisable for case-base verification. They will not guarantee you have built the system right, but they will help.

These steps should be repeated at intervals during the development of your CBR system. They should not be left until you think the system is complete. For a rough guide, repeat the steps when you estimate the case-base is one-third complete, two-thirds complete, and complete or ready to be released.

8.3.1 *Check Retrieval Accuracy*

Regardless of the CBR tool you are using or if you are using nearest-neighbor or inductive retrieval, a case should exactly match itself. Therefore, for a sample of cases in your case-base, check that if they are used as target cases, the source case retrieved is identical. If you are using nearest-neighbor, the similarity measurement should be 100%. Some tools, such as CBR3, let you perform this test automatically. With other tools, you will have to make a copy of the source case and use it as a target case. If a case does not retrieve itself or does not match exactly, there is something very wrong with the retrieval algorithm you are using.

8.3.2 *Check Retrieval Consistency*

Regardless of the CBR tool you are using or if you are using nearest-neighbor or inductive retrieval, if you perform exactly the same search twice, you should retrieve the same source cases with the same accuracy. If you do not, again, there is something wrong with the retrieval algorithm you are using. Some CBR tools limit retrieval to a set number of cases that fall within a given similarity. Thus, they do not search the entire case-base if they have already found a good-enough match. This can be affected by the order in which cases were entered in the case-base.

So repeat a set of searches several times and check for consistency. Inconsistency can be very disturbing to users who expect computers to give the same answer to the same question every time. You will be surprised how many users will perform this test when they first use a CBR system to see if it gives the same answer every time—it's as if they are trying to catch the computer out!

If your CBR system performs adaptation, you will also have to check the consistency of the adaptation rules or formulas.

8.3.3 *Check for Case Duplication*

A case should exactly match itself, but it should not be identical to other cases. Duplicate cases will not harm decision making but may slow the system down or cause other administrative problems. Some tools, like CBR3, support this, whereas for other tools you may have to remove each case in turn from the case-base and use it as a target case to search for duplicates.

8.3.4 *Check Case Coverage*

As was mentioned earlier, it is better to have an even distribution of cases across your problem area. This is actually hard to achieve, but you can be guided in several ways:

- If you have numerical features, check their standard deviation. It should be as low as possible. The mean of the feature value should also be near the middle of the feature range. Some tools, like ReMind, support this. If the standard deviation is high, then you have outlying cases. Either try to remove them or obtain more cases to improve the coverage for that feature. If the mean is toward one end of the range, you have too many cases at one end and not enough at the other. Of course, if there is a feature shift at one end of the range, it may be desirable to have more cases around the feature shift.

- If you have symbolic features, check the frequency of occurrence of each symbolic value in the case-base. Some tools, like ReMind, support this. Again, if the distribution is very uneven, then you have outlying cases. Either try to remove them or obtain more cases to improve the coverage for that feature. You may also need to consider combining features or dividing them if this is a problem.

- If you have a feature that will be used as the outcome of inductive retrieval, check its distribution very carefully. You will want cases to cover that feature value at regular intervals. For example, in the realtor case-base, we would ideally want to see houses with asking prices at perhaps $5,000 intervals. If there were a cluster of cases at $200,000 and then no cases until $250,000, and then none until $400,000, our case-base could not perform well in the $300,000 section of the market.

- Finally, if you are aware of a feature shift in your case-base, then pay particular attention to case coverage around the feature shift.

8.3.5 *Global System Verification Tests*

The steps described above have all concentrated on individual aspects of a CBR system and its performance, retrieval accuracy and consistency, and case coverage that will undoubtedly affect your system's performance. However, it is also vitally important to verify the overall performance of your system:

1. You should obtain a number of representative cases (perhaps 5% to 10% of your total case-base size). These cases should be representative of the full range of cases in your case-base. You may temporarily remove a sample of cases from the case-base or you may keep a separate permanent test set of cases.

2. You should then use each of your test cases as target cases.

3. You must then evaluate the performance of the system and you may require the help of domain experts to do this. The questions you should consider are

   ❑ Did the system retrieve a useful case or set of cases?

   ❑ Was the retrieval time acceptable?

   ❑ If relevant, was the adaptation successful?

4. You should record the results of these tests for comparison the next time you repeat them. Since by then the case-base will probably hold more cases, you will not get exactly the same answers, but you would hope to see an improvement.

If you follow these simple steps, you will build better, more reliable, and, most importantly, more useful CBR systems.

8.4 Maintaining Case-Bases

CBR systems can grow with time; indeed, this is one of the major benefits of the technology—their ability to learn and improve their performance by acquiring new cases. This learning process, though, should not be left to chance. To leverage continuing improvements from your CBR system, you will have to manage its maintenance.

This process is very closely linked to verification of the case-base, since in some ways the development of a CBR system is never completed; it is an ongoing process. I will now set out a series of steps you should follow to help the maintenance of your CBR system. As before, they will not guarantee success, but they will certainly help. These steps should be repeated at regular intervals. The precise period of the interval will depend on the usage that your CBR system gets and the numbers of new cases it acquires. Under no circumstances should the size of your CBR system increase by more than 20% without performing the following steps.

8.4.1 *Obtain Case Utilization Statistics*

If possible, obtain metrics from your CBR system on how many times each individual case is retrieved. Of the currently available CBR tools, only CaseAdvisor automatically provides a log of case usage (Figure 8-10).

You must try to log this vital information in some way. It may even have to be done manually until more software developers provide the functionality in CBR tools.

If a case was never retrieved over a period of time, you must ask whether it is needed. For example, if you have a diagnostic case-base for a product line, over the years certain products may no longer be supported, so no problems regarding an obsolete product will be encountered. Cases dealing with problems of obsolete products may need to be removed from the case-base. However, this is not a simple decision, since a new product could develop a fault that was *similar* to a fault in an old product. You may have to consult with domain experts and consider if the potentially redundant cases are harming the performance of the system. If not, you may be advised to leave them just in case they are useful in the future.

Alternatively, you may find that a particular case is retrieved very frequently. In this instance it is possible you have poor case coverage, and you should consider providing some near neighbors to the overused case.

Figure 8-10.
CaseAdvisor: 10 most commonly accessed cases

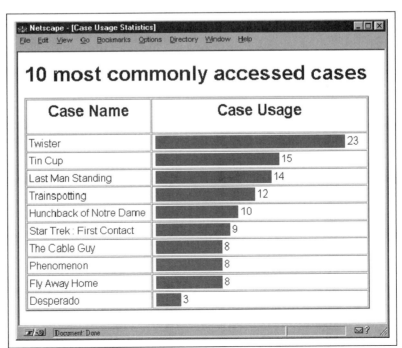

8.4.2 *Repeat the Verification Tests*

You should also repeat the verification tests described in Section 8.3. This might sound like a lot of work, but if you do not perform these tests, the usefulness of your system could degrade seriously over time. In particular, you should check for case duplication and case coverage. With time, you may acquire more cases than you actually need to provide acceptable solutions. In other words, the *granularity* of your case-base may become too fine. This may seriously affect the performance of your system, particularly if you are using nearest-neighbor retrieval. You may also acquire bizarre outlying cases that distort similarity metrics. You will need to find out if these outlying cases are really required.

At regular intervals, you should repeat the global system verification tests, preferably using the same test cases as you used the first time. You will want to see improvements in the three questions you are asking:

1. Did the system retrieve a useful case or set of cases?
2. Was the retrieval time acceptable?
3. If relevant, was the adaptation successful?

Thus, it might be useful to use a qualitative scale for the answer to each question from 1 to 6, where 1 = *totally unacceptable* and 6 = *perfect*. If you do this, you can then plot the results on a graph and monitor them over time. The only feature you may see decline with time is the retrieval time, which may get slower as the case-base increases in size. Monitoring these metrics will alert you to potential problems in your system.

Finally, do not ignore the users in this process. You should seek their opinion at regular intervals and ask them if they are still happy with the system. After all, there is no point in the system working perfectly if nobody uses it! For example, the graph in Figure 8-11 shows that the users' perception of the system's performance is closely linked to the retrieval speed. However, as the case-base size has increased to 2,000 cases, retrieval speed has declined. Despite the fact that the retrieval accuracy (i.e., the usefulness of retrieved cases) has increased with case-base size and the fact that adaptation accuracy has also improved with case-base size, the users are concerned by the decline in retrieval speed. This might suggest that unless retrieval speed can be improved (either by indexing or using inductive retrieval) perhaps the optimum size for the case-base is around 1,700 cases.

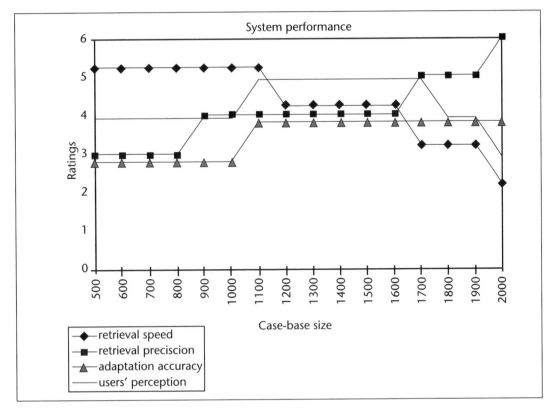

Figure 8-11. *A system performance graph*

8.5 **Summary**

This chapter has shown that developing a good case-base requires care. Homogenous case-bases are easier to develop than heterogeneous ones, particularly if a good historical record is not available, since *feature stabilization* cannot be guaranteed in a heterogeneous case-base. Case distribution is of vital importance, since it can affect how similarity measures work. Developers should, therefore, pay close attention to case distribution. Additionally, if there is a sudden *feature shift,* it could cause a CBR system to offer an incorrect solution unless cases are distributed closely around the point of the feature shift. Knowledge engineering may be required to identify points of feature shift.

This chapter has also shown that two popular tools, ReMind and CBR3, both address the problem of case distribution. ReMind's *Generalize* feature provides useful statistics to a developer. Inference's Tester module takes this further and provides a comprehensive range of features that analyze various aspects of case-base structure. It is perhaps no surprise that Inference, with their huge user base, is the first CBR tool developer to take case-base testing and metrics seriously. Other CBR tool developers would be well advised to follow suit.

Finally, this chapter has discussed issues concerning testing a CBR system and maintaining it. Practical steps you can take to improve the performance of your system and ensure that it learns successfully have been described. Regardless of the tool you use, you should not forget that creating a case-base is also a software engineering task. Consequently, you should follow your organization's usual software engineering practices. These may need to be modified slightly to accommodate the differences between creating a routine application, such as a database, and a case-based application.

Kitano and Shimazu (1996) describe a case study of developing a very large corporate-wide case-base at the NEC corporation, called SQUAD. They adapted the normal software quality-control activities (SWQC) to fit the case-based knowledge-engineering loop.

What is interesting in the diagram shown in Figure 8-12 is that this confirms the practice reported by many developers and maintainers of CBR systems. First, you should notice that knowledge engineering of the case-base is not a once-only activity. Case-bases are dynamic growing entities. Approximately 3,000 cases are acquired at NEC every year. These are passed onto a review committee, which decides which cases should be passed to the knowledge engineers for addition to the case-bases. The process of case acquisition may result in new case features being identified, which causes changes to the domain model and the case record structure (the case format) that employees use to capture cases. This loop is very similar to that at Legal & General (discussed in Chapter 5), where a case-base review meeting was held once a month to decide on changes to the case-bases.

Kitano and Shimazu (p. 267, 1996) conclude their case study with the following advice:

> [T]he successful corporate-wide deployment of an AI system must involve organizational efforts, as part of the algorithmic loop in the system in the broad sense. This includes a strong commitment from top-level management.

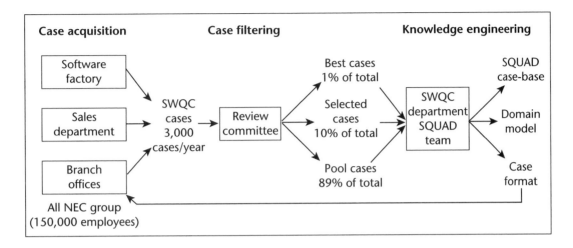

Figure 8-12. *The knowledge-engineering loop at NEC, after Kitano and Shimazu 1996*

I agree completely with this statement. Without strong management commitment, no amount of good practice and good technology will succeed.

The next chapter concludes the book by summarizing key points and discussing recent developments in CBR research.

8.6 Further Reading

CBR is a new discipline and, consequently, relatively little has been written about methodologies for designing, building, and maintaining CBR systems. Two of the few papers that explicitly discuss these issues within a corporate environment are

Curet, O., and Jackson, M. (1996). Towards a Methodology for Case-Based Systems. In *Research and Development in Expert Systems* XIII, 183–191, edited by J.L. Nealon and J. Hunt. Oxford: SGES Publications.

Kitano, H., and Shimazu, H. (1996). The Experience-Sharing Architecture: A Case Study in Corporate-Wide Case-Based Software Quality Control. In *Case-Based Reasoning: Experience, Lessons, & Future Directions*, 235–268, edited by D.B. Leake. Cambridge, MA: AAAI Press / MIT Press.

9

Conclusion

This chapter concludes the book with an overview, in particular, the differences between CBR and other decision support technologies and the benefits I believe CBR offers are discussed. The chapter ends with a look ahead to the future of CBR.

9.1 Learning Review

Chapter 1 introduced the concepts behind the representation and manipulation of data within a computer. It was made clear that the *meaning* we draw from data (i.e., its information) is not always a property of the data itself, but is more often a property of the relationship between data items in some form of structure. After a brief discussion of databases, the concepts behind logic programming and rule-based expert systems were introduced. These technologies allow a computer to make *inferences*—that is, to deduce new facts from existing facts. This technology underlies much of what has become known as *expert* or *knowledge-based* systems.

However, we do not always reason by using rules and first principles. Very often we solve problems by relying on our experience of similar problems we have encountered in the past. This problem-solving paradigm is one we all use and is perhaps used by other animals as well.

The first chapter showed that database technology, with its precise query languages, cannot support this reasoning based on remembering. We need a technology that can support imprecise fuzzy queries. This technology is *case-based reasoning*.

Chapter 2 briefly introduced the history and development of CBR and the cycle that describes CBR at a conceptual level. The CBR-cycle (Figure 9-1) is comprised of four processes, called the *four REs*:

1. *Retrieve* the most similar case(s) from the case-library or case-base.

2. *Reuse* the solution from the most similar case if appropriate.

3. *Revise* or adapt the proposed solution if necessary.

4. *Retain* the new case and its solution for future use.

Figure 9-1.
The CBR-cycle

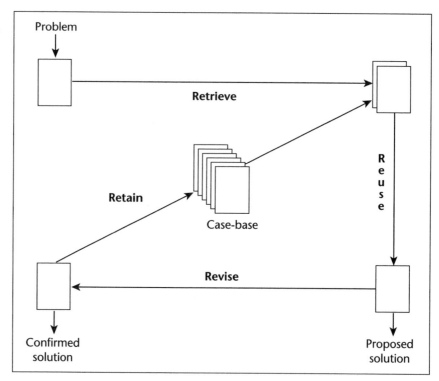

The implementational details that underlie each of the stages of the CBR-cycle were then described in some detail. In particular, the two retrieval techniques—*nearest-neighbor* and *induction*—were described, using simple examples. You should now be familiar with how these techniques work at a conceptual level and be able to understand the pros and cons of each approach.

Chapter 3 started to consider how CBR could be applied, by introducing you to a classification of CBR applications. Remember that *classification problems*, such as *diagnosis* or *assessment,* are easier to solve using CBR, because they fit the characteristics of CBR better than synthesis problems. Synthesis problems, such as design, can be solved using CBR, but often require more complex adaptation. Don't forget that adaptation is CBR's Achilles' heel and should be kept as simple as possible or even avoided entirely. The third chapter concluded by introducing you to a range of academic CBR demonstrators so you could see the wide range of potential applications of CBR, from legal reasoning to football coaching.

Chapter 4 described four influential commercial applications of CBR. Lockheed's CLAVIER program, in particular, showed how a CBR system could be built when a rule-based expert system had failed. This is because, to build a CBR system, you do not need to know how to solve a problem, you only have to *remember* if you have solved a similar problem in the past. The Wayland system showed how simple a CBR system can be yet still produce significant business benefits. British Airways' CASELine system showed how CBR could be used to support more complex diagnoses than that found on a customer help-desk—fault-finding on Jumbo Jets and Concorde. Finally, the Top Management Fraud Diagnosis Tool at Deloitte & Touche showed how CBR can be used to support *soft* problems that are based on careful consideration of often conflicting opinions and value judgments.

Chapter 5 dealt in detail with CBR's most successful application to date, namely, case-based help-desks. The Compaq SMART system was the first implementation of this and was complemented by the latest innovation of automated case-based help systems on the World Wide Web by Broderbund Software. Finally, Legal & General's SWIFT system described a methodology for developing successful CBR systems.

Chapter 6 reviewed all of the main CBR tools currently on the market, and some public domain ones as well. Regardless of your computing platform and your budget, there is a CBR tool to support your needs. The tools broadly fall into three categories:

1. Those designed specifically for help-desks—Case-1, CaseAdvisor, and CBR3
2. Tools combining nearest-neighbor and induction in a single environment—KATE, ReCall, ReMind, and Eclipse
3. Niche tools—ART*Enterprise*, CasePower, and ESTEEM

Chapter 7 then took one of these tools (CBR3) and showed you how easy it is to implement a simple diagnostic case-base for a help-desk. This chapter should have made the theory in Chapters 2 and 3 more concrete.

Finally, Chapter 8 gave you some step-by-step guidelines to help you design, test, and maintain better case-based reasoning systems.

The remainder of this chapter will revisit some of the issues raised in the preceding chapters and will make a strong argument for what I believe is a major breakthrough in computing.

9.2 Assumptions and Key Concepts

Before you finish this book, it is important that you clearly understand the assumptions and key concepts that underpin CBR. Janet Kolodner, in a recent paper, demonstrated that even experienced CBR researchers and developers often misunderstand some of these issues.

9.2.1 CBR Assumptions

CBR systems assume certain things to be true in the world (Kolodner 1996):

1. *Regularity*. The world is essentially a regular and predictable place. The same actions performed under the same conditions will normally have the same (or very similar) outcomes.
2. *Typicality*. Events tend to repeat. Thus, a CBR system's experiences are likely to be useful in the future.
3. *Consistency*. Small changes in the world only require small changes to our reasoning and need correspondingly small changes to our solutions.

Basically, this is saying that CBR expects the world to be a regular, consistent, and predictable place, in which things we have learned in the past will be useful in similar circumstances in the future. If you are designing a system for a problem that is not regular, consistent, or predictable, but is widely chaotic and unpredictable, then CBR is unlikely to be a useful approach. However, it must be said that most computing techniques, and particularly decision support technologies, also depend on these assumptions about the world.

9.2.2 *Similarity Is the Key*

CBR is primarily concerned with measuring or assessing *similarity* between cases. It is not important how similarity is measured. Chapter 2 described two ways of retrieving similar cases (i.e., nearest-neighbor and inductive indexing), but these are not the only ways. There is a belief held by some researchers that if a system does not use these or similar techniques then it cannot be a real CBR system. This is nonsense. For example, all of the following can be used to measure similarity: neural networks, fuzzy logics, statistical clustering algorithms, and rule-based systems. Providing that a system retrieves cases from its memory, assesses their similarity in some way, uses that measure to find a best or a good match, and then uses the retrieved case to suggest a solution, it is a CBR system. Precisely how the CBR-cycle is implemented is not important.

9.2.3 *Case-Bases Must Be Large to be Useful*

Two of the most common questions asked by delegates at a CBR conference or workshop are "How many cases does your system have?" and "How fast is the retrieval algorithm?" The answers that a developer should give are, "Enough cases to be useful" and "Fast enough to be used, thank you." There is a commonly held misconception that the more cases a system has, the better, and that *real* men build CBR systems with tens of thousands of cases with retrieval times of milliseconds. For many business applications, case-bases can be relatively small and retrieval times can be measured in seconds.

For example, I know of an insurance company that specializes in commercial vehicles. They use a CBR system with 300 cases to advise their underwriters. They found that the 300 cases cover the majority of commercial vehicles and their uses. Exceptions are handled by experienced underwriters. The company could have built a case-base containing all of the hundreds of thousands of vehicles they have ever insured, but this would only have resulted in a massive case-base that held many very similar cases. Moreover, with only 300 cases, the retrieval algorithm does not need to be very efficient, whereas with 300,000 cases it would have to be. Most of the CBR systems described in this book have case-bases that range from a couple of hundred cases to a couple of thousand. Very large case-bases—such as the 20,000-plus cases in SQUAD in use at NEC—are the exception, not the norm.

9.2.4 *CBR Is Just Hype*

It is true that there is some hype associated with CBR at the moment. To a degree I have been responsible in perpetuating some of this hype, by writing this book. You, in buying this book, may have succumbed to it. However, hype is necessary. Without it, people don't hear about a subject, governments don't fund research, and companies don't dare to use a new technology. The fear of the CBR community is that, as with the hype-surrounded expert systems in the early 1980s, CBR will fail to deliver and there will be a backlash.

This fear, I believe, is largely groundless because there is a significant difference between the two situations. The hype created around expert systems in the early 1980s preceded their successful commercial use. That is, exaggerated claims were made based on the findings of a small number of research prototypes and demonstrators. This is exactly the reverse of the situation with CBR. The hype has only recently started (many people, even in AI, have still not heard of CBR), but there have already been well over 100 successful commercial applications of CBR. In short, CBR has already proved itself to be commercially successful. It is not just hype.

9.3 The Case for Case-Based Reasoning

Case-based reasoning is different from the way computing has worked from the first days of computers. When you perform simple math using a calculator, it gives you a correct answer. If you then perform exactly the same sum again, the calculator will repeat the calculation, step for step, to give you the same answer. If the calculation was a long, complex one, you may have to wait several seconds for the answer. People don't work that way. If you are told, "The square root of 789 is 28.089," and then I ask you, "What is the square root of 789?", you know the answer—it's 28.089. You don't have to work it—you just remember it! Computers have always worked problems out from scratch, even if they just solved the same problem a few seconds ago. This seems odd, because computers have very good memories. If I asked you next week, "What is the square root of 789?", you may well have forgotten the answer by then. But if we had placed the answer in a database, the computer wouldn't have forgotten.

For the first time, CBR encourages computers to solve problems more like people do, by first asking, "Have I solved this problem or a similar one before? If I have, then I'll try to use that answer. If I haven't, then I guess I'll just have to work it out."

Case-based reasoning is not just about remembering answers to old problems, it is also fundamentally concerned with similarity. If I now ask, "What is the square root of 780?", one thing you can immediately tell me, before you get your calculator out, is that the answer must be *near* 28.089. You might also say that the answer is going to be slightly less than 28.089, perhaps 28. In fact, the correct answer is 27.928. So your guess wasn't too far out.

CBR, therefore, encourages computers to stop wasting time resolving problems they already may know the answer to. Of course, in some situations it may be quicker to solve the problem from scratch rather than search a massive case-base and then adapt the solution. This balance always has to be carefully considered. However, CBR has many potential benefits, outlined in the rest of this section.

9.3.1 *Corporate Memory*

As companies increasingly downsize and reengineer, the knowledge and experience of their employees becomes more vital to corporate success. Within a corporate environment, case-based reasoning can be used as a knowledge-management tool to help stop people from resolving problems someone else has already solved. Many companies already do this, and a good example of this is in case-based help-desks.

Case-based help-desks have several key benefits:

- Problem-solving knowledge is retained centrally and is available to all employees.

- Because of this, consistent advice and help is given to customers, regardless of which employee they talk to.

■ Case-based help-desks learn by acquiring new problems and their solutions as they arise.

Actually, these benefits are not unique to case-based help-desks. The CLAVIER system at Lockheed was not a help-desk, but it saw similar benefits—most important of which was the retention of experience. Companies across the world are beginning to realize that experience or knowledge is a corporate asset just as important as a company's more tangible assets, such as property or stock.

This concept is called *knowledge asset management*, and many companies are starting to implement CBR systems to help them retain and distribute their experience. For example:

■ NEC has implemented a corporate-wide case-base of problems that employees have encountered. SQUAD contains more than 20,000 cases and acquires around 3,000 new problems each year. Some of the problems have solutions, but others are there to help people avoid repeating mistakes.

■ Apple Computer also uses a corporate memory system, called NNable. In a similar way to the one at NEC, the case-base contains cases describing problem-solving experiences. These support what Apple terms a community of *knowledge workers*.

As we move further into the information age, knowledge becomes power and some people are arguing for a new corporate role for a "chief knowledge officer." This person would be a senior executive whose mission would be to manage the knowledge assets of the company. CBR is a crucial enabling technology behind these ideas.

9.3.2 *Case-Based Expert Systems*

Over the last 30 years, many expert systems have been developed that have an explicit model of the problem domain in which they operate. Usually the model is implemented by rules, and perhaps more recently using object technology. In second-generation systems, a deep underlying causal model exists that enables the system to reason from first principles in its application domain. There is little doubt that such expert systems (whether they use deep or shallow domain models) can be very successful. However, there are five major problems with the conventional expert systems approach:

1. Knowledge elicitation is acknowledged to be very difficult and time consuming.

2. Expert systems can be very complex and can take many years to develop.

3. Expert systems are frequently slow because of complex inferencing processes.

4. Expert systems are often poor at managing large volumes of information.

5. Once developed, they are notoriously difficult to maintain.

The first problem was recognized as soon as expert systems were built and was called the *knowledge-elicitation bottleneck*. The second problem is familiar to any expert system developer and has partially been responsible for the increasing interest in expert system development methodologies and of knowledge-modelling languages and ontologies. The third problem has partially been overcome by the ever-decreasing cost of processing power, while solutions to the fourth have been sought through the integration of AI techniques with database technology.

However, for many years practitioners believed that expert systems were easy to maintain. Almost all books on expert system development written during the 1980s contain a quote similar to this: "Maintaining a rule-base is easy, being simply a matter of adding or subtracting rules from the knowledge-base." Easier than maintaining procedural C or Fortran code, true, but not *easy*. Unfortunately, the experience of maintaining large rule-based systems such as XCON/R1 at Digital has shown that maintaining expert systems is not as simple as adding or subtracting rules. As a knowledge-base grows, it becomes a very complex debugging task.

However, there is a more fundamental problem that has been overlooked. Expert system practitioners did not consider how to build an expert system when there was no model or well-understood domain theory available. Overlooking this problem reflects the heritage of expert systems in academic research laboratories. The early expert systems (e.g., DENDRAL, MYCIN, PROSPECTOR) all operated in domains where there were good underlying models (either from first principles or statistics). Scientists are comfortable working with models: they build them for a living. Unfortunately, in a commercial environment and outside of universities, many people make decisions without reference to first principles and underlying causal or statistical models.

These people solve problems by using their own experience. It is no surprise that "expert" and "experience" derive from the same root. I believe that the expert system community was seduced by rules and neglected the truism that experts solve problems by applying their experience, while only novices attempt to solve problems by applying rules they have recently acquired. The application of experience to problem solving is the hallmark of CBR. Thus, CBR provides a reasoning paradigm that is close to the way people solve problems, and one that overcomes the problems of rule-based systems.

Hence, there are very strong arguments for case-based expert systems, since CBR has several advantages over rule-based reasoning:

- CBR systems can be built without passing through the knowledge-elicitation bottleneck, since elicitation becomes a simpler task of acquiring past cases. This is demonstrated by Lockheed's CLAVIER system. (Remember, they tried and failed to build a rule-based system.)

- CBR systems can be built where a model does not exist. This is also well demonstrated by the CLAVIER system.

- Implementation becomes a simpler task of identifying relevant case features.

- A CBR system can be rolled out with only a partial case-base, as happened with CLAVIER, CASELine, and SWIFT. Indeed, using CBR, a system need never be *complete*, since it will be continually growing. This removes one of the bugbears of rule-based systems—how to tell when a system is complete.

- CBR systems can propose a solution quickly by avoiding the need to infer an answer from first principles each time, important in CASELine and in most help-desk situations.

- Individual or generalized cases can be used to provide explanations that are sometimes more satisfactory than explanations generated by chains of rules.

- CBR systems can learn by acquiring new cases, making maintenance easier as demonstrated by CLAVIER, CASELine, and SWIFT.

- Finally, by acquiring new cases, CBR systems grow to reflect their organization's experience. If a rule-based system were delivered to six companies and used for six months, after that time each system would be identical, assuming no maintenance had taken place. If six identical CBR systems were used in a similar way after six months, there would be six *different* systems, as each would have acquired different cases.

The claim that CBR systems can be implemented faster than rule-based systems was supported by a study conducted by Cognitive Systems, which stated that it took two weeks to develop a case-based version of a system that took four months to build in rule-based form. Also, and more recently, developers at Digital Equipment Corp. confirmed that a rule-based system called CANASTA took over eight times longer to develop than CASCADE, a case-based system with the same functionality. DEC also claims that the maintenance of CANASTA is continual, whereas CASCADE needs almost no maintenance. Similar claims are provided by Lockheed regarding CLAVIER.

Thus, CBR offers solutions to many of the problems that have been associated with rule-based expert systems. It is certain the case-based expert systems will become more common over the next few years.

9.3.3 *Case-Based Information Retrieval*

When database developers are shown a CBR system, they often say, "So what, I could do that with a database." In some senses they are correct. As was discussed in Chapters 1 and 3, CBR has some similarities to database-retrieval and information-retrieval techniques. But I do not believe CBR will replace any of these techniques; it will complement them. SQL queries are a powerful and reliable technique; moreover, they are fast and, above all, widely used. However, in some situations, where a person is not sure how to phrase a query, CBR can be helpful. This is particularly true of exploratory searches. As ever-increasing amounts of digital information are made available (e.g., on the Internet), exploratory searching will become more important.

CBR is a technique that can complement both database- and information-retrieval technologies, and I believe that in the future a database system will seem incomplete without a form of nearest-neighbor or similarity-based retrieval.

9.3.4 *CBR Is a Complementary Technique*

CBR can also complement other computing techniques, not just databases. I was recently at a scientific conference where a professor was describing an intelligent computer system that could solve a complex mechanical design task. I asked him how long his system took to solve a problem. He proudly replied that his system could solve a task in four hours that used to take a team of people over a week. I then asked him, if his system were given exactly the same problem again, how long would it now take? Looking less proud he mumbled, "About four hours."

This state of affairs is ridiculous. The professor's system should have solved the problem the second time in seconds. We should rethink the way we design computers to solve problems. Before starting to solve a problem, we should check to see if we have solved the problem before. Only if we haven't should we start from scratch. What I'm saying is that CBR should be used to complement other computing approaches. After all, how can we say that a computer system is *intelligent,* if it has no memory!

9.4 **The Way Ahead**

Case-based reasoning is still a young technology, barely 10 years old. There is still a lot of work to be done to realize its full potential. This book has introduced you to the concepts of CBR and shown you how to apply it. I have shown how CBR addresses many of the shortcomings of rule-based expert systems: the knowledge-elicitation bottleneck and the ability of the systems to learn incrementally and to provide highly contextualized explanations. This is why over the last few years, this new way of building expert systems has grown from a specific and isolated research area to a field of widespread interest.

These developments have produced commercial CBR tools that use database and AI techniques that can help sift through large amounts of historical information in order to automate knowledge based on experience. This automation of historical experience required reasoning about previous cases that could complement other methods of problem solving. It is extremely natural, for example, to be reminded of something when trying to solve a particular problem. The goal of CBR systems is to be reminded of similar cases when faced with a new problem, and to retrieve those cases in order to help the user solve the new problem in a fashion similar to the way it was solved for a closely matching situation.

With all of its advantages in domains that are poorly understood or where there are many exceptions to rules, there are still problems that need to be worked out for CBR. If rule-based systems faced problems in eliciting and acquiring knowledge, there are also sensitive problems that face CBR, including

- How cases should be represented
- How indexes should be chosen for organizing memory efficiently
- How to structure relationships between cases and parts of different cases
- How to handle cases containing multimedia
- How to handle massive case-bases containing hundreds of thousands of cases
- How to develop general adaptation heuristics for modifying previous cases or their solutions to fit new cases

In the future, CBR systems may need to be able

- To *forget* unused cases in order to maintain case-base efficiency
- To learn about the emergence of case attributes that had not previously been thought significant

More immediately, it is necessary to integrate CBR fully with other reasoning paradigms and database information systems and to critically evaluate the effectiveness of CBR in commercial domains. Relying on previous experience, without validation, may result in inefficient or incorrect solutions being recommended, causing an increase in problem-solving time or errors that may have negative effects on the process of learning.

CBR is entering a period where people are exploring its potential and its limitations. This is largely being driven by the available tools, and we would be unwise to neglect the theoretical basis of CBR. In the next years we will see many more, hopefully successful applications using CBR. The majority of these will undoubtedly be in customer support help-desks. However, despite the shallow nature of these systems, the AI community should be proud that after all the hype surrounding expert systems, we are finally able to deliver a simple, effective solution that business can understand and benefit from.

Moreover, the acceptance of these systems, of CBR, and thus by implication, of AI techniques in general, may open the door to a more widespread use of AI and its integration with management information systems. Brightware's tool, ART*Enterprise*, for example, seems to be in the vanguard of corporate AI and may encourage the use of cases as a corporate resource and of knowledge as an asset to be managed.

Many CBR researchers are currently developing complex case representations, storage, and indexing mechanisms that are highly dependent on domain knowledge. This approach will never be commercially feasible. Within a university research lab it is acceptable to handcraft a case representation and retrieval mechanism for a few dozen cases. Within a commercial context, where you may have tens of thousands of cases, and may be building many systems a year to tight deadlines, case representations must be simple. These will usually be flat file structures based on relational database technology. This is why companies, like Inference, are storing their cases in conventional and widely used relational databases.

In a similar way, many CBR researchers believe there is one great challenge facing them—namely, adaptation. Relatively few commercial CBR systems adapt cases, and those that do usually do so in a simple way (e.g., the Wayland system). Many CBR tools, like Inference's CBR3, are purely case-retrieval systems, adaptation being left to human intervention. Adaptation is not a challenge for CBR, but is, in fact, a distraction. I firmly believe that the true power of CBR is retrieval. Adaptation inevitably involves using techniques that are not themselves case-based. In the words of Christopher Riesbeck, one of the early pioneers of CBR:

> Adaptation techniques are hard to generalize, hard to implement, and quick to break. Furthermore, adaptation is often unnecessary. The originally retrieved case is often as useful to a human as any half-baked adaptation of it.
>
> —Riesbeck 1996, p. 388

Moreover, Mark, Simoudis, and Hinkle (1996, p.293) collectively state about their experience:

> One of our consistent findings was that automated adaptation of cases was not feasible. The required depth of domain understanding consistently forced us into ad hoc approaches that had very limited coverage. . . . On the other hand, we found in CLAVIER that users are very willing to participate in the adaptation process.

Thus, the CBR-cycle should be redrawn to explicitly include people in the loop (Figure 9-2).

CBR will continue to be applied to a wider range of problem types as people experiment with its potential. Kristian Hammond, a pioneer of CBR in the United States, has proposed dividing CBR research into three categories according to their fundamental goals. Note that he intends that the categories should be inclusive, not exclusive, and should stimulate debate, not stifle it.

Figure 9-2.
*The real
CBR-cycle*

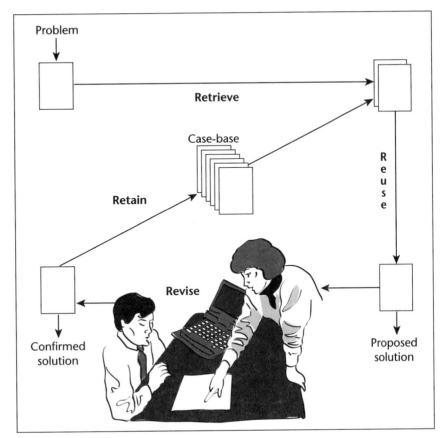

1. *True faith CBR.* Relating to the cognitive science and AI theoretical issues of CBR.

2. *Hard-core CBR.* Testing and refining true faith theories in challenging practical applications.

3. *CBR-lite.* Using selected CBR techniques, such as case retrieval, to solve particular problems (e.g., help-desks).

Kristian Hammond believes that research into each of these three categories is bona fide CBR research. CBR needs the cognitive science and AI theorists just as much as the hard-core researchers and those who apply CBR-lite for commercial profit. CBR is not rocket science, it is the application of relatively simple and well-understood techniques to support decisions.

Finally, this is the message I want to leave you with: The fundamental power and success of CBR is its simplicity. CBR is easy to understand, because it is how people have always solved problems. It is easy to implement, because the techniques are computationally straightforward. Therefore, if you are planning to build a CBR system, please, keep it simple.

9.5 Further Reading

One of the best books that describes the development of early expert systems and many of the problems encountered:

Hayes-Roth, F., Waterman, D.A., and Lenat, D.B. (1983). *Building Expert Systems*. Reading, MA: Addison-Wesley.

An excellent collection of papers, by many of the most influential people in CBR, that cover a lot of the issues raised in this chapter can be found in

Leake, D.B., ed. (1996). *Case-Based Reasoning: Experiences, Lessons, & Future Directions*. Cambridge, MA: AAAI Press / MIT Press.

The SQUAD system, in use at the NEC Corporation, is described in

Kitano, H., Shibata, A., Shimazu, H., Kajihara, J., and Sato, A. (1992). Building Large-Scale and Corporate Wide Case-Based Systems. In *Proceedings of AAAI-92*. Cambridge, MA: AAAI Press / MIT Press.

Kitano, H., and Shimazu, H. (1996). The Experience-Sharing Architecture: A Case Study in Corporate-Wide Case-Based Software Quality Control. In *Case-Based Reasoning: Experience, Lessons, & Future Directions*, 235–268, edited by D.B. Leake. Cambridge, MA: AAAI Press / MIT Press.

Apple Computer's NNable system is described in

Laffey, J., Machiraju, R., and Chandhok, R. (1991). Integrated Support and Learning Systems for Augmenting Knowledge Workers: A Focus on Case-Based Retrieval. In *Proceedings of the World Congress on Expert Systems*, Orlando, FL. Elmsford, NY: Pergamon Press.

A collective experience of building several CBR systems is described in

Mark, W., Simoudis, E., and Hinkle, D. (1996). Case-Based Reasoning: Expectations and Results. In *Case-Based Reasoning: Experiences, Lessons, & Future Directions*, 267–294, edited by D.B. Leake. Cambridge, MA: AAAI Press / MIT Press.

Janet Kolodner dispels several common misconceptions about CBR in

Kolodner, J. (1996). Making the Implicit Explicit: Clarifying the Principles of Case-Based Reasoning. In *Case-Based Reasoning: Experience, Lessons, & Future Directions*, 350–370, edited by D.B. Leake. Cambridge, MA: AAAI Press / MIT Press.

While, Christopher Riesbeck talks about the future of CBR in

Riesbeck, C.K. (1996). What Next? The Future of Case-Based Reasoning in Post Modern AI. In *Case-Based Reasoning: Experience, Lessons, & Future Directions*, 371–388, edited by D.B. Leake. Cambridge, MA: AAAI Press / MIT Press.

10

Bibliography

Although CBR is a relatively new discipline, there is an ever-increasing number of papers, reports, and books being published on the subject. In this context, the objective of this bibliography is to help guide an interested student or developer quickly through this literature, so you can easily identify references relevant to you. It is organized as follows:

- Section 10.1 presents the *essential* library of CBR publications. These works provide a comprehensive picture of the history, development, and application of CBR.

- Section 10.2 is devoted to papers that refer to the origins of CBR, the domains where CBR has succeeded, and the tasks it can perform, as well as to papers that give a background or survey of CBR.

- Section 10.3 covers CBR techniques, including case representation, indexing, case memory, case retrieval, and adaptation.

- Section 10.4 focuses on the practical application of CBR, including software tools, and lists papers that refer to applications. Both academic demonstrators and commercial systems are included.

- Section 10.5 lists papers on the cooperation between CBR and different reasoning methods, and papers relating to CBR and analogy.

- Finally, Section 10.6 lists Internet sites where information of relevance to CBR can be found.

Because a single work may refer to several subjects, I have decided to include the full reference to the work in all relevant categories, rather than referring readers to a single bibliography. I feel that this results in less work for the reader by making pertinent works easier to find. Note that this bibliography is a major update to the bibliography published by Marir and Watson in 1994 (Marir, F., and Watson, I. (1994). Case-Based Reasoning: A Categorised Bibliography. *The Knowledge Engineering Review*, 9(4)).

10.1 Essential Readings

The following works, presented in chronological order, will give you the essential CBR library.

These first two works are widely acknowledged as being the foundations of CBR:

Schank, R., and Abelson, R., eds. (1977). *Scripts, Plans, Goals and Understanding*. Hillsdale, NJ: Lawrence Erlbaum Associates.

Schank, R., ed. (1982). *Dynamic Memory: A Theory of Learning in Computers and People*. New York: Cambridge University Press.

There then followed two workshops, sponsored by DARPA, that established CBR as a research discipline in the United States:

Kolodner, J.L., ed. (1988). *Proceedings of the DARPA Case-Based Reasoning Workshop*. San Francisco: Morgan Kaufmann Publishers.

Hammond, K.J., ed. (1989). *Proceedings of the DARPA Case-Based Reasoning Workshop*. San Francisco: Morgan Kaufmann Publishers.

The following book presents the state of the art in CBR at this time and makes extensive use of the Micro-JUDGE program:

Riesbeck, C.K., and Schank, R. (1989). *Inside Case-Based Reasoning*. Northvale, NJ: Lawrence Erlbaum Associates.

The final workshop sponsored by DARPA:

Bareiss, E.R., ed. (1991). *Proceedings of the DARPA Case-Based Reasoning Workshop*. San Francisco: Morgan Kaufmann Publishers.

A series of introductory papers, special issues, and reviews presented CBR to a wider, mainly U.S., audience:

Barlet, S. (1991). An Introduction to Case-Based Reasoning. *AI Expert,* 6(8).

Simoudis, E. (1991). Special Issue on Case-Based Reasoning. *International Journal of Expert Systems,* 4(2).

Slade, S. (1991). Case-Based Reasoning: A Research Paradigm. *AI Magazine,* 42–55.

Harmon, P. (1992). Case-Based Reasoning III. *Intelligent Software Strategies,* 8(1).

IEEE Expert. (1992). *Special Issue on Case-Based Reasoning.* 7(5), October 1992.

Kolodner, J.L. (1992). An Introduction to Case-Based Reasoning. *Artificial Intelligence Review* 6(1), 3–34.

Janet Kolodner presented a very comprehensive study of CBR in

Kolodner, J.L. (1993). *Case-Based Reasoning.* San Francisco: Morgan Kaufmann Publishers.

The AAAI started to host a series of meetings on CBR:

Leake, D.B., ed. (1993). *Case-Based Reasoning.* AAAI Workshop Series WS-93-01.

Anick, P., and Simoudis, E., eds. (1993). *Case-Based Reasoning & Information Retrieval: Exploring Opportunities for Technology Sharing.* AAAI Spring Symposia SS-93-07.

Aha, D.W., ed. (1994). *Case-Based Reasoning.* AAAI Workshop Series WS-94-01.

CBR had now taken hold in Europe, and a series of workshops and review papers introduced a European audience to the subject:

Richter, M.M., Wess, S., Althoff, K.-D, and Maurer, F., eds. (1993). *EWCBR'93, Proceedings of the First European Workshop on Case-Based Reasoning.* Berlin: Springer-Verlag.

Aamodt, A., and Plaza, E. (1994). Case-Based Reasoning: Foundational Issues, Methodological Variations, and System Approaches. *AI Communications,* 7(i), 39–59.

Watson I., and Marir, F. (1994). Case-Based Reasoning: A Review. *The Knowledge Engineering Review,* 9(4), 355–381.

Watson, I., ed. (1995). *Progress in Case-Based Reasoning.* Lecture Notes in Artificial Intelligence 1020. Berlin: Springer-Verlag.

The first International Conference in CBR was held in Sesimbra, Portugal, in October 1995:

Veloso, M.M., and Aamodt, A., eds. (1995). *Case-Based Reasoning Research and Development, Proceedings of the First International Conference on Case-Based Reasoning.* Lecture Notes in Artificial Intelligence 1010. Berlin: Springer-Verlag.

While this symposium on adaptation was held in the United States:

Aha, D.W., and Ram, A., eds. (1995). *Adaptation of Knowledge for Reuse: Proceedings of the 1995 AAAI Fall Symposium.* AAAI Technical Report FS-95-04.

Many of the influential pioneers of CBR are able to reflect on their experience in this collection of papers:

Leake, D.B., ed. (1996). *Case-Based Reasoning: Experiences, Lessons, and Future Directions.* Cambridge, MA: AAAI Press / MIT Press.

European workshops are now a regular occurrence:

Smith, I., and Faltings, B., eds. (1996). *Advances in Case-Based Reasoning.* Lecture Notes in Artificial Intelligence 1186. Berlin: Springer-Verlag.

Watson, I., ed. (1996). *Progress in Case-Based Reasoning,* Proceedings of the Second U.K. Workshop on Case-Based Reasoning. Salford, UK: Salford University.

10.2 The Origins of CBR

10.2.1 *History*

This section contains references that describe the evolution of CBR and the conditions that led to its occurrence. It starts with a philosophical investigation of Wittgenstein published in 1953 and leads on to the work of Roger Schank on dynamic memory in 1982 and other associated memory models. It is also presents work and criticisms from both the cognitive and computer science communities that assisted the development of CBR theory. This includes psychological investigation and the relationship between human activity and reminding.

Bareiss, E.R., (1988). *PROTOS: A Unified Approach to Concept Representation, Classification, and Learning*. Ph.D. thesis, Dept. of Computer Science, University of Texas. Technical Report CS 88-10, Dept. of Computer Science, Vanderbilt University, Nashville, TN.

Bareiss, E.R. (1989). *Exemplar-Based Knowledge Acquisition: A Unified Approach to Concept Representation, Classification, and Learning*. Boston: Academic Press.

Cullingford, R. (1978). *Script Application: Computer Understanding of Newspaper Stories*. Technical Report No. 116., Dept. of Computer Science, Yale University.

Dyer, M. (1983). *In-Depth Understanding*. Cambridge, MA: MIT Press.

Gentner, D. (1983). Structure-Mapping: A Theoretical Framework for Analogy. *Cognitive Science, 7*(2).

Harmon, P. (1992). Case-Based Reasoning III. *Intelligent Software Strategies, 8*(1).

Keane, M. (1988). Where's the Beef? The Absence of Pragmatic Factors in Pragmatic Theories of Analogy. In*: Proceedings of ECCAI-88*, 327–332.

Klein, G.A., and Calderwood, R. (1988). How Do People Use Analogues to Make Decisions? In *Proceedings of the DARPA Case-Based Reasoning Workshop*, edited by J.L. Kolodner. San Francisco: Morgan Kaufmann Publishers.

Klein, G.A., Whitaker, L.A., and King, J.A. (1988). Using Analogues to Predict and Plan. In *Proceedings of the DARPA Case-Based Reasoning Workshop*, edited by J.L. Kolodner. San Francisco: Morgan Kaufmann Publishers.

Kolodner, J.L. (1983). Maintaining Organization in a Dynamic Long-Term Memory. *Cognitive Science, 7*, 243–280.

Kolodner, J.L. (1983). Reconstructive Memory, a Computer Model. *Cognitive Science, 7*(2), 281–328.

Koton, P. (1989). *Using Experience in Learning and Problem Solving*. Ph.D. thesis, October 1988, Laboratory of Computer Science, Massachusetts Institute of Technology, MIT/LCS/TR-441.

McDougal, T., Hammond, J.K., and Seifert, C. (1991). A Functional Perspective on Reminding. In *Proceedings of the DARPA Case-Based Reasoning Workshop*, edited by E.R. Bareiss. San Francisco: Morgan Kaufmann Publishers.

Porter, B.W., and Bareiss, E.R. (1986). PROTOS: An Experiment in Knowledge Acquisition for Heuristic Classification Tasks. In *Proceedings of the First International Meeting on Advances in Learning (IMAL)*, 159–174. Les Arcs, France.

Riesbeck, C.K., and Schank, R. (1989). *Inside Case-Based Reasoning*. Northvale, NJ: Lawrence Erlbaum Associates.

Schank, R., ed. (1982). *Dynamic Memory: A Theory of Learning in Computers and People.* New York: Cambridge University Press.

Schank, R., and Abelson, R., eds. (1977). *Scripts, Plans, Goals and Understanding.* Hillsdale, NJ: Lawrence Erlbaum Associates.

Seifert, C.M. (1988). Goals in Reminding. In *Proceedings of the DARPA Case-Based Reasoning Workshop,* edited by J.L. Kolodner. San Francisco: Morgan Kaufmann Publishers.

Smith, E.E., and Adams, N. (1978). Fact Retrieval and the Paradox of Interference. *Cognitive Psychology* 10, 438–64.

Smith, E.E., and Medin, D.L. (1981). *Categories and Concepts.* Cambridge, MA: Harvard University Press.

Strube, G. (1991). The Role of Cognitive Science in Knowledge Engineering. In *Contemporary Knowledge Engineering and Cognition,* 161–174, edited by F. Schmalhofer. New York: Springer-Verlag.

Tulving, E. (1977). Episodic and Semantic Memory. In *Organization of Memory,* 381–403, edited by E. Tulving and W. Donaldson. San Diego: Academic Press.

Wilensky, R. (1978). *Understanding Goal-Based Stories.* Technical Report No. 140, Dept. of Computer Science, Yale University.

Wittgenstein, L. (1953). *Philosophical Investigations.* United Kingdom: Blackwell.

10.2.2 *Feasibility and Uses of CBR*

This section contains references on works that consolidate the philosophical and psychological claims of the feasibility and the use of case-based reasoning to model realistic world problems as people do. In this context, it presents the advantages of CBR in relation to other reasoning paradigms, such as rule-based and model-based reasoning, through its success in performing complex tasks in various domains (e.g., legal, process control, history, planning, learning, tutoring, problem solving, explanation, and prediction in strategic domains such as health, agriculture, and education).

Aamodt, A. (1989). Towards Expert Systems That Learn from Experience. In *Proceedings of the DARPA Case-Based Reasoning Workshop,* edited by K.J. Hammond. San Francisco: Morgan Kaufmann Publishers.

Aleven, V., and Ashley, K.D. (1996). How Different Is Different? Arguing about the Significance of Similarities and Differences. In *Advances in Case-Based Reasoning,* edited by I. Smith and B. Faltings. Lecture Notes in Artificial Intelligence 1168. Berlin: Springer-Verlag.

Althoff, K.-D., Auriol, E., Barletta, R., and Manago, M. (1995). *A Review of Industrial Case-Based Reasoning Tools.* Oxford: AI Intelligence.

Althoff, K.-D., and Wess, S. (1992). Case-Based Reasoning and Expert System Development. In *Contemporary Knowledge Engineering and Cognition.* Lecture Notes in Computer Science 622, 146–160. Berlin: Springer-Verlag.

Baldwin, J.F. (1993). Evidential Support Logic, FRIL and Case-Based Reasoning. *International Journal of Intelligent Systems,* 8(9).

Barnden, J., and Srinivas, K. (1992). Overcoming Rule-Based Rigidity and Connectionist Limitation Through Massively Parallel Case-Based Reasoning. *International Journal of Man-Machine Studies,* 36(2), 221–246.

Berger, J. (1994). Roentgen: Radiation Therapy and Case-Based Reasoning. In *Proceedings of the Conference on Artificial Intelligence Applications,* 171–177.

Bradburn, C., and Zeleznikow, J. (1993). The Application of Case Based Reasoning to the Tasks of Health Care Planning. In *Proceedings of EWCBR'93,* edited by M.M. Richter et al. Berlin: Springer-Verlag.

Branting, L.K. (1988). The Role of Explanation in Reasoning from Legal Precedent. In *Proceedings of the DARPA Case-Based Reasoning Workshop,* edited by J.L. Kolodner. San Francisco: Morgan Kaufmann Publishers.

Chiriatti, K.C., and Plant, R.E. (1993). Case-Based Reasoning: Application to the Agricultural Domain, a Prototype. In *Proceeding of EWCBR'93,* edited by M.M. Richter et al. Berlin: Springer-Verlag.

Cunningham, P. (1993). Using CBR Techniques to Detect Plagiarism in Computing Assignments. In *Proceeding of EWCBR'93,* edited by M.M. Richter et al. Berlin: Springer-Verlag.

Curet, O., Jackson, M., and Killin, J. (1996). Implementing and Evaluating Case-Based Learning and Reasoning Applications: A Case Study. In *Proceedings of the Second U.K. Workshop on Case-Based Reasoning,* edited by I. Watson. Salford, UK: Salford University.

Dupuy, T. (1988). Military History and Case-Based Reasoning. In *Proceedings of the DARPA Case-Based Reasoning Workshop,* edited by J.L. Kolodner. San Francisco: Morgan Kaufmann Publishers.

Evans, C. (1993). Case-Based Learning of Dysmorphic Syndromes. In *Proceedings of EWCBR'93,* edited by M.M. Richter et al. Berlin: Springer-Verlag.

Farrell, R. (1988). Facilitating Self-Education by Questioning Assumptive Reasoning Using Paradigm Cases. In *Proceedings of the DARPA Case-Based Reasoning Workshop,* edited by J.L. Kolodner. San Francisco: Morgan Kaufmann Publishers.

Goodman, M. (1989). CBR in Battle Planning. In *Proceedings of the DARPA Case-Based Reasoning Workshop,* edited by K.J. Hammond. San Francisco: Morgan Kaufmann Publishers.

Griffiths, A.D., and Bridge, D.G. (1996). A Yardstick for the Evaluation of Case-Based Classifiers. In *Proceedings of the Second U.K. Workshop on Case-Based Reasoning*, edited by I. Watson. Salford, UK: Salford University.

Hammond, K.J. (1988). Case-Based Planning: Viewing Planning as a Memory Task. In *Proceedings of the DARPA Case-Based Reasoning Workshop*, edited by J.L. Kolodner. San Francisco: Morgan Kaufmann Publishers.

Klein, G.A., and Calderwood, R. (1988). How Do People Use Analogues to Make Decisions? In *Proceedings of the DARPA Case-Based Reasoning Workshop*, edited by J.L. Kolodner. San Francisco: Morgan Kaufmann Publishers.

Klein, G.A., Whitaker, L.A., and King, J.A. (1988). Using Analogues to Predict and Plan. In *Proceedings of the DARPA Case-Based Reasoning Workshop*, edited by J.L. Kolodner. San Francisco: Morgan Kaufmann Publishers.

Kolodner, J.L. (1992). *The Role of Experience in Natural Problem Solving*. College of Computing, Georgia Institute of Technology, Atlanta.

Kopeikina, L., Bandau, R., and Lemmon, A. (1988). Case-Based Reasoning for Continuous Control. In *Proceedings of the DARPA Case-Based Reasoning Workshop*, edited by J.L. Kolodner. San Francisco: Morgan Kaufmann Publishers.

Koton, P. (1988). Reasoning About Evidence in Causal Explanations. In *Proceedings of the DARPA Case-Based Reasoning Workshop*, edited by J.L. Kolodner. San Francisco: Morgan Kaufmann Publishers.

Marir, F., and Watson, I. (1995). Can CBR Imitate Human Intelligence and Are Such Systems Easy to Design and Maintain? A Critique. In *Progress in Case-Based Reasoning*, edited by I. Watson. Lecture Notes in Artificial Intelligence 1020. Berlin: Springer-Verlag.

Mark, W., Simoudis, E., and Hinkle, D. (1996). Case-Based Reasoning: Expectations and Results. In *Case-Based Reasoning: Experiences, Lessons, & Future Directions*, edited by D.B. Leake. Cambridge, MA: AAAI Press / MIT Press.

Marks, M., Hammond, K.A., and Converse, T. (1988). Planning in an Open World: A Pluralistic Approach. In *Proceedings of the DARPA Case-Based Reasoning Workshop*, edited by J.L. Kolodner. San Francisco: Morgan Kaufmann Publishers.

Mukhopadhyay, T., Vicinanaza, S.S, and Prieutula, M.J. (1992). Examining the Feasibility of a Case-Based Reasoning Model for Software Effort Estimation. *MIS Quarterly: Management Information Systems*, 16(2), 155–172.

Musgrove, P.B., Davies, J., and Izzard, D. (1996). A Comparison of Nearest Neighbour, Rule Induction and Neural Networks for the Recommendation of Treatment at Anticoagulant Out-Patient Clinics. In *Proceedings of the Second U.K. Workshop on Case-Based Reasoning*, edited by I. Watson. Salford, UK: Salford University.

Nakatani, Y., Tsukiyama, M., and Fukuda, T. (1992). Engineering Design Support Framework by Case-Based Reasoning. *ISA Transactions: A Publication of the Instrument Society of America,* 31(2).

Okamoto, S., and Satoh, K. (1995). An Average-Case Analysis of K-Nearest Neighbor Classifier. In *Case-Based Reasoning Research and Development,* edited by M. Veloso and A. Aamodt. Lecture Notes in Artificial Intelligence 1010. Berlin: Springer-Verlag.

Owens, C. (1988). Domain-Independent Prototype Cases for Planning. In *Proceedings of the DARPA Case-Based Reasoning Workshop,* edited by J.L. Kolodner. San Francisco: Morgan Kaufmann Publishers.

Pal, K., and Campbell, J.A. (1996). Suitability of Reasoning Methods in a Hybrid System. In *Proceedings of the Second U.K. Workshop on Case-Based Reasoning,* edited by I. Watson. Salford, UK: Salford University.

Richter, M.M., and Wess, S. (1991). Similarity, Uncertainty and Case-Based Reasoning in PATDEX. In *Automated Reasoning, Essays in Honour of Woody Beledsoe,* edited by R.S. Boyer.

Rougegrez, S. (1993). Case-Based Reasoning System that Avoids the Problem of the Case Identification. In *Proceedings of the IEEE International Conference on Systems, Man and Cybernetics,* 3, 182–186.

Schmitt, G., Baily, S.F., and Smith, I.F.C. (1994). Advances and Challenges in Case-Based Design. In *Proceedings of the First Congress Held in Conjunction with A/E/C Systems '94,* Vol. 1, edited by K. Khozeimeh.

Slade, S. (1991). Qualitative Decision Theory. In *Proceedings of the DARPA Case-Based Reasoning Workshop,* edited by R. Bareiss. San Francisco: Morgan Kaufmann Publishers.

Vargas, J.E., and Bourne, J.R. (1993). Scale-Guided Object Matching for Case-Based Reasoning. *Journal of Intelligent Robotic Systems,* 7(1).

Visser, W. (1995). Reuse of Knowledge: Empirical Studies. In *Case-Based Reasoning Research and Development,* edited by M. Veloso and A. Aamodt. Lecture Notes in Artificial Intelligence 1010. Berlin: Springer-Verlag.

Vo, D.P., and Macchion, D. (1993). Use of Case-Based Reasoning Technique in Building Expert Systems. In *Future Generation Computer Systems,* 9(4), 311–319.

Wall, R.S., Donahue, D., and Hill, S. (1988). The Use of Domain Semantics for Retrieval and Explanation in Case-Based Reasoning. In *Proceedings of the DARPA Case-Based Reasoning Workshop,* edited by J.L. Kolodner. San Francisco: Morgan Kaufmann Publishers.

Wendel, O. (1993). Case-Based Reasoning in a Simulation Environment for Biological Neural Networks. In *Proceedings of EWCBR'93,* edited by M.M. Richter et al. Berlin: Springer-Verlag.

Yavner, J., Alterman, R., and Sherman, F. (1989). Diachronic Analysis of Political-Event Cases. In *Proceedings of the DARPA Case-Based Reasoning Workshop*, edited by K.J. Hammond. San Francisco: Morgan Kaufmann Publishers.

Ziarko, W. (1989). Data Analysis and Case-Based Expert System Development Tool "Rough." In *Proceedings of the DARPA Case-Based Reasoning Workshop*, edited by K.J. Hammond. San Francisco: Morgan Kaufmann Publishers.

10.2.3 **Background and Review of CBR**

This section presents references on papers that give a survey or overview of CBR.

Aamodt, A., and Plaza, E. (1994). Case-Based Reasoning: Foundational Issues, Methodological Variations, and System Approaches. *AI Communications*, 7(i), 39–59.

Althoff, K.-D., Auriol, E., Barletta, R., and Manago, M. (1995). *A Review of Industrial Case-Based Reasoning Tools*. Oxford: AI Intelligence.

Bareiss, E.R., ed. (1991). *Proceedings of the DARPA Workshop on Case-Based Reasoning*. San Francisco: Morgan Kaufmann Publishers.

Barlet, S. (1991). An Introduction to Case-Based Reasoning. *AI Expert*, 6(8).

Domeshek, E., and Kolodner, J.L. (1991). Toward a Case-Based Aid for Conceptual Design. *International Journal of Expert Systems*, 4(2), 201–220.

Domeshek, E., and Kolodner, J.L. (1992). A Case-Based Design Aid for Architecture. In *Artificial Intelligence in Design*, edited by J. Gero. Boston: Kluwer.

Hammond, K.J. (1988). Case-Based Planning: Viewing Planning as a Memory Task. In *Proceedings of the DARPA Case-Based Reasoning Workshop*, edited by J.L. Kolodner. San Francisco: Morgan Kaufmann Publishers.

Hammond, K.J., ed. (1989). *Proceedings of the DARPA Workshop on Case-Based Reasoning*. San Francisco: Morgan Kaufmann Publishers.

Harmon, P. (1992). Case-Based Reasoning III. *Intelligent Software Strategies*, 8(1).

IEEE Expert. (1992). *Special Issue on Case-Based Reasoning*, 7(5), October 1992.

Kolodner, J.L., ed. (1988). *Proceedings of the DARPA Workshop on Case-Based Reasoning*. San Francisco: Morgan Kaufmann Publishers.

Kolodner, J.L. (1991). Improving Human Decision Making Through Case-Based Decision Aiding. *AI Magazine*, 12(ii), 52–68.

Kolodner, J.L. (1992). An Introduction to Case-Based Reasoning. *Artificial Intelligence Review*, 6(1), 3–34.

Kolodner, J.L. (1993). *Case-Based Reasoning.* San Francisco: Morgan Kaufmann Publishers.

Kolodner, J.L. (1996). Making the Implicit Explicit: Clarifying the Principles of Case-Based Reasoning. In *Case-Based Reasoning: Experiences, Lessons, & Future Directions*, edited by D.B. Leake. Cambridge, MA: AAAI Press / MIT Press.

Kolodner, J.L., and Leake, D.B. (1996). A Tutorial Introduction to Case-Based Reasoning. In *Case-Based Reasoning: Experiences, Lessons, and Future Directions*, edited by D.B. Leake. Cambridge, MA: AAAI Press / MIT Press.

Leake, D.B., ed. (1996). *Case-Based Reasoning: Experiences, Lessons, & Future Directions.* Cambridge, MA: AAAI Press / MIT Press.

Leake, D.B. (1996). CBR in Context: The Present and Future. In *Case-Based Reasoning: Experiences, Lessons, & Future Directions*, edited by D.B. Leake. Cambridge, MA: AAAI Press / MIT Press.

Lewis, L., et al. (1992). A Case-Based Reasoning Solution to the Problem of Redundant Engineering in Large-Scale Manufacturing. *International Journal of Expert Systems,* 4(ii), 189–200.

Maher, M.L., Balachandran, M.B., and Zhang, D.M. (1995). *Case-Based Reasoning in Design.* Northvale, NJ: Lawrence Erlbaum Associates.

Richter, M.M, Wess, S., Althoff, K.-D, and Maurer, F., eds. (1993). *First European Workshop on Case-Based Reasoning, (EWCBR'93).* Berlin: Springer-Verlag.

Riesbeck, C.K. (1996). What Next? The Future of Case-Based Reasoning in Postmodern AI. In *Case-Based Reasoning: Experiences, Lessons, & Future Directions*, edited by D.B. Leake. Cambridge, MA: AAAI Press / MIT Press.

Riesbeck, C.K., and Schank, R. (1989). *Inside Case-Based Reasoning.* Northvale, NJ: Lawrence Erlbaum Associates.

Simoudis, E. (1991). Special Issue on Case-Based Reasoning. *International Journal of Expert Systems,* 4(2).

Slade, S. (1991). Case-Based Reasoning: A Research Paradigm. *Al Magazine,* 42–55.

Vargas, J.E., and Raj, S. (1993). Developing Maintainable Expert Systems Using Case-Based Reasoning. *Expert Systems,* 10(4), 219–225.

Watson, I. (1995). An Introduction to Case-Based Reasoning. In *Progress in Case-Based Reasoning*, 3–16, edited by I. Watson. Lecture Notes in Artificial Intelligence 1020. Berlin: Springer-Verlag.

Watson, I., and Marir, F. (1994). Case-Based Reasoning: A Review. *The Knowledge Engineering Review,* 9(4), 355–381.

10.3 CBR Techniques

This section covers theoretical contributions to CBR techniques, along with application papers that present different ways of representing, indexing, retrieving, and adapting cases.

10.3.1 *Representation*

The case-representation process is one of the most important phases in designing a CBR system. The case representation should contain information that has a direct impact on the outcome or the solution of a problem situation. Depending on the complexity of the situation, cases can be represented in a flat form or a complex hierarchical form. This section lists papers that present a wide range of representational formalisms, including frames, semantic nets, rules, and relational database techniques, or a combination of different knowledge representations.

Aha, D.W. (1991). Case-Based Learning Algorithms. In *Proceedings of the DARPA Case-Based Reasoning Workshop*, edited by E.R. Bareiss. San Francisco: Morgan Kaufmann Publishers.

Aleven, V., and Ashley, K.D. (1996). How Different Is Different? Arguing About the Significance of Similarities and Differences. In *Advances in Case-Based Reasoning,* edited by I. Smith and B. Faltings. Lecture Notes in Artificial Intelligence 1168. Berlin: Springer-Verlag.

Alexander, P., Millden, G., Tsatsonlis, C., and Holtzman, J. (1989). Storing Design Knowledge in Cases. In *Proceedings of the DARPA Case-Based Reasoning Workshop*, edited by K.J. Hammond. San Francisco: Morgan Kaufmann Publishers.

Alterman, R. (1989). Panel Discussion on Case Representation. In *Proceedings of the DARPA Case-Based Reasoning Workshop*, edited by K.J. Hammond. San Francisco: Morgan Kaufmann Publishers.

Alterman, R. (1991). A Concept Space for Reasoning About Cases Involving Event Structures. In *Proceedings of the DARPA Case-Based Reasoning Workshop*, edited by E.R. Bareiss. San Francisco: Morgan Kaufmann Publishers.

Alterman, R., and Wentworth, M. (1989). Determining the Important Features of a Case. In *Proceedings of the DARPA Case-Based Reasoning Workshop*, edited by K.J. Hammond. San Francisco: Morgan Kaufmann Publishers.

Althoff, K.-D., Auriol, E., Barletta, R., and Manago, M. (1995). *A Review of Industrial Case-Based Reasoning Tools*. Oxford: AI Intelligence.

Bareiss, E.R. (1989). *Exemplar-Based Knowledge Acquisition: A Unified Approach to Concept Representation, Classification, and Learning.* Boston: Academic Press.

Bergmann, R., and Wilke, W. (1996). On the Role of Abstraction in Case-Based Reasoning. In *Advances in Case-Based Reasoning,* edited by I. Smith and B. Faltings. Lecture Notes in Artificial Intelligence 1168. Berlin: Springer-Verlag.

Blau, L., Bonissone, P.P., and Ayub, S. (1991). Planning with Dynamic Cases. In *Proceedings of the DARPA Case-Based Reasoning Workshop*, edited by E.R. Bareiss. San Francisco: Morgan Kaufmann Publishers.

Brandau, R., Lemmon, A., and Lafond, C. (1991). Experience with Extended Episodes: Cases with Complex Temporal Structure. In *Proceedings of the DARPA Case-Based Reasoning Workshop*, edited by E.R. Bareiss. San Francisco: Morgan Kaufmann Publishers.

Branting, K. (1989). Integrating Generalizations with Exemplar-Based Reasoning. In *Proceedings of the DARPA Case-Based Reasoning Workshop*, edited by K.J. Hammond. San Francisco: Morgan Kaufmann Publishers.

Branting, K. (1991). Exploiting the Complementarity of Rules and Precedents with Reciprocity and Fairness. In *Proceedings of the DARPA Case-Based Reasoning Workshop*, edited by E.R. Bareiss. San Francisco: Morgan Kaufmann Publishers.

Brown, M., Watson, I., and Filer, N. (1995). Separating the Cases from the Data: Towards More Flexible Case-Based Reasoning. In *Case-Based Reasoning Research and Development*, edited by M. Veloso and A. Aamodt. Lecture Notes in Artificial Intelligence 1010. Berlin: Springer-Verlag.

Carbonell, J.G., and Veloso, M.M. (1988). Integrating Derivational Analogy into a General Problem Solving Architecture. In *Proceedings of the DARPA Case-Based Reasoning Workshop*, edited by J.L. Kolodner. San Francisco: Morgan Kaufmann Publishers.

David, B.S. (1991). Principles for Case Representation in a Case-Based Aiding System for Lesson Planning. In *Proceedings of the DARPA Case-Based Reasoning Workshop*, edited by E.R. Bareiss. San Francisco: Morgan Kaufmann Publishers.

Domeshek, E., and Kolodner, J.L. (1993). Finding the points of large cases. In *Artificial Intelligence for Engineering Design, Analysis and Manufacturing,* 7(2), 87–96.

Faltings, B., Hua, K., Schmitt, G., and Shih, S.-G. (1991). Case-Based Representation of Architectural Design Knowledge. In *Proceedings of the DARPA Case-Based Reasoning Workshop*, edited by E.R. Bareiss. San Francisco: Morgan Kaufmann Publishers.

Garner, B.J., Larkiu, C., and Tsui, E. (1989). Prototypical Knowledge for Case-Based Reasoning. In *Proceedings of the DARPA Case-Based Reasoning Workshop*, edited by K.J. Hammond. San Francisco: Morgan Kaufmann Publishers.

Goel, A.K., and Murdock, J.W. (1996). Meta Cases: Explaining Case-Based Reasoning. In *Advances in Case-Based Reasoning*, edited by I. Smith and B. Faltings. Lecture Notes in Artificial Intelligence 1168. Berlin: Springer-Verlag.

Grimnes, M., and Aamodt, A. (1996). A Two-Layer Case-Based Reasoning Architecture for Medical Image Understanding. In *Advances in Case-Based Reasoning*, edited by I. Smith and B. Faltings. Lecture Notes 1168 in Artificial Intelligence. Berlin: Springer-Verlag.

Hendler, J.A. (1988). Refitting Plans for Case-Based Reasoning. In *Proceedings of the DARPA Case-Based Reasoning Workshop*, edited by J.L. Kolodner. San Francisco: Morgan Kaufmann Publishers.

Huang, Y. (1996). An Evolutionary Agent Model of Case-Based Classification. In *Advances in Case-Based Reasoning*, edited by I. Smith and B. Faltings. Lecture Notes in Artificial Intelligence 1168. Berlin: Springer-Verlag.

Hunt, J., and Fellows, A. (1996). Introducing an Immune Response into a CBR System for Data Mining. In *Research & Development in Expert Systems XIII*, edited by J.L. Nealon and J. Hunt. Oxford: SGES Publications.

Jones, E.K. (1989). Case-Based Analogical Reasoning Using Proverbs. In *Proceedings of the DARPA Case-Based Reasoning Workshop*, edited by K.J. Hammond. San Francisco: Morgan Kaufmann Publishers.

Kambhampati, S. (1989). Representational Requirements for Plan Reuse. In *Proceedings of the DARPA Case-Based Reasoning Workshop*, edited by K.J. Hammond. San Francisco: Morgan Kaufmann Publishers.

Kamp, G. (1996). Using Description Logics for Knowledge-Intensive Case-Based Reasoning. In *Advances in Case-Based Reasoning*, edited by I. Smith and B. Faltings. Lecture Notes in Artificial Intelligence 1168. Berlin: Springer-Verlag.

Kass, A. M., and Leake, D.B. (1988). Case-Based Reasoning Applied to Constructing Explanations. In *Proceedings of the DARPA Case-Based Reasoning Workshop*, edited by J.L. Kolodner. San Francisco: Morgan Kaufmann Publishers.

Kolodner, J.L. (1988). Extending Problem Solving Capabilities Through Case-Based Inference. In *Proceedings of the DARPA Case-Based Reasoning Workshop*, edited by J.L. Kolodner. San Francisco: Morgan Kaufmann Publishers.

Kolodner, J.L. (1988). Retrieving Events from a Case Memory: A Parallel Implementation. In *Proceedings of the DARPA Case-Based Reasoning Workshop*, edited by J.L. Kolodner. San Francisco: Morgan Kaufmann Publishers.

Kopeikina, L., Bandau, R., and Lemmon, A. (1988). Case-Based Reasoning for Continuous Control. In *Proceedings of the DARPA Case-Based Reasoning Workshop*, edited by J.L. Kolodner. San Francisco: Morgan Kaufmann Publishers.

Koton, P. (1988). Reasoning About Evidence in Causal Explanations. In *Proceedings of the DARPA Case-Based Reasoning Workshop*, edited by J.L. Kolodner. San Francisco: Morgan Kaufmann Publishers.

Marir, F., and Watson, I. (1995). Representing and Indexing Building Refurbishment Cases for Multiple Retrieval of Adaptable Pieces of Cases. In *Case-Based Reasoning Research and Development*, edited by M. Veloso and A. Aamodt. Lecture Notes in Artificial Intelligence 1010. Berlin: Springer-Verlag.

Montazeri, M.A. (1996). The Effect of Standardized Case Representation and Cross-Structural Similarity on Retrieval Robustness. In *Research & Development in Expert Systems XIII*, edited by J.L. Nealon and J. Hunt. Oxford: SGES Publications.

Navinchandra, D. (1988). Case-Based Reasoning in CYCLOPS, a Design Problem Solver. In *Proceedings of the DARPA Case-Based Reasoning Workshop*, edited by J.L. Kolodner. San Francisco: Morgan Kaufmann Publishers.

Osborne, H.R., and Bridge, D.G. (1996). A Case Base Similarity Framework. In *Advances in Case-Based Reasoning*, edited by I. Smith and B. Faltings. Lecture Notes in Artificial Intelligence 1168. Berlin: Springer-Verlag.

Owens, C. (1988). Domain-Independent Prototype Cases for Planning. In *Proceedings of the DARPA Case-Based Reasoning Workshop*, edited by J.L. Kolodner. San Francisco: Morgan Kaufmann Publishers.

Oxman, R. (1994). Precedents in Design: A Computational Model for Organization of Case Knowledge. In *Proceedings of the First Congress Held in Conjunction with A/E/C Systems '94*, vol. 2., edited by K. Khozeimeh.

Perera, R.S., and Watson, I. (1995). A Case-Based Design Approach for the Integration of Design and Estimating. In *Progress in Case-Based Reasoning*, edited by I. Watson. Lecture Notes in Artificial Intelligence 1020. Berlin: Springer-Verlag.

Plaza, E. (1995). Cases as Terms: A Feature Term Approach to the Structured Representation of Cases. In *Case-Based Reasoning, Research, and Development*, edited by M. Veloso and A. Aamodt. Lecture Notes in Artificial Intelligence 1010. Berlin: Springer-Verlag.

Plaza, E., de Mántaras, L., and Armengol, E. (1996). On the Importance of Similitude: An Entropy-Based Assessment. In *Advances in Case-Based Reasoning*, edited by I. Smith and B. Faltings. Lecture Notes in Artificial Intelligence 1168. Berlin: Springer-Verlag.

Raphael, B., Kumar, B., and McLeod, A. (1994). Representing Design Cases Based on Methods. In *Proceedings of the First Congress Held in Conjunction with A/E/C Systems '94*, vol. 2., edited by K. Khozeimeh.

Redmond, R. (1989). Learning from Others' Experience: Creating Cases from Examples. In *Proceedings of the DARPA Case-Based Reasoning Workshop*, edited by K.J. Hammond. San Francisco: Morgan Kaufmann Publishers.

Riesbeck, C.K. (1988). An Interface for Case-Based Knowledge Acquisition. In *Proceedings of the DARPA Case-Based Reasoning Workshop*, edited by J.L. Kolodner. San Francisco: Morgan Kaufmann Publishers.

Sanders, K.E. (1991). Within the Letter of the Law: Reasoning Among Multiple Cases. In *Proceedings of the DARPA Case-Based Reasoning Workshop*, edited by E.R. Bareiss. San Francisco: Morgan Kaufmann Publishers.

Schmidt, R., Heindl, B., Pollwein, B., and Gierl, L. (1996). Abstractions of Data and Time for Multiparametric Time Course Prognoses. In *Advances in Case-Based Reasoning*, edited by I. Smith and B. Faltings. Lecture Notes in Artificial Intelligence 1168. Berlin: Springer-Verlag.

Shinn, H.S. (1988). Abstractional Analogy: A Model of Analogical Reasoning. In *Proceedings of the DARPA Case-Based Reasoning Workshop*, edited by J.L. Kolodner. San Francisco: Morgan Kaufmann Publishers.

Skalak, D.B. (1992). Representing Cases as Knowledge Sources That Apply Local Similarity Metrics. In *Proceedings of the Fourteenth Annual Conference of the Cognitive Science Society*. Northvale, NJ: Lawrence Erlbaum Associates.

Smith, D.B. (1991). Principles for Case Representation in a Case-Based Aiding System for Lesson Planning. In *Proceedings of the DARPA Case-Based Reasoning Workshop*, edited by E.R. Bareiss. San Francisco: Morgan Kaufmann Publishers.

Strube, G. (1991). The Role of Cognitive Science in Knowledge Engineering. In *Contemporary Knowledge Engineering and Cognition: First Joint Workshop Proceedings*, 161–174, edited by F. Schmalhofer and G. Strube. Berlin: Springer-Verlag.

Sycara, K.P., and Navinchandra, D. (1991). Influences: A Thematic Abstraction for Creative Use of Multiple Cases. In *Proceedings of the DARPA Case-Based Reasoning Workshop*, edited by E.R. Bareiss. San Francisco: Morgan Kaufmann Publishers.

Tirri, H., Kontkanen, P., and Myllymäki, P. (1996). A Bayesian Framework for Case-Based Reasoning. In *Advances in Case-Based Reasoning*, edited by I. Smith and B. Faltings. Lecture Notes in Artificial Intelligence 1168. Berlin: Springer-Verlag.

Turner, R.M. (1988). Organizing and Using Schematic Knowledge for Medical Diagnosis. In *Proceedings of the DARPA Case-Based Reasoning Workshop*, edited by J.L. Kolodner. San Francisco: Morgan Kaufmann Publishers.

Weber-Lee, R., Barcia, R.M., Martins, A., and Pacheco, R.C. (1996). Using Typicality Theory to Select the Best Match. In *Advances in Case-Based Reasoning,* edited by I. Smith and B. Faltings. Lecture Notes in Artificial Intelligence 1168. Berlin: Springer-Verlag.

Zarri, G.P. (1993). Using a High-Level, Conceptual Knowledge Representation Language for Visualizing Efficiently the Internal Structure of Complex "Cases." In *Proceedings of EWCBR'93,* edited by M.M. Richter et al. Berlin: Springer-Verlag.

10.3.2 *Indexing*

This section includes papers that describe different techniques used to index cases. Papers presenting case studies of indexing techniques and analysis of these techniques are also included.

Alterman, R., and Wentworth, M. (1989). Determining the Important Features of a Case. In *Proceedings of the DARPA Case-Based Reasoning Workshop,* edited by K.J. Hammond. San Francisco: Morgan Kaufmann Publishers.

Althoff, K.-D., Auriol, E., Barletta, R., and Manago, M. (1995). *A Review of Industrial Case-Based Reasoning Tools.* Oxford: AI Intelligence.

Ashley, K.D. (1989). Indexing and Analytic Models. In *Proceedings of the DARPA Case-Based Reasoning Workshop,* edited by K.J. Hammond. San Francisco: Morgan Kaufmann Publishers.

Barletta, R., and Kerber, R. (1989). Improving Explanation-Based Indexing with Empirical Learning. *Proceeding of the 1989 International Machine Learning Workshop.*

Barletta, R., and Mark, W. (1988). Explanation-Based Indexing of Cases. *In Proceedings of the Seventh National Conference on Artificial Intelligence.* Palo Alto, CA: AAAI.

Chang, L.W., and Harrison, P. (1995). A Testbed for Experiments in Adaptive Memory Retrieval and Indexing. In *Adaptation of Knowledge for Reuse: Proceedings of the 1995 AAAI Fall Symposium.,* edited by D.W. Aha and A. Ram. AAAI Technical Report FS-95-04.

Daengdej, J., Lukose, D., Tsui, E., Beinat, P., and Prophet, P. (1996). Dynamically Creating Indices for Two Million Cases: A Real World Problem. In *Advances in Case-Based Reasoning,* edited by I. Smith and B. Faltings. Lecture Notes in Artificial Intelligence 1168. Berlin: Springer-Verlag.

Domeshek, E. (1989). Parallelism for Index Generation and Reminding. In *Proceedings of the DARPA Case-Based Reasoning Workshop,* edited by K.J. Hammond. San Francisco: Morgan Kaufmann Publishers.

Domeshek, E. (1991). *Do the Right Thing: A Component Theory for Indexing Stories as Social Advice*. Technical Report No. 26, Institute for the Learning Sciences, Northwestern University.

Domeshek, E. (1991). Indexing Stories as Social Advice. In *Proceedings of AAAI-91*. Cambridge, MA: AAAI Press / MIT Press.

Domeshek, E. (1991). What Abby Cares About. In *Proceedings of the DARPA Case-Based Reasoning Workshop*, edited by E.R. Bareiss. San Francisco: Morgan Kaufmann Publishers.

Domeshek, E. (1993). A Case Study of Case Indexing: Designing Index Feature Sets to Suit Task Demands and Support Parallelism. *In Advances in Connectionist and Neural Computation Theory, Vol. 2: Analogical Connections,* edited by J. Bamden and K. Holyoak. Norwood, NJ: Ablex.

Fox, S., and Leake, D.B. (1995). Learning to Refine Indexing by Introspective Reasoning. In *Case-Based Reasoning Research and Development*, edited by M. Veloso and A. Aamodt. Lecture Notes in Artificial Intelligence 1010. Berlin: Springer-Verlag.

Goodman, M. (1989). CBR in Battle Planning. In *Proceedings of the DARPA Case-Based Reasoning Workshop*, edited by K.J. Hammond. San Francisco: Morgan Kaufmann Publishers.

Hammond, K.J. (1988). Case-Based Planning: Viewing Planning as a Memory Task. In *Proceedings of the DARPA Case-Based Reasoning Workshop*, edited by J.L. Kolodner. San Francisco: Morgan Kaufmann Publishers.

Hammond, K.J., and Hurwits, N. (1988). Extracting Diagnostic Features from Explanations. In *Proceedings of the DARPA Case-Based Reasoning Workshop*, edited by J.L. Kolodner. San Francisco: Morgan Kaufmann Publishers.

Kolodner, J.L. (1989). Selecting the Best Case for a Case-Based Reasoner. In *Proceedings of the Eleventh Annual Conference of the Cognitive Science Society*. Northvale, NJ: Lawrence Erlbaum Associates.

Lebowitz, M. (1987). Experimental with Incremental Concept Formation: UNIMEM. *Machine Learning, 2*(ii), 103–138.

Macedo, L., Pereira, F.C., Grilo, C., and Cardoso, A. (1996). Plans as Structured Networks of Hierarchically and Temporally Related Case Pieces. In *Advances in Case-Based Reasoning,* edited by I. Smith and B. Faltings. Lecture Notes in Artificial Intelligence 1168. Berlin: Springer-Verlag.

Malek, M. (1995). A Connectionist Indexing Approach for CBR Systems. In *Case-Based Reasoning Research and Development*, edited by M. Veloso and A. Aamodt. Lecture Notes in Artificial Intelligence 1010. Berlin: Springer-Verlag.

Marir, F., and Watson, I. (1995). Representing and Indexing Building Refurbishment Cases for Multiple Retrieval of Adaptable Pieces of Cases. In *Case-Based Reasoning Research and Development*, edited by M. Veloso and A. Aamodt. Lecture Notes in Artificial Intelligence 1010. Berlin: Springer-Verlag.

Martin, C. (1989). Complex Indices: A Metaphorical Example. In *Proceedings of the DARPA Case-Based Reasoning Workshop*, edited by K.J. Hammond. San Francisco: Morgan Kaufmann Publishers.

Martin, C. (1989). Indexing Using Complex Features. In *Proceedings of the DARPA Case-Based Reasoning Workshop*, edited by K.J. Hammond. San Francisco: Morgan Kaufmann Publishers.

Oehlmann, R., Edwards, P., and Sleeman, D. (1995). Self-Questioning and Experimentation: An Index Vocabulary of Situated Interaction. In *Progress in Case-Based Reasoning*, edited by I. Watson. Lecture Notes in Artificial Intelligence 1020. Berlin: Springer-Verlag.

Owens, C. (1989). Integrating Feature Extraction and Memory Search. In *Proceedings of the Eleventh Annual Conference of the Cognitive Science Society*. Northvale, NJ: Lawrence Erlbaum Associates.

Pazzani, M. (1989). Indexing Strategies for Goal-Specific Retrieval of Cases. In *Proceedings of the DARPA Case-Based Reasoning Workshop*, edited by K.J. Hammond. San Francisco: Morgan Kaufmann Publishers.

Riesbeck, C.K. (1988). An Interface for Case-Based Knowledge Acquisition. In *Proceedings of the DARPA Case-Based Reasoning Workshop*, edited by J.L. Kolodner. San Francisco: Morgan Kaufmann Publishers.

Schank, R. (1988). Reminding and Memory. In *Proceedings of the DARPA Case-Based Reasoning Workshop*, edited by J.L. Kolodner. San Francisco: Morgan Kaufmann Publishers.

Simoudis, E. (1991). *Retrieving Justifiably Relevant Cases from a Case Base Using Validation Models*. Ph.D. thesis., Dept. of Computer Science, Brandeis University.

Simoudis, E. (1992). Using Case-Based Retrieval for Customer Technical Support. *IEEE Expert*, 7(5), 7–13.

Smith, D.B. (1991). Principles for Case Representation in a Case-Based Aiding System for Lesson Planning. In *Proceedings of the DARPA Case-Based Reasoning Workshop*, edited by E.R. Bareiss. San Francisco: Morgan Kaufmann Publishers.

Stanfill, C. (1988). Learning to Read: A Memory-Based Model. In *Proceedings of the DARPA Case-Based Reasoning Workshop*, edited by J.L. Kolodner. San Francisco: Morgan Kaufmann Publishers.

Stanfill, C., and Waltz, D.L. (1988). The Memory-Based Reasoning Paradigm. In *Proceedings of the DARPA Case-Based Reasoning Workshop*, edited by J.L. Kolodner. San Francisco: Morgan Kaufmann Publishers.

Sycara, K.P., and Navinchandra, D. (1989). Index Transformation and Generation for Case Retrieval. In *Proceedings of the DARPA Case-Based Reasoning Workshop*, edited by K.J. Hammond. San Francisco: Morgan Kaufmann Publishers.

Sycara, K.P., and Navinchandra, D. (1991). Influences: A Thematic Abstraction for Creative Use of Multiple Cases. In *Proceedings of the DARPA Case-Based Reasoning Workshop*, edited by E.R. Bareiss. San Francisco: Morgan Kaufmann Publishers.

Thagard, P., and Holyoak, K.J. (1989). Why Indexing Is the Wrong Way to Think about Analogical Retrieval. In *Proceedings of the DARPA Case-Based Reasoning Workshop*, edited by K.J. Hammond. San Francisco: Morgan Kaufmann Publishers.

Waltz, D. (1989). Panel Discussion on "Indexing Algorithms." In *Proceedings of the DARPA Case-Based Reasoning Workshop*, edited by K.J. Hammond. San Francisco: Morgan Kaufmann Publishers.

Waltz, D. (1991). Is Indexing Used for Retrieval? In *Proceedings of the DARPA Case-Based Reasoning Workshop*, edited by K.J. Hammond. San Francisco: Morgan Kaufmann Publishers.

Williams, R.S. (1988). Learning to Program by Examining and Modifying Cases. In *Proceedings of the DARPA Case-Based Reasoning Workshop*, edited by J.L. Kolodner. San Francisco: Morgan Kaufmann Publishers.

10.3.2.1 Indexing Vocabulary

Barletta, R., and Mark, W. (1988). Explanation-Based Indexing of Cases. In *Proceedings of the DARPA Case-Based Reasoning Workshop*, edited by J.L. Kolodner. San Francisco: Morgan Kaufmann Publishers.

Birnbaum, L. (1991). Panel Discussion on "Indexing Vocabulary." In *Proceedings of the DARPA Case-Based Reasoning Workshop*, edited by K.J. Hammond. San Francisco: Morgan Kaufmann Publishers.

Birnbaum, L., and Collins G. (1989). Reminding and Engineering Design Themes: A Case Study in Indexing Vocabulary. In *Proceedings of the DARPA Case-Based Reasoning Workshop*, edited by K.J. Hammond. San Francisco: Morgan Kaufmann Publishers.

Hammond, K.J. (1989). On Functionally Motivated Vocabularies: An Apologia. In *Proceedings of the DARPA Case-Based Reasoning Workshop*, edited by K.J. Hammond. San Francisco: Morgan Kaufmann Publishers.

Hunt, J., and Fellows, A. (1996). Introducing an Immune Response into a CBR System for Data Mining. In *Research & Development in Expert Systems XIII*, edited by J.L. Nealon and J. Hunt. Oxford: SGES Publications.

Hunter, L. (1989). Finding Paradigm Cases, or, When Is a Case Worth Remembering? In *Proceedings of the DARPA Case-Based Reasoning Workshop*, edited by K.J. Hammond. San Francisco: Morgan Kaufmann Publishers.

Marir, F., and Watson, I. (1995). Representing and Indexing Building Refurbishment Cases for Multiple Retrieval of Adaptable Pieces of Cases. In *Case-Based Reasoning Research and Development*, edited by M. Veloso and A. Aamodt. Lecture Notes in Artificial Intelligence 1010. Berlin: Springer-Verlag.

Oehlmann, R., Edwards, P., and Sleeman, D. (1995). Self-Questioning and Experimentation: An Index Vocabulary of Situated Interaction. In *Progress in Case-Based Reasoning*, edited by I. Watson. Lecture Notes in Artificial Intelligence 1020. Berlin: Springer-Verlag.

Ortony, A., Glore, G., and Collins, A. (1988). *The Cognitive Structure of Emotions*. Cambridge: Cambridge University Press.

Owens, C. (1989). Plan Transformation as Abstract Indices. In *Proceedings of the DARPA Case-Based Reasoning Workshop*, edited by K.J. Hammond. San Francisco: Morgan Kaufmann Publishers.

Perera, R.S., and Watson, I. (1995). A Case-Based Design Approach for the Integration of Design and Estimating. In *Progress in Case-Based Reasoning*, edited by I. Watson. Lecture Notes in Artificial Intelligence 1020. Berlin: Springer-Verlag.

Schank, R., and Osgood, R. (1990). *A Content Theory of Memory Indexing*. Technical Report No. 2, Institute for the Learning Sciences, Northwestern University.

Wettschereck, D., and Aha, D.W. (1995). Weighting Features. In *Case-Based Reasoning Research and Development*, edited by M. Veloso and A. Aamodt. Lecture Notes in Artificial Intelligence 1010. Berlin: Springer-Verlag.

Wilke, W., and Bergmann, R. (1996). Considering Decision Cost During Learning of Feature Weights. In *Advances in Case-Based Reasoning,* edited by I. Smith and B. Faltings. Lecture Notes in Artificial Intelligence 1168. Berlin: Springer-Verlag.

10.3.2.2 Analysis of Indexing Methods

Althoff, K.-D., Auriol, E., Barletta, R., and Manago, M. (1995). *A Review of Industrial Case-Based Reasoning Tools*. Oxford: AI Intelligence.

Bradtke, S., and Lehnert, W.G. (1988). Some Experiments with Case-Based Search. In *Proceedings of the DARPA Case-Based Reasoning Workshop*, edited by J.L. Kolodner. San Francisco: Morgan Kaufmann Publishers.

Griffiths, A.D., and Bridge, D.G. (1996). A Yardstick for the Evaluation of Case-Based Classifiers. In *Proceedings of the Second U.K. Workshop on Case-Based Reasoning*, edited by I. Watson. Salford, UK: Salford University.

Ruby, D., and Kibler, D. (1988). Exploration of Case-Based Problem Solving. In *Proceedings of the DARPA Case-Based Reasoning Workshop*, edited by J.L. Kolodner. San Francisco: Morgan Kaufmann Publishers.

Tirri, H., Kontkanen, P., and Myllymäki, P. (1996). A Bayesian Framework for Case-Based Reasoning. In *Advances in Case-Based Reasoning,* edited by I. Smith and B. Faltings. Lecture Notes in Artificial Intelligence 1168. Berlin: Springer-Verlag.

10.3.3 *Memory Organization*

The memory organization, or case memory, is an important aspect in designing efficient case-based reasoners. It should reflect and translate into the computer the conceptual view of what is represented in the case, taking into account the indexes that characterize the case. It should also organize cases into a manageable structure that allows efficient search and retrieval of relevant cases. Extensive references to this important phase of CBR design are presented below.

Alterman, R. (1988). An Adaptive Planner. In *Proceedings of the DARPA Case-Based Reasoning Workshop*, edited by J.L. Kolodner. San Francisco: Morgan Kaufmann Publishers.

Althoff, K.-D., Auriol, E., Barletta, R., and Manago, M. (1995). *A Review of Industrial Case-Based Reasoning Tools*. Oxford: AI Intelligence.

Bareiss, E.R. (1988). *PROTOS: A Unified Approach to Concept Representation, Classification, and Learning*. Ph.D. thesis, Dept. of Computer Science, University of Texas. Technical Report CS 88-10, Dept. of Computer Science, Vanderbilt University, Nashville, TN.

Basu, C. (1989). Organizing Multiple Points of View in Episodic Memory. In *Proceedings of the DARPA Case-Based Reasoning Workshop*, edited by K.J. Hammond. San Francisco: Morgan Kaufmann Publishers.

Brown, M.G. (1993). An Under-Lying Memory Model to Support Case Retrieval. In *Proceedings of EWCBR'93*, edited by M.M. Richter et al. Berlin: Springer-Verlag.

Dearden, A. (1995). Improving the Interfaces to Interactive Case Memories. In *Progress in Case-Based Reasoning*, edited by I. Watson. Lecture Notes in Artificial Intelligence 1020. Berlin: Springer-Verlag.

Dubitzky, W., Hughes, J.G., and Bell, D.A. (1996). Case Memory and the Behaviouristic Model of Concepts and Cognition. In *Advances in Case-Based Reasoning,* edited by I. Smith and B. Faltings. Lecture Notes in Artificial Intelligence 1168. Berlin: Springer-Verlag.

Dzeng, R.-J., and Tommelein, I.D. (1994). Case Storage of Planning Knowledge for Power Plant Construction. In *Proceedings of the First Congress Held in Conjunction with A/E/C Systems '94*, vol. 1., edited by K. Khozeimeh.

Feigenbaum, E.A. (1963). The Simulation of Natural Learning Behavior. In *Computers and Thought*, edited by E.A. Feigenbaum and J. Feldman. New York: McGraw-Hill.

Gentner, D. (1983). Structure-Mapping: A Theoretical Framework for Analogy. *Cognitive Science, 7*(2).

Griffiths, A.D., and Bridge, D.G. (1995). Formalising the Knowledge Content of Case Memory Systems. In *Progress in Case-Based Reasoning*, edited by I. Watson. Lecture Notes in Artificial Intelligence 1020. Berlin: Springer-Verlag.

Hammond, K.J. (1988). Opportunistic Memory: Storing and Recalling Suspended Goals. In *Proceedings of the DARPA Case-Based Reasoning Workshop*, edited by J.L. Kolodner. San Francisco: Morgan Kaufmann Publishers.

Hunt, J., and Fellows, A. (1996). Introducing an Immune Response into a CBR System for Data Mining. In *Research & Development in Expert Systems XIII*, edited by J.L. Nealon and J. Hunt. Oxford: SGES Publications.

Hunt, J.E., Cooke, D.E., and Holstein, H. (1995). Case memory and retrieval based on the immune system. In *Case-Based Reasoning Research and Development*, edited by M. Veloso and A. Aamodt. Lecture Notes in Artificial Intelligence 1010. Berlin: Springer-Verlag.

Kass, A.M., and Leake, D.B. (1988). Case-Based Reasoning Applied to Constructing Explanations. In *Proceedings of the DARPA Case-Based Reasoning Workshop*, edited by J.L. Kolodner. San Francisco: Morgan Kaufmann Publishers.

Kolodner, J.L. (1983). Maintaining Organization in a Dynamic Long-Term Memory. *Cognitive Science, 7*(4), 243–280.

Kolodner, J.L. (1983). Reconstructive Memory: A Computer Model. *Cognitive Science, 7*(4), 281–328.

Kolodner, J.L. (1984). *Retrieval and Organization Strategies in Conceptual Memory: A Computer Model*. Northvale, NJ: Lawrence Erlbaum Associates.

Kolodner, J.L. (1988). *Design and Implementation of a Case Memory*. Cambridge, MA: Thinking Machine Corp.

Kolodner, J.L. (1988). Retrieving Events from a Case Memory: A Parallel Implementation. In *Proceedings of the DARPA Case-Based Reasoning Workshop*, edited by J.L. Kolodner. San Francisco: Morgan Kaufmann Publishers.

Kolodner, J.L., and Thau, R. (1988). *Design and Implementation of a Case Memory*. Technical Report No. GIT-ICS-88/34, School of Information and Computer Science, Georgia Institute of Technology.

Koton, P. (1989). *Using Experience in Learning and Problem Solving*. Ph.D. thesis MIT/LCS/TR-441, Laboratory of Computer Science, Massachusetts Institute of Technology.

Lebowitz, M. (1983). Generalization from Natural Language Text. *Cognitive Science*, 7(1).

Lewis, L. (1996). Managing Computer Networks—Case-Based Reasoning Approach. Boston, MA: Artech House Inc.

Maher, M.L. (1994). Representation of Case Memory for Structural Design. In *Proceedings of the First Congress Held in Conjunction with A/E/C Systems '94*, vol. 1, edited by K. Khozeimeh.

Marir, F., and Watson, I. (1995). Representing and Indexing Building Refurbishment Cases for Multiple Retrieval of Adaptable Pieces of Cases. In *Case-Based Reasoning Research and Development*, edited by M. Veloso and A. Aamodt. Lecture Notes in Artificial Intelligence 1010. Berlin: Springer-Verlag.

Owens, C. (1988). Domain-Independent Prototype Cases for Planning. *In Proceedings of the DARPA Case-Based Reasoning Workshop*, edited by J.L. Kolodner. San Francisco: Morgan Kaufmann Publishers.

Perera, R.S., and Watson, I. (1995). A Case-Based Design Approach for the Integration of Design and Estimating. In *Progress in Case-Based Reasoning*, edited by I. Watson. Lecture Notes in Artificial Intelligence 1020. Berlin: Springer-Verlag.

Porter, B., Bareiss, E.R., and Holte, R. (1990). Concept Learning and Heuristic Classification in Weak Theory Domains. *Artificial Intelligence*, 45(1/2), 229–263.

Porter, B.W., and Bareiss, E.R. (1986). PROTOS: An Experiment in Knowledge Acquisition for Heuristic Classification Tasks. In *Proceedings of the First International Meeting on Advances in Learning (IMAL)*, 159–174.

Rissland, E.L., and Ashley, K.D. (1988). Credit Assignment and the Problem of Competing Factors in Case-Based Reasoning. In *Proceedings of the DARPA Case-Based Reasoning Workshop*, edited by J.L. Kolodner. San Francisco: Morgan Kaufmann Publishers.

Schank, R. (1988). Reminding and Memory. In *Proceedings of the DARPA Case-Based Reasoning Workshop*, edited by J.L. Kolodner. San Francisco: Morgan Kaufmann Publishers.

Selfridge, M., and Cuthill, B. (1989). Retrieving Relevant Out-of-Context Cases: A Dynamic Memory Approach to Case-Based Reasoning. In *Proceedings of the DARPA Case-Based Reasoning Workshop*, edited by K.J. Hammond. San Francisco: Morgan Kaufmann Publishers.

Shinn, H.S. (1988). Abstractional Analogy: A Model of Analogical Reasoning. In *Proceedings of the DARPA Case-Based Reasoning Workshop*, edited by J.L. Kolodner. San Francisco: Morgan Kaufmann Publishers.

Stanfill, C., and Waltz, D.L. (1986). Toward Memory-Based Reasoning. *Communications of the ACM, 29*(12).

Stanfill, C., and Waltz, D.L. (1988). The Memory-Based Reasoning Paradigm. In *Proceedings of the DARPA Case-Based Reasoning Workshop*, edited by J.L. Kolodner. San Francisco: Morgan Kaufmann Publishers.

Tanaka, M., et al. (1993). Integration of Multiple Knowledge Representation for Classification Problems. In *Proceedings of the International Conference on Tools with Artificial Intelligence 1993,* 448–449.

Tirri, H., Kontkanen, P., and Myllymäki, P. (1996). A Bayesian Framework for Case-Based Reasoning. In *Advances in Case-Based Reasoning,* edited by I. Smith and B. Faltings. Lecture Notes in Artificial Intelligence 1168. Berlin: Springer-Verlag.

Tompson, K., and Langley, P. (1989). Organization and Retrieval of Composite Concepts. In *Proceedings of the DARPA Case-Based Reasoning Workshop*, edited by K.J. Hammond. San Francisco: Morgan Kaufmann Publishers.

Turner, R.M. (1988). Organizing and Using Schematic Knowledge for Medical Diagnosis. In *Proceedings of the DARPA Case-Based Reasoning Workshop*, edited by J.L. Kolodner. San Francisco: Morgan Kaufmann Publishers.

10.3.4 *Retrieval*

Given a description of a problem, the retrieval algorithm should retrieve the most similar cases to the current problem. The retrieval algorithm relies heavily on the indexes and the structure and organization of the case memory to direct search to appropriate cases. Many retrieval algorithms are presented in the following papers, including heuristic search and matching techniques that are used to retrieve an ordered set of useful cases from the case-base, as well as concept refinement and parallel search techniques. The issue of choosing and ranking a best matching case is addressed, using many approaches such as analogy, similarity metrics, combinations of analytical and similarity-based CBR, and qualitative and multiattribute similarity.

Aamodt, A. (1993). Explanation-Driven Retrieval, Reuse, and Learning of Cases. In *Proceedings of EWCBR'93*, edited by M.M. Richter et al., 279–284. Berlin: Springer-Verlag.

Althoff, K.-D., Auriol, E., Barletta, R., and Manago, M. (1995). *A Review of Industrial Case-Based Reasoning Tools*. Oxford: AI Intelligence.

Bento, C., and Costa, E. (1993). A Similarity Metric for Retrieval of Cases— Imperfectly Described and Explained. In *Proceedings of EWCBR'93*, edited by M.M. Richter et al. Berlin: Springer-Verlag.

Bonissone, P.P., and Ayub, S. (1992). Similarity Measures for Case-Based Reasoning Systems. In *IPMU'92—Advanced Methods in AI, the Fourth International Conference on Information Processing and Management of Uncertainty in KBS*, edited by Bouchon-Meunier et al. Lecture Notes in Artificial Intelligence 682. Berlin: Springer-Verlag.

Brown, M., and Filer, N. (1995). Beauty vs. the Beast: The Case Against Massively Parallel Retrieval. In *Progress in Case-Based Reasoning*, edited by I. Watson. Lecture Notes in Artificial Intelligence 1020. Berlin: Springer-Verlag.

Brown, M.G. (1993). An Under-Lying Memory Model to Support Case Retrieval. In *Proceedings of EWCBR'93*, edited by M.M. Richter et al. Berlin: Springer-Verlag.

Burke, R. (1989). Understanding and Responding in Conversation: Case Retrieval with Natural Language. In *Proceedings of the DARPA Case-Based Reasoning Workshop*, edited by K.J. Hammond. San Francisco: Morgan Kaufmann Publishers.

Callan, J.P., Fawcett, T.E., and Rissland, E.L. (1991). Adaptive Case-Based Reasoning. In *Proceedings of the DARPA Case-Based Reasoning Workshop*, edited by E.R. Bareiss. San Francisco: Morgan Kaufmann Publishers.

Collins, B., and Cunningham, P. (1996). Adaptation Guided Retrieval in EBMT: A Case-Base Approach to Machine Translation. In *Advances in Case-Based Reasoning*, edited by I. Smith and B. Faltings. Lecture Notes in Artificial Intelligence 1168. Berlin: Springer-Verlag.

Domeshek, E. (1989). Parallelism for Index Generation and Reminding. In *Proceedings of the DARPA Case-Based Reasoning Workshop*, edited by K.J. Hammond. San Francisco: Morgan Kaufmann Publishers.

Domeshek, E. (1991). Indexing Stories as Social Advice. In *Proceedings of AAAI-91*. Cambridge, MA: AAAI Press / MIT Press.

Domeshek, E. (1991). What Abby Cares About. In *Proceedings of the DARPA Case-Based Reasoning Workshop*, edited by E.R. Bareiss. San Francisco: Morgan Kaufmann Publishers.

Donahue, D. (1989). OGRE: Generic Reasoning from Experience. In *Proceedings of the DARPA Case-Based Reasoning Workshop*, edited by K.J. Hammond. San Francisco: Morgan Kaufmann Publishers.

Falkeneheimer, B., Forbus, K.D., and Gentner, D. (1986). The Structure Mapping Engine. In *Proceedings of the Sixth National Conference on Artificial Intelligence*, Cambridge, MA: AAAI Press / MIT Press.

Farrell, R. (1988). Facilitating Self-Education by Questioning Assumptive Reasoning Using Paradigm Cases. In *Proceedings of the DARPA Case-Based Reasoning Workshop*, edited by J.L. Kolodner. San Francisco: Morgan Kaufmann Publishers.

Gentner, D., and Forbus, K.D. (1991). MAC/FAC: A Model of Similarity-Based Access and Mapping. In *Proceedings of the Thirteenth Annual Conference of the Cognitive Science Society*. Northvale, NJ: Lawrence Erlbaum Associates.

Gentner, D., Ratternann, M.J., and Forbus, K.D. (1993). The Roles of Similarity in Transfer: Separating Retrievability from Inferential Soundness. *Cognitive Psychology*.

Kitano, H. (1993). Challenges for Massive Parallelism. In *IJCAI-93, Proceedings of the Thirteenth International Conference on Artificial Intelligence*, 813–834. San Francisco: Morgan Kaufmann Publishers.

Kolodner, J.L. (1988). Retrieving Events from a Case Memory: A Parallel Implementation. In *Proceedings of the DARPA Case-Based Reasoning Workshop*, edited by J.L. Kolodner. San Francisco: Morgan Kaufmann Publishers.

Kolodner, J.L. (1989). Selecting the Best Case for a Case-Based Reasoner. In *Proceedings of the Eleventh Annual Conference of the Cognitive Science Society*. Northvale, NJ: Lawrence Erlbaum Associates.

Lenz, M., Burkhard, H.-D., and Brückner, S. (1996). Applying Case Retrieval Nets to Diagnostic Tasks in Technical Domains. In *Advances in Case-Based Reasoning,* edited by I. Smith and B. Faltings. Lecture Notes in Artificial Intelligence 1168. Berlin: Springer-Verlag.

Marir, F., and Watson, I. (1995). Representing and Indexing Building Refurbishment Cases for Multiple Retrieval of Adaptable Pieces of Cases. In *Case-Based Reasoning Research and Development*, edited by M. Veloso and A. Aamodt. Lecture Notes in Artificial Intelligence 1010. Berlin: Springer-Verlag.

Mehl, M. (1993). Retrieval in Case-Based Reasoning Using Preferred Sub-Theories. In *Nonmonotonic and Inductive Logic*, edited by G. Brewka et al. Lecture Notes in Artificial Intelligence 659. Berlin: Springer-Verlag.

Schank, R. (1988). Reminding and Memory, from Dynamic Memory. In *Proceedings of the DARPA Case-Based Reasoning Workshop*, edited by J.L. Kolodner. San Francisco: Morgan Kaufmann Publishers.

Seifert, C.M. (1988). Goals in Reminding. In *Proceedings of the DARPA Case-Based Reasoning Workshop*, edited by J.L. Kolodner. San Francisco: Morgan Kaufmann Publishers.

Selfridge, M., and Cuthill, B. (1989). Retrieving Relevant Out-of-Context Cases: A Dynamic Memory Approach to Case-Based Reasoning. In *Proceedings of the DARPA Case-Based Reasoning Workshop*, edited by K.J. Hammond. San Francisco: Morgan Kaufmann Publishers.

Simoudis, E. (1991). *Retrieving Justifiably Relevant Cases from a Case Base Using Validation Models*. Ph.D. thesis, Dept. of Computer Science, Brandeis University.

Simoudis, E. (1992). Using Case-Based Retrieval for Customer Technical Support. *IEEE Expert* 7(5), 7–13.

Smail, M. (1993). Case-Based Information Retrieval. In *Proceedings of EWCBR'93*, edited by M.M. Richter et al. Berlin: Springer-Verlag.

Smyth, B., and Keane, M.T. (1993). Retrieving Adaptable Cases: The Role of Adaptation Knowledge in Case Retrieval. In *Proceedings of EWCBR'93*, edited by M.M. Richter et al. Berlin: Springer-Verlag.

Smyth, B., and Keane, M.T. (1996). Adaptation-Guided Retrieval: Using Adaptation Knowledge to Guide the Retrieval of Adaptable Cases. In *Proceedings of the Second U.K. Workshop on Case-Based Reasoning*, edited by I. Watson. Salford, UK: Salford University.

Thompson, K., and Langley, P. (1989). Organization and Retrieval of Composite Concepts. In *Proceedings of the DARPA Case-Based Reasoning Workshop*, edited by K.J. Hammond. San Francisco: Morgan Kaufmann Publishers.

Tirri, H., Kontkanen, P., and Myllymäki, P. (1996). A Bayesian Framework for Case-Based Reasoning. In *Advances in Case-Based Reasoning*, edited by I. Smith and B. Faltings. Lecture Notes in Artificial Intelligence 1168. Berlin: Springer-Verlag.

Veloso, M.M, and Carbonell, J.G. (1991). Variable-Precision Case Retrieval in Analogical Problem Solving. In *Proceedings of the DARPA Case-Based Reasoning Workshop*, edited by E.R. Bareiss. San Francisco: Morgan Kaufmann Publishers.

Wall, R.S., Donahue, D., and Hill, S. (1988). The Use of Domain Semantics for Retrieval and Explanation in Case-Based Reasoning. In *Proceedings of the DARPA Case-Based Reasoning Workshop*, edited by J.L. Kolodner. San Francisco: Morgan Kaufmann Publishers.

Wess, S., Althoff, K.-D., and Derwand, G. (1993). Improving the Retrieval Step in Case-Based Reasoning. In *Proceedings of EWCBR'93*, edited by M.M. Richter et al. Berlin: Springer-Verlag.

10.3.4.1 Matching and Ranking

Ashley, K., and Rissland, E.L. (1988). Compare and Contrast, a Test of Expertise. In *Proceedings of the DARPA Case-Based Reasoning Workshop*, edited by J.L. Kolodner. San Francisco: Morgan Kaufmann Publishers.

Collins, A., and Burstein, M. (1989). A Framework for a Theory of Mapping. In *Similarity, Analogy, and Thought*, edited by A. Vosniadou and A. Ortony. New York: Cambridge University Press.

Falkenhainer, B. (1988). *Learning From Physical Analogies: A Study in Analogy and the Explanation Process*. Ph.D. thesis, University of Illinois.

Gentner, D. (1983). Structure-Mapping: A Theoretical Framework for Analogy. *Cognitive Science* 7(2).

Gentner, D. (1988). Analogical Inference and Analogical Access. In *Analogica*, edited by A. Prieditis. San Francisco: Morgan Kaufmann Publishers.

Hinrichs, T.R. (1992). *Problem Solving in Open Worlds*. Northvale, NJ: Lawrence Erlbaum Associates.

Holyoak, K.J. (1984). Analogical Thinking and Human Intelligence. In *Advances in the Psychology of Human Intelligence,* vol. 2, edited by R.J. Stemberg. Northvale, NJ: Lawrence Erlbaum Associates.

Holyoak, K., and Thagard, P.R. (1989). A Computational Model of Analogical Problem Solving. In *Similarity, Analogy, and Thought,* edited by A. Vosniadou and A. Ortony. New York: Cambridge University Press.

Kopeilkina, L., Bandau, R., and Lemmon, A. (1988). Case-Based Reasoning for Continuous Control. In *Proceedings of the DARPA Case-Based Reasoning Workshop*, edited by J.L. Kolodner. San Francisco: Morgan Kaufmann Publishers.

Koton, P. (1988). Reasoning About Evidence in Causal Explanations. In *Proceedings of the DARPA Case-Based Reasoning Workshop*, edited by J.L. Kolodner. San Francisco: Morgan Kaufmann Publishers.

Martin, J.D. (1989). Retrieving Reasonable Predictions from Case Bases. In *Proceedings of the DARPA Case-Based Reasoning Workshop*, edited by K.J. Hammond. San Francisco: Morgan Kaufmann Publishers.

Rissland, E.L., and Ashley, K.D. (1988). Credit Assignment and the Problem of Competing Factors in Case-Based Reasoning. In *Proceedings of the DARPA Case-Based Reasoning Workshop*, edited by J.L. Kolodner. San Francisco: Morgan Kaufmann Publishers.

Shavlik, J.W. (1991). Finding Genes by Case-Based Reasoning in the Presence of Noisy Case Boundaries. In *Proceedings of the DARPA Case-Based Reasoning Workshop*, edited by E.R. Bareiss. San Francisco: Morgan Kaufmann Publishers.

Smyth, B., and Keane, M.T. (1996). Adaptation-Guided Retrieval: Using Adaptation Knowledge to Guide the Retrieval of Adaptable Cases. In *Proceedings of the Second U.K. Workshop on Case-Based Reasoning*, edited by I. Watson. Salford, UK: Salford University.

Tirri, H., Kontkanen, P., and Myllymäki, P. (1996). A Bayesian Framework for Case-Based Reasoning. In *Advances in Case-Based Reasoning*, edited by I. Smith and B. Faltings. Lecture Notes in Artificial Intelligence 1168. Berlin: Springer-Verlag.

Veloso, M.M. (1991). Efficient Nonlinear Planning Using Casual Commitment and Analogical Reasoning. *In Proceedings of the Thirteenth Annual Conference of the Cognitive Science Society.* Northvale, NJ: Lawrence Erlbaum Associates.

Veloso, M.M. (1992). *Learning by Analogical Reasoning in General Problem Solving.* Technical Report No. CMU-CS-92-174, School of Computer Science, Carnegie Mellon University.

10.3.4.2 Similarity

Ashley, K.D. (1989). Assessing Similarities Among Cases: A Position Paper. In *Proceedings of the DARPA Case-Based Reasoning Workshop*, edited by K.J. Hammond. San Francisco: Morgan Kaufmann Publishers.

Borner, K. (1993). Structural Similarity as Guidance in Case-Based Design. In *Proceedings of EWCBR'93*, edited by M.M. Richter et al. Berlin: Springer-Verlag.

Cain, T., Pazzani, M.J., and Silverstein, G. (1991). Domain Knowledge to Influence Similarity Judgment. In *Proceedings of the DARPA Case-Based Reasoning Workshop*, edited by E.R. Bareiss. San Francisco: Morgan Kaufmann Publishers.

Golding, A.R., and Rosenbloom, P.S. (1989). Combining Analytical and Similarity-Based CBR. In *Proceedings of the DARPA Case-Based Reasoning Workshop*, edited by K.J. Hammond. San Francisco: Morgan Kaufmann Publishers.

Janetzko, D., and Melis, S.W. (1993). System and Processing View in Similarity Assessment. In *Proceedings of EWCBR'93*, edited by M.M. Richter et al. Berlin: Springer-Verlag.

King, J., and Bareiss, R. (1989). Similarity Assessment and Case-Based Reasoning. In *Proceedings of the DARPA Case-Based Reasoning Workshop*, edited by K.J. Hammond. San Francisco: Morgan Kaufmann Publishers.

Knauff, M., and Schlieder, C. (1993). Similarity Assessment and Case Representation in Case-Based Design. In *Proceedings of EWCBR'93*, edited by M.M. Richter et al. Berlin: Springer-Verlag.

Kolodner, J.L. (1989). Judging Which Is the "Best" Case for a Case-Based Reasoner. In *Proceedings of the DARPA Case-Based Reasoning Workshop*, edited by K.J. Hammond. San Francisco: Morgan Kaufmann Publishers.

Leake, D.B. (1988). ACCEPTER: A Program for Dynamic Similarity Assessment in Case-Based Explanation. In *Proceedings of the DARPA Case-Based Reasoning Workshop*, edited by E.R. Bareiss. San Francisco: Morgan Kaufmann Publishers.

Muñoz-Avila, H., and Hüllen, J. (1996). Feature Weighting by Explaining Case-Based Planning Episodes. In *Advances in Case-Based Reasoning,* edited by I. Smith and B. Faltings. Lecture Notes in Artificial Intelligence 1168. Berlin: Springer-Verlag.

Musgrove, P.B., Davies, J., and Izzard, D. (1996). A Comparison of Nearest Neighbour, Rule Induction and Neural Networks for the Recommendation of Treatment at Anticoagulant Out-Patient Clinics. In *Proceedings of the Second U.K. Workshop on Case-Based Reasoning,* edited by I. Watson. Salford, UK: Salford University.

Myllymäki, P., and Tirri, H. (1993). Massively Parallel Case-Based Reasoning with Probabilistic Similarity Metrics. In *Proceedings of EWCBR'93,* edited by M.M. Richter et al. Berlin: Springer-Verlag.

Netten, B.D., and Vingerhoeds, R.A. (1996). Retrieval and Reuse of Conceptual Designs in EADOCS. In *Advances in Case-Based Reasoning,* edited by I. Smith and B. Faltings. Lecture Notes in Artificial Intelligence 1168. Berlin: Springer-Verlag.

Osborne, H.R., and Bridge, D.G. (1996). A Case-Base Similarity Framework. In *Advances in Case-Based Reasoning,* edited by I. Smith and B. Faltings. Lecture Notes in Artificial Intelligence 1168. Berlin: Springer-Verlag.

Osborne, H.R., and Bridge, D.G. (1996). Parallel Retrieval from Case Bases. In *Proceedings of the Second U.K. Workshop on Case-Based Reasoning,* edited by I. Watson. Salford, UK: Salford University.

Perera, R.S., and Watson, I. (1995). A Case-Based Design Approach for the Integration of Design and Estimating. In *Progress in Case-Based Reasoning,* edited by I. Watson. Lecture Notes in Artificial Intelligence 1020. Berlin: Springer-Verlag.

Plaza, E., and Arcos, J.L. (1993). Reflection and Analogy in Memory-Based Learning. In *Proceedings of the Multi-Strategy Learning Workshop,* 42–49.

Plaza, E., de Mántaras, L., and Armengol, E. (1996). On the Importance of Similitude: An Entropy-Based Assessment. In *Advances in Case-Based Reasoning,* edited by I. Smith and B. Faltings. Lecture Notes in Artificial Intelligence 1168. Berlin: Springer-Verlag.

Poole, J. (1993). Similarity in Legal Case-Based Reasoning as Degree of Matching Between Conceptual Graphs. In *Proceedings of EWCBR '93,* edited by M.M. Richter et al. Berlin: Springer-Verlag.

Porter, B. (1989). Similarity Assessment: Computation vs. Representation. In *Proceedings of the DARPA Case-Based Reasoning Workshop,* edited by K.J. Hammond. San Francisco: Morgan Kaufmann Publishers.

Ricci, F., and Avesani, P. (1995). Learning a Local Similarity Metric for Case-based Reasoning. In *Case-Based Reasoning Research and Development,* edited by M. Veloso and A. Aamodt. Lecture Notes in Artificial Intelligence 1010. Berlin: Springer-Verlag.

Richter, M.M., and Weiss, S. (1991). Similarity, Uncertainty and Case-Based Reasoning in PATDEX. *In Automated Reasoning, Essays in Honour of Woody Beledsoe*, edited by R.S. Boyer, 249–265. Norwell, MA: Kluwer.

Rissland, E.L., Basu, C., Daniels, J.J., McCarthy, J., Rubinstein, B., and Skalak, D.B. (1991). A Blackboard-Based Architecture for CBR: An Initial Report. In *Proceedings of the DARPA Case-Based Reasoning Workshop*, edited by E.R. Bareiss. San Francisco: Morgan Kaufmann Publishers.

Rougegrez, S. (1993). A Similarity-Assessment Algorithm Based on Comparisons Between Events. In *Proceedings of EWCBR'93*, edited by M.M. Richter et al. Berlin: Springer-Verlag.

Schaaf, J.W. (1995). Fish and Sink: An Anytime Algorithm to Retrieve Adequate Cases. In *Case-Based Reasoning Research and Development*, edited by M. Veloso and A. Aamodt. Lecture Notes in Artificial Intelligence 1010. Berlin: Springer-Verlag.

Schaaf, J.W. (1996). Fish and Shrink: A Next Step Towards Efficient Case Retrieval in Large-Scale Case Bases. In *Advances in Case-Based Reasoning*, edited by I. Smith and B. Faltings. Lecture Notes in Artificial Intelligence 1168. Berlin: Springer-Verlag.

Sebag, M., and Schoenauer, M. (1993). A Rule-Based Similarity Measure. In *Proceedings of EWCBR '93*, edited by M.M. Richter et al. Berlin: Springer-Verlag.

Smyth, B., and Keane, M.T. (1996). Adaptation-Guided Retrieval: Using Adaptation Knowledge to Guide the Retrieval of Adaptable Cases. In *Proceedings of the Second U.K. Workshop on Case-Based Reasoning*, edited by I. Watson. Salford, UK: Salford University.

Thagard, P., and Holyoak, K.J. (1989). How to Compute Semantic Similarity. In *Proceedings of the DARPA Case-Based Reasoning Workshop*, edited by K.J. Hammond. San Francisco: Morgan Kaufmann Publishers.

Tirri, H., Kontkanen, P., and Myllymäki, P. (1996). A Bayesian Framework for Case-Based Reasoning. In *Advances in Case-Based Reasoning*, edited by I. Smith and B. Faltings. Lecture Notes in Artificial Intelligence 1168. Berlin: Springer-Verlag.

Weber-Lee, R., Barcia, R.M., Martins, A., and Pacheco, R.C. (1996). Using Typicality Theory to Select the Best Match. In *Advances in Case-Based Reasoning*, edited by I. Smith and B. Faltings. Lecture Notes in Artificial Intelligence 1168. Berlin: Springer-Verlag.

Whitaker, L., Wiggins, S., and Klein, G. (1989). Using Qualitative or Multi-Attribute Similarity to Retrieve Useful Cases from a Case Base. In *Proceedings of the DARPA Case-Based Reasoning Workshop*, edited by K.J. Hammond. San Francisco: Morgan Kaufmann Publishers.

Wolverton, M. (1995). An Investigation of Marker-Passing Algorithms for Analogue Retrieval. In *Case-Based Reasoning Research and Development*, edited by M. Veloso and A. Aamodt. Lecture Notes in Artificial Intelligence 1010. Berlin: Springer-Verlag.

10.3.5 *Adaptation and Repair*

Once cases are retrieved, a CBR system may adapt the solution stored in a retrieved case to better meet the needs of the current case. Several types of adaptation are presented in the following references. These include: *structural adaptation*, where adaptation rules are applied directly to the solution stored in cases and *derivational adaptation*, where the rules that generated the original solution are re-run to produce a new solution to the problem.

Aha, D.W., and Ram, A., eds. (1995). *Adaptation of Knowledge for Reuse: Proceedings of the 1995 AAAI Fall Symposium*. AAAI Technical Report FS-95-04.

Alterman, R. (1986). An Adaptive Planner. In *Proceedings of AAAI-86*. Cambridge, MA: AAAI Press/MIT Press.

Ashley, K., and Rissland, E. (1987). Compare and Contrast, a Test of Expertise. In *Proceedings of AAAI-87*. Cambridge, MA: AAAI Press/MIT Press.

Barletta, R., and Hennessy, D. (1989). Case Adaptation in Autoclave Layout Design. In *Proceedings of the DARPA Case-Based Reasoning Workshop*, edited by K.J. Hammond. San Francisco: Morgan Kaufmann Publishers.

Callan, J.P., Fawcett, T.E., and Rissland, E.L. (1991). Adaptive Case-Based Reasoning. In *Proceedings of the DARPA Case-Based Reasoning Workshop*, edited by E.R. Bareiss. San Francisco: Morgan Kaufmann Publishers.

Carbonell, J.G. (1986). Derivational Analogy: A Theory of Reconstructive Problem Solving and Expertise Acquisition. In *Machine Learning—An Artificial Intelligence Approach*, vol. 2, edited by R.S. Michalski, J.G. Carbonell, and T.M. Mitchell, 371–392. San Francisco: Morgan Kaufmann Publishers.

Carbonell, J.G., and Veloso, M. (1988). Integrating Derivational Analogy into a General Problem Solving Architecture. In *Proceedings of the DARPA Case-Based Reasoning Workshop*, edited by J.L. Kolodner. San Francisco: Morgan Kaufmann Publishers.

Chang, L.W., and Harrison, P. (1995). A Testbed for Experiments in Adaptive Memory Retrieval and Indexing. In *Adaptation of Knowledge for Reuse: Proceedings of the 1995 AAAI Fall Symposium*, edited by D.W. Aha and A. Ram. AAAI Technical Report FS-95-04. Cambridge, MA: AAAI Press / MIT Press.

Chattergee, N., and Campbell, J.A. (1993). Adaptation Through Interpolation for Time-Critical Case-Based-Reasoning. In *Proceedings of EWCBR'93*, edited by M.M. Richter et al. Berlin: Springer-Verlag.

Collins, B., and Cunningham, P. (1996). Adaptation Guided Retrieval in EBMT: A Case-Base Approach to Machine Translation. In *Advances in Case-Based Reasoning,* edited by I. Smith and B. Faltings. Lecture Notes in Artificial Intelligence 1168. Berlin: Springer-Verlag.

Collins, G. (1989). Plan Adaptation: A Transformational Approach. In *Proceedings of the DARPA Case-Based Reasoning Workshop*, edited by K.J. Hammond. San Francisco: Morgan Kaufmann Publishers.

Fuchs, B., Mille, A., and Chiron, B. (1995). Operator Decision Aiding by Adaptation of Supervision Strategies. In *Case-Based Reasoning Research and Development*, edited by M. Veloso and A. Aamodt. Lecture Notes in Artificial Intelligence 1010. Berlin: Springer-Verlag.

Gennari, J., Altman, R.B., and Musen, M.A. (1995). Reuse and PROTÉGÉ-II: Adapting Problem Solving Methods with Mapping Relations. In *Adaptation of Knowledge for Reuse: Proceedings of the 1995 AAAI Fall Symposium,* edited by D.W. Aha and A. Ram. AAAI Technical Report FS-95-04. Cambridge, MA: AAAI Press / MIT Press.

Goel, A., and Chandrasekaran, B. (1989). Use of Device Models in Adaptation of Design Cases. In *Proceedings of the DARPA Case-Based Reasoning Workshop*, edited by K.J. Hammond. San Francisco: Morgan Kaufmann Publishers.

Hammond, K.J. (1988). Case-Based Planning: Viewing Planning as a Memory Task. In *Proceedings of the DARPA Case-Based Reasoning Workshop*, edited by J.L. Kolodner. San Francisco: Morgan Kaufmann Publishers.

Hammond, K.J. (1989). Adaptation of Cases. In *Proceedings of the DARPA Case-Based Reasoning Workshop*, edited by K.J. Hammond. San Francisco: Morgan Kaufmann Publishers.

Hammond, K.J., Converse, T., and Marks, M. (1989). Learning Modification Rules from Expectation Failure. In *Proceedings of the DARPA Case-Based Reasoning Workshop*, edited by K.J. Hammond. San Francisco: Morgan Kaufmann Publishers.

Hanney, K., Keane, M.T., Smyth, B., and Cunningham, P. (1995). Systems, Tasks and Adaptation Knowledge: Revealing Some Revealing Dependencies. In *Case-Based Reasoning Research and Development*, edited by M. Veloso and A. Aamodt. Lecture Notes in Artificial Intelligence 1010. Berlin: Springer-Verlag.

Hanney, K., Keane, M.T., Smyth, B., and Cunningham, P. (1995). What Kind of Adaptation Do CBR Systems Need? A Review of Current Practice. In *Adaptation of Knowledge for Reuse: Proceedings of the 1995 AAAI Fall Symposium,* edited by D.W. Aha and A. Ram. AAAI Technical Report FS-95-04. Cambridge, MA: AAAI Press / MIT Press.

Hastings, J.D., and Branting, K. (1995). Global and Case-Specific Model-Based Adaptation. In *Adaptation of Knowledge for Reuse: Proceedings of the 1995 AAAI Fall Symposium*, edited by D.W. Aha and A. Ram. AAAI Technical Report FS-95-04. Cambridge, MA: AAAI Press / MIT Press.

Hastings, J.D., Branting, L.K., and Lockwood, J.A. (1995). Case Adaptation Using an Incomplete Causal Model. In *Case-Based Reasoning Research and Development*, edited by M. Veloso and A. Aamodt. Lecture Notes in Artificial Intelligence 1010. Berlin: Springer-Verlag.

Hendler, J.A. (1988). Refitting Plans for Case-Based Reasoning. In *Proceedings of the DARPA Case-Based Reasoning Workshop*, edited by J.L. Kolodner. San Francisco: Morgan Kaufmann Publishers.

Hinrichs, T.R. (1989). Strategies for Adaptation and Recovery in a Design Problem Solver. In *Proceedings of the DARPA Case-Based Reasoning Workshop*, edited by K.J. Hammond. San Francisco: Morgan Kaufmann Publishers.

Hinrichs, T.R., and Kolodner, J.L. (1991). The Roles of Adaptation in Case-Based Design. In *Proceedings of the DARPA Case-Based Reasoning Workshop*, edited by E.R. Bareiss. San Francisco: Morgan Kaufmann Publishers.

Hunt, J. (1995). Evolutionary Case Based Design. In *Progress in Case-Based Reasoning*, edited by I. Watson. Lecture Notes in Artificial Intelligence 1020. Berlin: Springer-Verlag.

Kass, A. (1989). Strategies for Adapting Explanations. In *Proceedings of the DARPA Case-Based Reasoning Workshop*, edited by K.J. Hammond. San Francisco: Morgan Kaufmann Publishers.

Kass, A.M., and Leake, D.B. (1988). Case-Based Reasoning Applied to Constructing Explanations. In *Proceedings of the DARPA Case-Based Reasoning Workshop*, edited by J.L. Kolodner. San Francisco: Morgan Kaufmann Publishers.

Koehler, J. (1995). Correct Adaptation of Complex Plans. In *Adaptation of Knowledge for Reuse: Proceedings of the 1995 AAAI Fall Symposium*, edited by D.W. Aha and A. Ram. AAAI Technical Report FS-95-04. Cambridge, MA: AAAI Press / MIT Press.

Kolbe, T., and Walther, C. (1995). Adaptation of Proofs for Reuse. In *Adaptation of Knowledge for Reuse: Proceedings of the 1995 AAAI Fall Symposium*, edited by D.W. Aha and A. Ram. AAAI Technical Report FS-95-04. Cambridge, MA: AAAI Press / MIT Press.

Kolodner, J.L. (1988). Extending Problem Solving Capabilities Through Case-Based Inference. In *Proceeding of the 4th Annual International Machine Learning Workshop*. Cambridge, MA: AAAI Press / MIT Press.

Kopeikina, L., Bandau, R., and Lemmon, A. (1988). Case-Based Reasoning for Continuous Control. In *Proceedings of the DARPA Case-Based Reasoning Workshop*, edited by J.L. Kolodner. San Francisco: Morgan Kaufmann Publishers.

Koton, P. (1988). Reasoning About Evidence in Causal Explanations. In *Proceedings of the DARPA Case-Based Reasoning Workshop*, edited by J.L. Kolodner. San Francisco: Morgan Kaufmann Publishers.

Leake, D.B., Kinley, A., and Wilson, D. (1995). Learning to improve case adaptation by introspective reasoning and CBR. In *Case-Based Reasoning Research and Development*, edited by M. Veloso and A. Aamodt. Lecture Notes in Artificial Intelligence 1010. Berlin: Springer-Verlag.

Marir, F., and Watson, I. (1995). Representing and Indexing Building Refurbishment Cases for Multiple Retrieval of Adaptable Pieces of Cases. In *Case-Based Reasoning Research and Development*, edited by M. Veloso and A. Aamodt. Lecture Notes in Artificial Intelligence 1010. Berlin: Springer-Verlag.

Mostow, G., and Fisher, G. (1989). Replaying Transformational Derivations of Heuristic Search Algorithms in DIOGENES. In *Proceedings of the DARPA Case-Based Reasoning Workshop*, edited by K.J. Hammond. San Francisco: Morgan Kaufmann Publishers.

Mulvehill, A.M. (1995). Reusing Force Deployment Plans. In *Adaptation of Knowledge for Reuse: Proceedings of the 1995 AAAI Fall Symposium*, edited by D.W. Aha and A. Ram. AAAI Technical Report FS-95-04. Cambridge, MA: AAAI Press/MIT Press.

Oehlmann, R. (1995). Metacognitive Adaptation: Regulating the Plan Transformation Process. In *Adaptation of Knowledge for Reuse: Proceedings of the 1995 AAAI Fall Symposium*, edited by D.W. Aha and A. Ram. AAAI Technical Report FS-95-04. Cambridge, MA: AAAI Press / MIT Press.

O'Hara, S., and Indurkhya, B. (1995). Adaptation and Re-Description in the Context of Geometric Proportional Analogies. In *Adaptation of Knowledge for Reuse: Proceedings of the 1995 AAAI Fall Symposium*, edited by D.W. Aha and A. Ram. AAAI Technical Report FS-95-04. Cambridge, MA: AAAI Press / MIT Press.

Orsvarn, K. (1995). Adaptation of Generic Models in Model-Driven Knowledge Acquisition. In *Adaptation of Knowledge for Reuse: Proceedings of the 1995 AAAI Fall Symposium*, edited by D.W. Aha and A. Ram. AAAI Technical Report FS-95-04. Cambridge, MA: AAAI Press / MIT Press.

Petridis, V., and Paraschidis, K. (1993). Structural Adaptation Based on a Simple Learning Algorithm. In *Proceedings of the International Joint Conference on Neural Networks 1993*, vol. 1, 621–623.

Purvis, L., and Pu, P. (1995). Adaptation Using Constraint Satisfaction Techniques. In *Case-Based Reasoning Research and Development*, edited by M. Veloso and A. Aamodt. Lecture Notes in Artificial Intelligence 1010. Berlin: Springer-Verlag.

Rousu, J., and Aarts, R.J. (1996). Adaptation Cost as a Criterion for Solution Evaluation. In *Advances in Case-Based Reasoning,* edited by I. Smith and B. Faltings. Lecture Notes in Artificial Intelligence 1168. Berlin: Springer-Verlag.

Shinn, H.S. (1988). Abstractional Analogy: A Model of Analogical Reasoning. In *Proceedings of the DARPA Case-Based Reasoning Workshop*, edited by J.L. Kolodner. San Francisco: Morgan Kaufmann Publishers.

Simmons, R.G. (1988) A Theory of Debugging. In *Proceedings of the DARPA Case-Based Reasoning Workshop*, edited by J.L. Kolodner. San Francisco: Morgan Kaufmann Publishers.

Smyth, B., and Keane, M.T. (1995). Experiments on Adaptation-Guided Retrieval in Case-Based Design. In *Case-Based Reasoning Research and Development*, edited by M. Veloso and A. Aamodt. Lecture Notes in Artificial Intelligence 1010. Berlin: Springer-Verlag.

Smyth, B., and Keane, M.T. (1995). Retrieval and Adaptation in Deja Vu. In *Adaptation of Knowledge for Reuse: Proceedings of the 1995 AAAI Fall Symposium*, edited by D.W. Aha and A. Ram. AAAI Technical Report FS-95-04. Cambridge, MA: AAAI Press / MIT Press.

Smyth, B., and Keane, M.T. (1996). Adaptation-Guided Retrieval: Using Adaptation Knowledge to Guide the Retrieval of Adaptable Cases. In *Proceedings of the Second U.K. Workshop on Case-Based Reasoning*, edited by I. Watson. Salford, UK: Salford University.

Smyth, B., and Keane, M.T. (1996). Design à la Deja Vu: Reducing the Adaptation Overhead. In *Case-Based Reasoning: Experiences, Lessons, & Future Directions*, edited by D.B. Leake. Cambridge, MA: AAAI Press / MIT Press.

Sussman, G.J. (1975). *A Computer Model of Skill Acquisition*. New York: Elsevier.

Sycara, K. (1988). Using Case-Based Reasoning for Plan Adaptation and Repair. In *Proceedings of the DARPA Case-Based Reasoning Workshop*, edited by J.L. Kolodner. San Francisco: Morgan Kaufmann Publishers.

Veloso, M.M., and Carbonell, J.G. (1993). Derivational analogy in PRODIGY. In *Machine Learning* 10(3), 249–278.

Voss, A. (1996). Principles of Case Reusing Systems. In *Advances in Case-Based Reasoning,* edited by I. Smith and B. Faltings. Lecture Notes in Artificial Intelligence 1168. Berlin: Springer-Verlag.

Weiss, M., and Zeyer, F. (1994). Redesign of Local Area Networks Using Similarity-Based Adaptation. In *Proceedings of the Conference on Artificial Intelligence Applications 1994*, 284–290.

Zeyer, F., and Weiss, M. (1993). Similarity-Based Adaptation and Its Application to the Case-Based Redesign of Local Area Networks. In *Proceedings of EWCBR '93*, edited by M.M. Richter et al. Berlin: Springer-Verlag.

10.3.5.1 Evaluation of Adaptation

Bareiss, E.R. (1989). The Experimental Evaluation of a Case-Based Learning Apprentice. In *Proceedings of the DARPA Case-Based Reasoning Workshop*, edited by K.J. Hammond. San Francisco: Morgan Kaufmann Publishers.

Börner, K., Pippig, E., Tammer, E., and Coulon, C.-H. (1996). Structural Similarity and Adaptation. In *Advances in Case-Based Reasoning*, edited by I. Smith and B. Faltings. Lecture Notes in Artificial Intelligence 1168. Berlin: Springer-Verlag.

Cohen, P. (1989). Evaluation and Case-Based Reasoning. In *Proceedings of the DARPA Case-Based Reasoning Workshop*, edited by K.J. Hammond. San Francisco: Morgan Kaufmann Publishers.

Funk, P., and Robertson, D. (1995). Capturing and Matching Dynamic Behaviour in Case-Based Reasoning. In *Progress in Case-Based Reasoning*, edited by I. Watson. Lecture Notes in Artificial Intelligence 1020. Berlin: Springer-Verlag.

Hanney, K., and Keane, M.T. (1996). Learning Adaptation Rules from a Case-Base. In *Advances in Case-Based Reasoning*, edited by I. Smith and B. Faltings. Lecture Notes in Artificial Intelligence 1168. Berlin: Springer-Verlag.

Hurley, N. (1995). Evaluating the Application of CBR in Mesh Design for Simulation Problems. In *Case-Based Reasoning Research and Development*, edited by M. Veloso and A. Aamodt. Lecture Notes in Artificial Intelligence 1010. Berlin: Springer-Verlag.

Koton, P. (1989). Applications and Validation: Case-Based Reasoning in the Real World. In *Proceedings of the DARPA Case-Based Reasoning Workshop*, edited by K.J. Hammond. San Francisco: Morgan Kaufmann Publishers.

Koton, P. (1989). Evaluating Case-Based Problem Solving. In *Proceedings of the DARPA Case-Based Reasoning Workshop*, edited by K.J. Hammond. San Francisco: Morgan Kaufmann Publishers.

Mark, W. (1989). Case-Based Reasoning for Autoclave Management. In *Proceedings of the DARPA Case-Based Reasoning Workshop*, edited by K.J. Hammond. San Francisco: Morgan Kaufmann Publishers.

Rousu, J., and Aarts, R.J. (1996). Adaptation Cost as a Criterion for Solution Evaluation. In *Advances in Case-Based Reasoning*, edited by I. Smith and B. Faltings. Lecture Notes in Artificial Intelligence 1168. Berlin: Springer-Verlag.

Smyth, B., and Cunningham, P. (1996). The Utility Problem Analysed: A Case-Based Reasoning Perspective. In *Advances in Case-Based Reasoning*, edited by I. Smith and B. Faltings. Lecture Notes in Artificial Intelligence 1168. Berlin: Springer-Verlag.

10.4 Applied CBR

10.4.1 CBR Software Tools

The following papers and reports describe CBR software tools.

Althoff, K.-D., Auriol, E., Barletta, R., and Manago, M. (1995). *A Review of Industrial Case-Based Reasoning Tools.* Oxford: AI Intelligence.

Harmon, P. (1992). Case-Based Reasoning III. *Intelligent Software Strategies,* 8(1).

Pegler, I., and Price, C.J. (1996). CASPIAN: A Freeware Case-Based Reasoning Shell. In *Proceedings of the Second U.K. Workshop on Case-Based Reasoning,* edited by I. Watson. Salford, UK: Salford University.

Watson, I. (1996). Case-Based Reasoning Tools: An Overview. In *Proceedings of the Second U.K. Workshop on Case-Based Reasoning,* edited by I. Watson. Salford, UK: Salford University.

Watson, I., and Marir, F. (1994). Case-Based Reasoning: A Review. *The Knowledge Engineering Review,* 9(4), 355–381.

10.4.2 CBR Demonstrators

This section covers CBR demonstrators. These systems are used in a wide range of tasks, such as knowledge acquisition and refinement, legal reasoning, explanation of anomalies, diagnosis, arbitration, design, adaptation and repair, tutoring, planning, help-desks, and so on.

10.4.2.1 Adaptation and Repair

Alterman, R. (1986). An adaptive planner. In *Proceedings of AAAI-86.* Cambridge, MA: AAAI Press / MIT Press.

Alterman, R. (1988). Adaptive planning. *Cognitive Science* 12, 393–422.

Collins, G. (1987). *Plan Creation: Using Strategies as Blueprints.* Ph.D. thesis, Dept. of Computer Science, Yale University, New Haven, CT.

Deugo, D., and Oppacher, F. (1989). Applications of Case-Based Reasoning Using Knowledge Base and Genetic Techniques. In *Proceedings of the DARPA Case-Based Reasoning Workshop,* edited by K.J. Hammond. San Francisco: Morgan Kaufmann Publishers.

Hammond, K.J. (1986). CHEF: A Model of Case-Based Planning. In *Proceedings of AAAI-86, August 1986.* Cambridge, MA: AAAI Press / MIT Press.

Hammond, K.J. (1987). Explaining and Repairing Plans That Fail. In *Proceedings International Joint Conference on Artificial Intelligence, IJCAI-87.*

Sycara, K. (1988). Using Case-Based Reasoning for Plan Adaptation and Repair. In *Proceedings of the DARPA Case-Based Reasoning Workshop*, edited by J.L. Kolodner. San Francisco: Morgan Kaufmann Publishers.

10.4.2.2 Arbitration

Simpson, R.L. (1985). *A Computer Model of Case-Based Reasoning in Problem Solving: An Investigation in the Domain of Dispute Mediation*. Technical Report No. GIT-ICS-85/18, School of Information and Computer Science. Atlanta: Georgia Institute of Technology.

Sycara, E.P. (1987). Finding Creative Solutions in Adversarial Impasses. In *Proceedings of the Ninth Annual Conference of the Cognitive Science Society*. Northvale, NJ: Lawrence Erlbaum Associates.

Sycara, E.P. (1987). *Resolving Adversarial Conflicts: An Approach to Integrating Case-Based and Analytic Methods*. Technical Report No. GIT-ICS-87/26, School of Information and Computer Science. Georgia Institute of Technology.

10.4.2.3 Data Mining

Heider, R. (1996). Troubleshooting CFM 56-3 Engines for the Boeing 737—Using CBR and Data-Mining. In *Advances in Case-Based Reasoning*, edited by I. Smith and B. Faltings. Lecture Notes in Artificial Intelligence 1168. Berlin: Springer-Verlag.

Hunt, J., and Fellows, A. (1996). Introducing an Immune Response into a CBR System for Data Mining. In *Research & Development in Expert Systems XIII*, edited by J.L. Nealon and J. Hunt. Oxford: SGES Publications.

Milne, R., and Nelson, C. (1994). Knowledge Guided Data Mining. In *Proceedings of the IEE Colloquium on Case-Based Reasoning: Prospects for Applications*, Digest No. 1994/057, 10/1–10/3.

10.4.2.4 Design

Bakhtar, S., and Bartsch-Sporl, B. (1993). Our Perspective on Using CBR in Design Problem Solving. In *Proceedings of EWCBR'93*, edited by M.M. Richter et al. Berlin: Springer-Verlag.

Bardasz, B., and Zeid, I. (1993). Dejavu: Case-Based Reasoning for Mechanical Design. In *Artificial Intelligence for Engineering Design, Analysis and Manufacturing*, 7(2), 111–124.

Bartsch-Sporl, B. (1995). Towards the Integration of Case-Based, Schema-Based and Model-Based Reasoning for Supporting Complex Design Tasks. In *Case-Based Reasoning Research and Development*, edited by M. Veloso and A. Aamodt. Lecture Notes in Artificial Intelligence 1010. Berlin: Springer-Verlag.

Daube, F., and Hayes-Roth, B. (1989). A Case-Based Mechanical Redesign System. In *Proceeding of the 1989 International Joint Conference on Artificial Intelligence*, 1402–1407. San Francisco: Morgan Kaufmann Publishers.

Domeshek, E., and Kolodner, J.L. (1993). Finding the Points of Large Cases. *Artificial Intelligence for Engineering Design, Analysis and Manufacturing (AIEDAM)*, 7(2), 87–96.

Domeshek, E., Zimring, G.M., and Kolodner, J.L. (1994). Scaling Up is Hard to Do—Experiences in Preparing a Case-Based Design Aid Prototype for Field Trial. In *Proceedings of the First Congress Held in Conjunction with A/E/C Systems '94*, vol. 2, edited by K. Khozeimeh.

Flemming, U., Coyne, R., and Snyder, J. (1994). Case-Based Design in the SEED System. *In Proceedings of the First Congress Held in Conjunction with A/E/C Systems '94*, vol. 2, edited by K. Khozeimeh.

Geffraye, F., Wybo, J.L., and Russeil, A. (1995). PROFIL: A Decision Support Tool for Metallic Sections Design Using a CBR Approach. In *Case-Based Reasoning Research and Development*, edited by M. Veloso and A. Aamodt. Lecture Notes in Artificial Intelligence 1010. Berlin: Springer-Verlag.

Goel, A.K., and Chandrasekaran, B. (1992). Case-Based Design: A Task Analysis. In *Artificial Intelligence Approaches to Engineering Design, Vol. 2: Innovative Design*, edited by C. Tong and D. Sriram. San Diego: Academic Press.

Goel, A.K., Kolodner, J.L., Pearce, M., Billington, R., and Zimring, C. (1991). Towards a Case-Based Tool for Aiding Conceptual Design Problem Solving. In *Proceedings of the DARPA Case-Based Reasoning Workshop*, edited by E.R. Bareiss. San Francisco: Morgan Kaufmann Publishers.

Griffith, A.L., and Domeshek, E. (1996). Indexing Evaluations of Buildings to Aid Conceptual Design. In *Case-Based Reasoning: Experiences, Lessons, & Future Directions*, edited by D.B. Leake. Cambridge, MA: AAAI Press / MIT Press.

Hinrichs, T.R. (1992). *Problem Solving in Open Worlds*. Northvale, NJ: Lawrence Erlbaum Associates.

Hinrichs, T.R. (1995). Some Limitations of Feature-Based Recognition in Case-Based Design. In *Case-Based Reasoning Research and Development*, edited by M. Veloso and A. Aamodt. Lecture Notes in Artificial Intelligence 1010. Berlin: Springer-Verlag.

Hinrichs, T.R., and Kolodner, J.L. (1991). The Roles of Adaptation in Case-Based Design. In *Proceedings of AAAI-91*. Cambridge, MA: AAAI Press / MIT Press.

Hua, K., Smith, I., and Faltings, B. (1993). Integrated Case-Based Building Design. In *Proceedings of EWCBR'93*, edited by M.M. Richter et al. Berlin: Springer-Verlag.

Hunt, J., and Miles, R. (1995). Towards an Intelligent Architectural Design Aid. *Expert Systems*, 12(3), 209–218.

Maher, M.L. (1994). Creative Design Using a Genetic Algorithm. *ASCE*, 2014–2021.

Maher, M.L. (1994). Representation of Case Memory for Structural Design, *ASCE*, 2030–2037.

Maher, M.L., and Balachandran, B. (1994). Flexible Retrieval Strategies for Case-Based Design. In *Artificial Intelligence in Design '94*, 163–180, edited by J.S. Gero and F. Sudweeks. Netherlands: Kluwer Academic Publishers.

Maher, M.L., and Balachandran, B. (1994). Multimedia Approach to Case-Based Structural Design. *The Journal of Computing in Civil Engineering*, 8(3), 359–376.

Maher, M.L., Balachandran, B., and Zhang, D.M. (1995). *Case-Based Reasoning in Design*. Northvale, NJ: Lawrence Erlbaum Associates.

Maher, M.L., and Zhang, D.M. (1991). CADSYN: Using Case and Decomposition Knowledge for Design Synthesis. In *Artificial Intelligence in Design*, edited by J.S. Gero. Oxford: Butterworth-Heinmann.

Maiden, N.A.M. (1993). Case-Based Reasoning in Complex Design Tasks. In *Proceedings of EWCBR '93*, edited by M.M. Richter et al. Berlin: Springer-Verlag.

Moore, C.J., Lehane, M.S., and Price, C.J. (1994). Case-Based Reasoning for Decision Support in Engineering Design. In *Proceeding of the IEE Colloquium on Case-Based Reasoning: Prospects for Applications*, Digest No. 1994/057, 4/1–4/4.

Mostow, J., Barley, M., and Weinrich, T. (1992). Automated Reuse of Design Plans in BOGART. In *Artificial Intelligence in Engineering Design*, edited by C. Tong and D. Sriram. San Diego: Academic Press.

Navinchandra, D. (1988). Case-Based Reasoning in CYCLOPS, a Design Problem Solver. In *Proceedings of the DARPA Case-Based Reasoning Workshop*, edited by J.L. Kolodner. San Francisco: Morgan Kaufmann Publishers.

Netten, B.D., and Vingerhoeds, R.A. (1996). Retrieval and Reuse of Conceptual Designs in EADOCS. In *Advances in Case-Based Reasoning*, edited by I. Smith and B. Faltings. Lecture Notes in Artificial Intelligence 1168. Berlin: Springer-Verlag.

Oxman, R. (1994). Precedents in Design: A Computational Model for Organization of Case Knowledge. In *Proceedings of the First Congress Held in Conjunction with A/E/C Systems '94*, vol. 2, edited by K. Khozeimeh.

Oxman, R. (1995). Design Case Bases: Graphic Knowledge Bases for the Design Workspace. *International Conference on Computer Aided Architectural Design—CAAD Futures*, Singapore.

Pearce, M., Ashok, K.G., Kolodner, J.L., Zimring, C., and Billington, R. (1992). Case-Based Support—A Case Study in Architectural Design. *IEEE Expert*, October 1992.

Perera, R.S., and Watson, I. (1995). A Case-Based Design Approach for the Integration of Design and Estimating. In *Progress in Case-Based Reasoning*, edited by I. Watson. Lecture Notes in Artificial Intelligence 1020. Berlin: Springer-Verlag.

Ram, A., and Hunter, L. (1992). Goals for Learning and Understanding. *Journal of Applied Intelligence*, 2, 47–73.

Raphael, B., Kumar, B., and McLeod, A. (1994). Representing Design Cases Based on Methods. In *Proceedings of the First Congress Held in Conjunction with A/E/C Systems '94*, vol. 1, edited by K. Khozeimeh.

Santamaria, J.C., and Ram, A. (1996). Systematic Evaluation of Design Decisions in Case-Based Reasoning Systems. In *Case-Based Reasoning: Experiences, Lessons, & Future Directions*, edited by D.B. Leake. Cambridge, MA: AAAI Press/MIT Press.

Smith, I., Lottaz, C., and Faltings, B. (1995). Spatial Composition Using Cases: IDIOM. In *Case-Based Reasoning Research and Development*, edited by M. Veloso and A. Aamodt. Lecture Notes in Artificial Intelligence 1010. Berlin: Springer-Verlag.

Stehr, J. (1995). CBR and Machine Learning for Combustion System Design. In *Case-Based Reasoning Research and Development*, edited by M. Veloso and A. Aamodt. Lecture Notes in Artificial Intelligence 1010. Berlin: Springer-Verlag.

Surma, J., and Braunschweig, B. (1996). REPRO: Supporting Flowsheet Design by Case-Base Retrieval. In *Advances in Case-Based Reasoning*, edited by I. Smith and B. Faltings. Lecture Notes in Artificial Intelligence 1168. Berlin: Springer-Verlag.

Sycara, K. (1992). CADET: A Case-Based Synthesis Tool for Engineering Design. *International Journal for Expert Systems* 4(2), 157–188.

Sycara, K., and Navinchandra, D. (1992). Retrieval Strategies in a Case-Based Design System. In *Artificial Intelligence in Engineering Design*, vol. 2, edited by C. Tong and D. Sriram. San Diego: Academic Press.

Trousse, B., and Visser, W. (1994). Use of Case-Based Reasoning Techniques for Intelligent Computer-Aided-Design Systems. In *Proceedings of the IEEE International Conference on Systems, Man and Cybernetics 1993*, 3, 513–517.

Watson, I., and Perera, R.S. (1995). NIRMANI: A Case-Based Expert System for Integrated Design & Estimating. In *Applications and Innovations in Expert Systems III*, 335–348, edited by A. Macintosh and C. Cooper. Proceedings of Expert Systems '95. Oxford: SGES Publications.

Wills, L.M., and Kolodner, J.L. (1996). Towards More Creative Case-Based Design Systems. In *Case-Based Reasoning: Experiences, Lessons, & Future Directions*, edited by D.B. Leake. Cambridge, MA: AAAI Press / MIT Press.

Yamamato, H., and Fujimoto, H. (1992). *Case-Based Reasoning in Expert Systems Assisting Production Line Design.* Lecture Notes in Computer Science, 604, 49–58. Berlin: Springer-Verlag.

Zdrahal, Z., and Motta, E. (1996). Case-Based Problem Solving Methods for Parametric Design Tasks. In *Advances in Case-Based Reasoning,* edited by I. Smith and B. Faltings. Lecture Notes in Artificial Intelligence 1168. Berlin: Springer-Verlag.

10.4.2.5 Diagnosis

Acorn, T., and Walden, S. (1992). SMART: Support Management Cultivated Reasoning Technology for Compaq Customer Service. In *Proceedings of AAAI-92.* Cambridge, MA: AAAI Press / MIT Press.

Allen, J.R.C., Patterson, D., Mulvenna, M.D., and Hughes, J.G. (1995). Integration of Case-Based Retrieval with a Relational Database System in Aircraft Technical Support. In *Case-Based Reasoning Research and Development,* edited by M. Veloso and A. Aamodt. Lecture Notes in Artificial Intelligence 1010. Berlin: Springer-Verlag.

Bub, R., et al. (1994). A Case-Based Reasoning System for Troubleshooting. In *Proceedings of the IEE Colloquium on Case-Based Reasoning: Prospects for Applications,* Digest No. 1994/057, 5/1–5/8.

Cook, L.K. (1989). Teaching Expertise: Using Case-Based Systems to Transfer Real World Experience. In *Proceedings of the DARPA Case-Based Reasoning Workshop,* edited by K.J. Hammond. San Francisco: Morgan Kaufmann Publishers.

Dattani, I., and Bramer, M. (1995). Case-Based Reasoning: A Technique for "Decision Support Systems" in Residential Valuation and the Construction of Residential Housing. In *Progress in Case-Based Reasoning,* edited by I. Watson. Lecture Notes in Artificial Intelligence 1020. Berlin: Springer-Verlag.

Deters, R. (1995). Case-Based Diagnosis of Multiple Faults. In *Case-Based Reasoning Research and Development,* edited by M. Veloso and A. Aamodt. Lecture Notes in Artificial Intelligence 1010. Berlin: Springer-Verlag.

Georgin, E., et al. (1994). The Use of Cases in Diagnostic Explanations. In *Proceedings of the IEE Colloquium on Case-Based Reasoning: Prospects for Applications,* Digest No. 1994/057, 2/1–2/3.

Koton, P. (1989). *Using Experience in Learning and Problem Solving.* Ph.D. thesis MIT/LCS/TR-441, Laboratory of Computer Science, Massachusetts Institute of Technology.

Lenz, M., Burkhard, H.-D., and Brückner, S. (1996). Applying Case Retrieval Nets to Diagnostic Tasks in Technical Domains. In *Advances in Case-Based Reasoning,* edited by I. Smith and B. Faltings. Lecture Notes in Artificial Intelligence 1168. Berlin: Springer-Verlag.

Netten, B.D., and Vingerhoeds, R.A. (1995). Large-Scale Fault Diagnosis for On-Board Train Systems. In *Case-Based Reasoning Research and Development*, edited by M. Veloso and A. Aamodt. Lecture Notes in Artificial Intelligence 1010. Berlin: Springer-Verlag.

Okuda, K., Watanabe, H., Yamazaki, K., and Baba, T. (1990). Fault Restoration Operation Scheme in Secondary Power Systems Using Case-Based Reasoning. *In Electrical Engineering in Japan,* 110(2).

Opiyo, E.T.O. (1995). Case-Based Reasoning for Expertise Relocation in Support of Rural Health Workers in Developing Countries. In *Case-Based Reasoning Research and Development*, edited by M. Veloso and A. Aamodt. Lecture Notes in Artificial Intelligence 1010. Berlin: Springer-Verlag.

Porter, B.W., and Bareiss, E.R. (1986). PROTOS: An Experiment in Knowledge Acquisition for Heuristic Classification Tasks. *In Proceedings of the First International Meeting on Advances in Learning (IMAL)*, 159–174.

Ram, A., and Hunter, L. (1992). Goals for Learning and Understanding. *Journal of Applied Intelligence, 2,* 47–73.

Redmond, M.A. (1992). *Learning by Observing and Understanding Expert Problem Solving*. Technical Report No. GIT-CC-92/43, College of Computing. Atlanta: Georgia Institute of Technology.

Simoudis, E. (1992). Using Case-Based Retrieval for Customer Technical Support. *IEEE Expert, 7*(5), 7–13.

Simoudis, E., Mendall, A., and Miller, P. (1993). Automated Support for Developing Retrieve-and-Propose Systems. In *Proceedings of Artificial Intelligence XI Conference*, Orlando, Florida.

Turner, R.M. (1988). Organizing and Using Schematic Knowledge for Medical Diagnosis. In *Proceedings of the DARPA Case-Based Reasoning Workshop*, edited by J.L. Kolodner. San Francisco: Morgan Kaufmann Publishers.

Watson, I., and Abdullah, S. (1994). Developing Case-Based Reasoning Systems: A Case Study in Diagnosing Building Defects. In *Proceedings of the IEE Colloquium on Case-Based Reasoning: Prospects for Applications*, Digest No. 1994/057, l/1–1/3.

10.4.2.6 Explanation

Kass, A.M., and Leake, D.B. (1988). Case-Based Reasoning Applied to Constructing Explanations. In *Proceedings of the DARPA Case-Based Reasoning Workshop*, edited by J.L. Kolodner. San Francisco: Morgan Kaufmann Publishers.

Kass, A.M., Leake, D.B., and Owens, C. (1986). SWALE: A Program That Explains. In *Explanation Patterns: Understanding Mechanically and Creatively,* edited by R. Schank. Northvale, NJ: Lawrence Erlbaum Associates.

Leake, D.B. (1988). ACCEPTER: A Program for Dynamic Similarity Assessment in Case-Based Explanation. In *Proceedings of the DARPA Case-Based Reasoning Workshop*, edited by J.L. Kolodner. San Francisco: Morgan Kaufmann Publishers.

Leake, D.B. (1991). Goal-Based Explanation Evaluation. *Cognitive Science*, 15, 509–545.

10.4.2.7 Help-Desks and Advice Giving

Allen, B. (1994). Case-Based Reasoning: Business Applications. *Communications of the ACM*, 37(3), 40–42.

Bonzano, A., Cunningham, P., and Meckiff, C. (1996). ISAC: A CBR System for Decision Support in Air Traffic Control. In *Advances in Case-Based Reasoning*, edited by I. Smith and B. Faltings. Lecture Notes in Artificial Intelligence 1168. Berlin: Springer-Verlag.

Borron, J., Morales, D., and Klahr, P. (1996). Developing and Deploying Knowledge on a Global Scale. In *Innovative Applications of Artificial Intelligence 8, Proceedings of AAAI-96*. Cambridge, MA: AAAI Press / MIT Press.

Brandau, R., Lemmon, A., and Lafond, C. (1991). Experience with Extended Episodes: Cases with Complex Temporal Structure. In *Proceedings of the DARPA Case-Based Reasoning Workshop*, edited by E.R. Bareiss. San Francisco: Morgan Kaufmann Publishers.

Davies, J., and May, R. (1995). The Development of a Prototype "Correctly Dressed" Case-Based Reasoner: Efficacy of CBR Express. In *Progress in Case-Based Reasoning*, edited by I. Watson. Lecture Notes in Artificial Intelligence 1020. Berlin: Springer-Verlag.

Dearden, A.M., and Bridge, D.G. (1993). Choosing a Reasoning Style for a Knowledge-Based System: Lessons from Supporting a Help Desk. *The Knowledge Engineering Review*, 8(3), 210–222.

Domeshek, E. (1991). What Abby Cares About. In *Proceedings of the DARPA Case-Based Reasoning Workshop*, edited by E.R. Bareiss. San Francisco: Morgan Kaufmann Publishers.

Domeshek, E. (1993). A Case Study of Case Indexing: Designing Index Feature Sets to Suit Task Demands and Support Parallelism. In *Advances in Connectionist and Neural Computation Theory, Vol. 2: Analogical Connections*, edited by J. Bamden and K. Holyoak. Norwood, NJ: Ablex.

Dutton, D., and Maun, K. (1996). CBR for the Selection of Appropriate Timber in Design. In *Proceedings of the Second U.K. Workshop on Case-Based Reasoning*, edited by I. Watson. Salford, UK: Salford University.

Hamza, M., Lees, B., and Irgens, C. (1996). Applying Case-Based Reasoning in Software Quality Assessment. In *Proceedings of the Second U.K. Workshop on Case-Based Reasoning*, edited by I. Watson. Salford, UK: Salford University.

Kitano, H., Shibata, A., Shimazu, H., Kajihara, J., and Sato, A. (1992). Building Large-Scale and Corporate Wide Case-Based Systems. In *Proceedings of AAAI-92*. Cambridge, MA: AAAI Press / MIT Press.

Klahr, P. (1996). Global Case-Based Development and Deployment. In *Advances in Case-Based Reasoning*, 519–530, edited by I. Smith and B. Faltings. Lecture Notes in Artificial Intelligence 1168. Berlin: Springer-Verlag.

Maguire, P., Shankaraman, V., Szegfue, R., and Moriss, L. (1995). Application of Case-Based Reasoning (CBR) to Software Reuse. In *Progress in Case-Based Reasoning*, edited by I. Watson. Lecture Notes in Artificial Intelligence 1020. Berlin: Springer-Verlag.

McCarthy, D. (1994). Automation of Help Desks Using Case-Based Reasoning. In *Proceedings of the IEE Colloquium on Case-Based Reasoning: Prospects for Applications*, Digest No. 1994/057, 9/1–9/3.

Rahmer, J., and Voss, A. (1996). Case-Enhanced Configuration by Resource Balancing. In *Advances in Case-Based Reasoning*, edited by I. Smith and B. Faltings. Lecture Notes in Artificial Intelligence 1168. Berlin: Springer-Verlag.

Simoudis, E. (1992). Using Case-Based Reasoning for Customer Technical Support. *IEEE Expert 7(5)*, 7–13.

Simoudis, E., and Miller, J.S. (1988). The Application of CBR to Help Desk Applications. In *Proceedings of the DARPA Case-Based Reasoning Workshop*, edited by J.L. Kolodner. San Francisco: Morgan Kaufmann Publishers.

Simoudis, E., and Miller, J.S. (1991). The Application of CBR to Help Desk Applications. In *Proceedings of the DARPA Workshop on Case-Based Reasoning*, edited by E. R. Bareiss. San Francisco: Morgan Kaufmann Publishers.

Slator, B.M., and Riesbeck, C.K. (1992). TaxOps: A Case-Based Advisor. *International Journal for Expert Systems*, 4(2), 117–140.

10.4.2.8 Heuristic Search and Classification

Goodman, M. (1990). Prism: A Case-Based Telex Classifier. In *Innovative Applications of Artificial Intelligence*, vol. 2, edited by A. Rappaport and R. Smith. Cambridge, MA: MIT Press.

Hickman, A.K., and Lovett, M.C. (1991). Partial Match and Search Control via Internal Analogy. In *Proceedings of the Thirteenth Annual Conference of the Cognitive Science Society*. Northvale, NJ: Lawrence Erlbaum Associates.

Napoli, A., Lieber, J., and Curien, R. (1996). Classification-Based Problem-Solving in Case-Based Reasoning. In *Advances in Case-Based Reasoning*, edited by I. Smith and B. Faltings. Lecture Notes in Artificial Intelligence 1168. Berlin: Springer-Verlag.

Porter, B.W., Bareiss, E.R., and Holte, R.C. (1990). Concept Learning and Heuristic Classification in Weak Theory Domains. *Artificial Intelligence* 45, 229–263.

10.4.2.9 **Interpretation**

The references in this section refer to the interpretative or precedent-based approach of CBR. It includes argumentation to decide whether a new situation should or should not be treated like a past experience based on similarities or differences. These types of CBR are mostly used in precedent-based fields like law or where the explanation or justification of a solution or the interpretation or assessment of a situation is required. The section also includes papers that treat the subject of checking the appropriateness of results from interpretation.

Ashley, K. (1991). *Modelling Legal Arguments: Reasoning with Cases and Hypotheticals*. Cambridge, MA: MIT Press.

Ashley, K., and Rissland, E. (1987). Compare and Contrast, a Test of Expertise. In *Proceedings of the Sixth National Conference on AI (AAAI-87)*, 273–284. Cambridge, MA: AAAI Press/MIT Press.

Barletta, R., and Mark, W. (1988). Explanation-Based Indexing of Cases. In *Proceedings of the DARPA Case-Based Reasoning Workshop*, edited by J.L. Kolodner. San Francisco: Morgan Kaufmann Publishers.

Birnbaum, L., and Collins, G. (1988). The Transfer of Experience Across Planning Domains Through the Acquisition of Abstract Strategies. In *Proceedings of the DARPA Case-Based Reasoning Workshop*, edited by J.L. Kolodner. San Francisco: Morgan Kaufmann Publishers.

Branting, L.K. (1988). The Role of Explanation in Reasoning from Legal Precedent. In *Proceedings of the DARPA Case-Based Reasoning Workshop*, edited by J.L. Kolodner. San Francisco: Morgan Kaufmann Publishers.

Branting, L.K. (1991). Exploiting the Complementarity of Rules and Precedents with Reciprocity and Fairness. In *Proceedings of the DARPA Case-Based Reasoning Workshop*, edited by E.R. Bareiss. San Francisco: Morgan Kaufmann Publishers.

Carbonell, J.G., and Veloso, M.M. (1988). Integrating Derivational Analogy into a General Problem Solving Architecture. In *Proceedings of the DARPA Case-Based Reasoning Workshop*, edited by J.L. Kolodner. San Francisco: Morgan Kaufmann Publishers.

Hammond, K.J. (1987). Explaining and Repairing Plans That Fail. In *Proceedings of the International Joint Conference on Artificial Intelligence, IJCAI-87*.

Hammond, K.J., and Hurwitz, N. (1988). Extracting Diagnostic Features from Explanations. In *Proceedings of the DARPA Case-Based Reasoning Workshop*, edited by J.L. Kolodner. San Francisco: Morgan Kaufmann Publishers.

Kass, A.M., and Leake, D.B. (1988). Case-Based Reasoning Applied to Constructing Explanations. In *Proceedings of the DARPA Case-Based Reasoning Workshop*, edited by J.L. Kolodner. San Francisco: Morgan Kaufmann Publishers.

Koton, P. (1988). Reasoning About Evidence in Causal Explanations. In *Proceedings of the DARPA Case-Based Reasoning Workshop*, edited by J.L. Kolodner. San Francisco: Morgan Kaufmann Publishers.

Rissland, E.L. (1983). Examples in Legal Reasoning: Legal Hypotheticals. In *Proceedings of the Eighth International Joint Conference on Artificial Intelligence, IJCAI-83*.

Rissland, E.L., and Ashley, K.D. (1988). Credit Assignment and the Problem of Competing Factors in Case-Based Reasoning. In *Proceedings of the DARPA Case-Based Reasoning Workshop*, edited by J.L. Kolodner. San Francisco: Morgan Kaufmann Publishers.

Skalak, C.B., and Rissland, E.L. (1992). Arguments and Cases: An Inevitable Twining. *Artificial Intelligence and Law,* 1(i), 3–48.

Sycara, K. (1988). Using Case-Based Reasoning for Plan Adaptation and Repair. In *Proceedings of the DARPA Case-Based Reasoning Workshop*, edited by J.L. Kolodner. San Francisco: Morgan Kaufmann Publishers.

Wall, R.S., Donahue, D., and Hill, S. (1988). The Use of Domain Semantics for Retrieval and Explanation in Case-Based Reasoning. In *Proceedings of the DARPA Case-Based Reasoning Workshop*, edited by J.L. Kolodner. San Francisco: Morgan Kaufmann Publishers.

10.4.2.10 Knowledge Acquisition and Learning

This section contains references on case-based learning algorithms and CBR systems that focus on the learning of a topic. They can be used for knowledge acquisition and to improve future problem solving or interpretation. The result of this learning process is the creation and storage of new cases that can be used to help solve or interpret new problems.

Aamodt, A. (1989). Towards Expert Systems That Learn from Experience. In *Proceedings of the DARPA Case-Based Reasoning Workshop*, edited by K.J. Hammond. San Francisco: Morgan Kaufmann Publishers.

Agre, G. (1995). KBS Maintenance as Learning Two-Tiered Domain Representation. In *Case-Based Reasoning Research and Development*, edited by M. Veloso and A. Aamodt. Lecture Notes in Artificial Intelligence 1010, Berlin: Springer-Verlag.

Aha, D.W. (1991). Case-Based Learning Algorithms. In *Proceedings of the DARPA Case-Based Reasoning Workshop*, edited by E.R. Bareiss. San Francisco: Morgan Kaufmann Publishers.

Aha, D.W., ed. (1997). *Artificial Intelligence Review* (special issue on Lazy Learning). Norwell, MA: Kluwer.

Althoff, K.-D. (1989). Knowledge Acquisition in the Domain of CNC Machine Centers: The MOLTKE Approach. In *EKAW-89 Third European Workshop on Knowledge-Based Systems*, edited by J. Boose, B. Gaines, and J.-G. Ganascia, 180–195.

Althoff, K.-D. (1992). Machine Learning and Knowledge Acquisition in a Computational Architecture for Fault Diagnosis in Engineering Systems. In *Proceedings of the ML-92 Workshop on Computational Architectures for Machine Learning and Knowledge Acquisition*.

Bareiss, E.R. (1989). *Exemplar-Based Knowledge Acquisition: A Unified Approach to Concept Representation Classification and Learning*. Boston: Academic Press.

Beck, H.W. (1991). Language Acquisition from Cases. In *Proceedings of the DARPA Case-Based Reasoning Workshop*, edited by E.R. Bareiss. San Francisco: Morgan Kaufmann Publishers.

Becker, L., and Guay, T. (1991). Measures for the Evaluation of Case-Based Suggestion. In *Proceedings of the DARPA Case-Based Reasoning Workshop*, edited by E.R. Bareiss. San Francisco: Morgan Kaufmann Publishers.

Bichindaritz, I. (1995). Incremental Concept Learning and Case-Based Reasoning: For a Co-operative Approach. In *Progress in Case-Based Reasoning*, edited by I. Watson. Lecture Notes in Artificial Intelligence 1020. Berlin: Springer-Verlag.

Birnbaum, L., and Collins, G. (1988). The Transfer of Experience Across Planning Domains Through the Acquisition of Abstract Strategies. In *Proceedings of the DARPA Case-Based Reasoning Workshop*, edited by J.L. Kolodner. San Francisco: Morgan Kaufmann Publishers.

Cain, T., Pazzani, M.J., and Silverstein, G. (1991). Domain Knowledge to Influence Similarity Judgment. In *Proceedings of the DARPA Case-Based Reasoning Workshop*, edited by E.R. Bareiss. San Francisco: Morgan Kaufmann Publishers.

Callan, J.P., Fawcett, T.E., and Rissland, E.L. (1991). Adaptive Case-Based Reasoning. In *Proceedings of the DARPA Case-Based Reasoning Workshop*, edited by E.R. Bareiss. San Francisco: Morgan Kaufmann Publishers.

Carbonell, J.G., and Veloso, M.M. (1988). Integrating Derivational Analogy into a General Problem Solving Architecture. In *Proceedings of the DARPA Case-Based Reasoning Workshop*, edited by J.L. Kolodner. San Francisco: Morgan Kaufmann Publishers.

El-Gamel, S., et al. (1993). Case-Based Algorithms Applied in a Medical Acquisition Tool. *Medical Informatics (Medicine Et Informatique)*, 18(ii), 149–162.

Farrell, R. (1988). Facilitating Self-Education by Questioning Assumptive Reasoning Using Paradigm Cases. In *Proceedings of the DARPA Case-Based Reasoning Workshop*, edited by J.L. Kolodner. San Francisco: Morgan Kaufmann Publishers.

Hammond, K.J. (1988). Opportunistic Memory: Storing and Recalling Suspended Goals. In *Proceedings of the DARPA Case-Based Reasoning Workshop*, edited by J.L. Kolodner. San Francisco: Morgan Kaufmann Publishers.

Hammond, K.J., and Hurwitz, N. (1988). Extracting Diagnostic Features from Explanations. In *Proceedings of the DARPA Case-Based Reasoning Workshop*, edited by J.L. Kolodner. San Francisco: Morgan Kaufmann Publishers.

Kerner, Y., and Bar-Ilan (1995). Learning Strategies for Explanation Patterns: Basic Game Patterns with Applications to Chess. In *Case-Based Reasoning Research and Development*, edited by M. Veloso and A. Aamodt. Lecture Notes in Artificial Intelligence 1010. Berlin: Springer-Verlag.

Kolodner, J.L. (1987). Extending Problem Solving Capabilities Through Case-Based Inference. In *Proceedings of the Fourth Annual International Machine Learning Workshop, 1987*.

Lopez, B., and Plaza, E. (1990). Case-Based Learning of Strategic Knowledge. In *Machine Learning EWSML-91*, 398–411. Lecture Notes in Computer Science 689. Berlin: Springer-Verlag.

Manago, M., Althoff, K.-D., and Traphoner, R. (1993). Induction and reasoning from cases. In *ECML—European Conference on Machine Learning Workshop on Intelligent Learning Architectures*.

Oehlmann, R. (1992). Learning Causal Models by Self-Questioning and Experimentation. *AAAI-92 Workshop on Communicating Scientific and Technical Knowledge*. Menlo Park, CA: AAAI Press.

Plaza, E., and Arcos, J.L. (1993). Reflection and Analogy in Memory-Based Learning. In *Proceedings of the Multi-Strategy Learning Workshop*, 42–49.

Plaza, E., and Lopez de Mantaras, R. (1990). A Case-Based Apprentice That Learns from Fuzzy Examples. In *Methodologies for Intelligent Systems*, 5, edited by Z. Ras, M. Zemankova, and M.L. Emrich. Amsterdam: North-Holland.

Redmond, R. (1989). Learning from Others' Experience: Creating Cases from Examples. In *Proceedings of the DARPA Case-Based Reasoning Workshop*, edited by K.J. Hammond. San Francisco: Morgan Kaufmann Publishers.

Riesbeck, C.K. (1988). An Interface for Case-Based Knowledge Acquisition. In *Proceedings of the DARPA Case-Based Reasoning Workshop*, edited by J.L. Kolodner. San Francisco: Morgan Kaufmann Publishers.

Schank, R. (1988). Reminding and Memory. In *Proceedings of the DARPA Case-Based Reasoning Workshop*, edited by J.L. Kolodner. San Francisco: Morgan Kaufmann Publishers.

Sharma, S., and Sleeman, D. (1988). REFINER: A Case-Based Differential Diagnosis Aide for Knowledge Acquisition and Knowledge Refinement. In *EWSL 88; Proceedings of the European Working Session on Learning*, 201–210.

Shinn, H.S. (1988). Abstractional Analogy: A Model of Analogical Reasoning. In *Proceedings of the DARPA Case-Based Reasoning Workshop*, edited by J.L. Kolodner. San Francisco: Morgan Kaufmann Publishers.

Simon, G., and Grandbastien, M. (1996). Case-Based Reasoning for Knowledge Capitalization. In *Applications & Innovations in Expert Systems IV*, edited by A. Macintosh and C. Cooper. Oxford: SGES Publications.

Stanfill, C. (1988). Learning to Read: A Memory-Based Model. In *Proceedings of the DARPA Case-Based Reasoning Workshop*, edited by J.L. Kolodner. San Francisco: Morgan Kaufmann Publishers.

Stanfill, C., and Walts, D.L. (1988). The Memory-Based Reasoning Paradigm. In *Proceedings of the DARPA Case-Based Reasoning Workshop*, edited by J.L. Kolodner. San Francisco: Morgan Kaufmann Publishers.

Ting, K.M. (1995). Towards Using a Single Uniform Metric in Instance-Based Learning. In *Case-Based Reasoning Research and Development*, edited by M. Veloso and A. Aamodt. Lecture Notes in Artificial Intelligence 1010. Berlin: Springer-Verlag.

Tsatsoulis, C., and Kashyap, R.L. (1994). Case-Based Reasoning and Learning in Manufacturing with the TOTLEC Planner. In *IEEE Transactions on Systems, Man and Cybernetics 1993*, 23(4), 1010–1023.

Veloso, M.M. (1996). Flexible Strategy Learning Using Analogical Replay of Problem Solving Episodes. In *Case-Based Reasoning: Experiences, Lessons, & Future Directions*, edited by D.B. Leake. Cambridge, MA: AAAI Press / MIT Press.

Williams, R.S. (1988). Learning to Program by Examining and Modifying Cases. In *Proceedings of the DARPA Case-Based Reasoning Workshop*, edited by J.L. Kolodner. San Francisco: Morgan Kaufmann Publishers.

Zito-Wolf, R.J., and Alterman, R. (1992). Multicases: A Case-Based Representation for Procedural Knowledge. In *Proceedings of the Fourteenth Annual Conference of the Cognitive Science Society*. Northvale, NJ: Lawrence Erlbaum Associates.

10.4.2.11 Legal Reasoning

Ashley, K.D. (1988). Arguing by Analogy in Law: A Case-Based Model. In *Analogical Reasoning: Perspectives of Artificial Intelligence, Cognitive Science, and Philosophy*. Norwell, MA: D. Reidel.

Ashley, K.D. (1991). Reasoning with Cases and Hypothetical in Hypo. *International Journal of Man Machine Studies*, 34, 753–796.

Ashley, K.D., and McLaren, B.M. (1995). Reasoning with Reasons in Case-Based Comparisons. In *Case-Based Reasoning Research and Development*, edited by M. Veloso and A. Aamodt. Lecture Notes in Artificial Intelligence 1010. Berlin: Springer-Verlag.

Bain, W.M. (1986). *Case-Based Reasoning: A Computer-Model of Subjective Assessment*. Ph.D. thesis, Yale University, Yale, CT.

Branting, L.K. (1991). Exploiting the Complementarity of Rules and Precedents with Reciprocity and Fairness. In *Proceedings of the DARPA Case-Based Reasoning Workshop*, edited by E.R. Bareiss. San Francisco: Morgan Kaufmann Publishers.

Branting, L.K., and Porter, B.W. (1991). Rules and Precedents as Complementary Warrants. In *Proceedings of AAAI-91*. Cambridge, MA: AAAI Press / MIT Press.

Huang, W.-B., and Cross, G.R. (1989). Reasoning About Trademark Infringement Cases. In *Proceedings of the DARPA Case-Based Reasoning Workshop*, edited by K.J. Hammond. San Francisco: Morgan Kaufmann Publishers.

Pal, K. (1995). A Hybrid System for Decision Making in English Divorce Cases. In *Progress in Case-Based Reasoning*, edited by I. Watson. Lecture Notes in Artificial Intelligence 1020. Berlin: Springer-Verlag.

Rissland, E.L., and Skalak, D.B. (1991). CABARET: Rule interpretation in a hybrid architecture. *International Journal of Man-Machine Studies*, 34, 839–887.

Rissland, E.L., Skalak, D.B., and Friedmann, M.T. (1996). Using Heuristic Search to Retrieve Cases That Support Arguments. In *Case-Based Reasoning: Experiences, Lessons, & Future Directions*, edited by D.B. Leake. Cambridge, MA: AAAI Press / MIT Press.

Sanders, K.E. (1991). Within the Letter of the Law: Reasoning Among Multiple Cases. In *Proceedings of the DARPA Case-Based Reasoning Workshop*, edited by E.R. Bareiss. San Francisco: Morgan Kaufmann Publishers.

Skalak, D.B., and Rissland, E.L. (1992). Arguments and Cases: An Inevitable Intertwining. *Artificial Intelligence and Law*, 1, 3–48.

Yang, S., and Robertson, D. (1994). A Case-Based Reasoning System for Regulatory Information. In *Proceedings of the IEE Colloquium on Case-Based Reasoning: Prospects for Applications*, Digest No. 1994/057, 3/1–3/3.

10.4.2.12 **Planning**

Aarts, R.J., and Rousu, J. (1996). Towards CBR for Bioprocess Planning. In *Advances in Case-Based Reasoning*, edited by I. Smith and B. Faltings. Lecture Notes in Artificial Intelligence 1168. Berlin: Springer-Verlag.

Alexander, P., and Tsatsoulis, C. (1992). Using Sub-cases for Skeletal Planning and Partial Case Reuse. *International Journal for Expert Systems,* 4(2), 117–140.

Blau, L., Bonissone, P.P., and Ayub, S. (1991). Planning with Dynamic Cases. In *Proceedings of the DARPA Case-Based Reasoning Workshop,* edited by E.R. Bareiss. San Francisco: Morgan Kaufmann Publishers.

Brandau, R., Lemmon, A., and Lafond, C. (1991). Experience with Extended Episodes: Cases with Complex Temporal Structure. In *Proceedings of the DARPA Case-Based Reasoning Workshop,* edited by E.R. Bareiss. San Francisco: Morgan Kaufmann Publishers.

Costas, T., and Kashyap, N. (1993). Case-Based Reasoning and Learning in Manufacturing with TOLTEC Planner. *IEEE Transactions on Systems, Man, and Cybernetics,* 23(iv), July/August 1993.

Goodman, M. (1989). CBR in Battle Planning. In *Proceedings of the DARPA Case-Based Reasoning Workshop,* edited by K.J. Hammond. San Francisco: Morgan Kaufmann Publishers.

Haigh, K.Z., and Veloso, M. (1995). Route Planning by Analogy. In *Case-Based Reasoning Research and Development,* edited by M. Veloso and A. Aamodt. Lecture Notes in Artificial Intelligence 1010. Berlin: Springer-Verlag.

Hammond, K.J. (1989). *Case-Based Planning: Viewing Planning as a Memory Task.* Boston: Academic Press.

Kambhampati, S. (1989). Integrating Planning and Reuse: A Framework for Flexible Plan Reuse. In *Proceedings of the DARPA Case-Based Reasoning Workshop,* edited by K.J. Hammond. San Francisco: Morgan Kaufmann Publishers.

Kambhampati, S., Cutkosky, M.R., Tenenbaum, J.M., and Lee, S.H. (1993). Integrating General Purpose Planners and Specialized Reasoners: Case Study of a Hybrid Planning Architecture. *IEEE Transactions on Systems, Man and Cybernetics,* 23.

Kambhampati, S., and Hendler, J.A. (1992). A Validation Structure-Based Theory of Plan Modification and Reuse. *Artificial Intelligence Journal,* 55, 193–258.

Khemani, D., and Bhanu Prasad, P.V.S.R. (1995). A Memory-Based Hierarchical Planner. In *Case-Based Reasoning Research and Development,* edited by M. Veloso and A. Aamodt. Lecture Notes in Artificial Intelligence 1010. Berlin: Springer-Verlag.

Klein, G.A., Whitaker, L.A., and King, J.A. (1988). Using Analogues to Predict and Plan. In *Proceedings of the DARPA Case-Based Reasoning Workshop,* edited by J.L. Kolodner. San Francisco: Morgan Kaufmann Publishers.

Kolodner, J.L., and Simpson, R.L. (1989). The MEDIATOR: Analysis of an Early Case-Based Problem Solver. *Cognitive Science* 13(4), 507–549.

Krovvidy, W., and Wee, W.G. (1993). Wastewater Treatment System from Case-Based Reasoning. *Machine Learning,* 10(iii).

Lopez, B., and Plaza, E. (1993). Case-Base Planning for Medical Diagnosis. In *Methodologies for Intelligent Systems, Seventh International Symposium, ISMIS-93.* Lecture Notes in Artificial Intelligence 689. Berlin: Springer-Verlag.

Macedo, L., Pereira, F.C., Grilo, C., and Cardoso, A. (1996). Plans as Structured Networks of Hierarchically and Temporally Related Case Pieces. In *Advances in Case-Based Reasoning,* edited by I. Smith and B. Faltings. Lecture Notes in Artificial Intelligence 1168. Berlin: Springer-Verlag.

McCartney, R., and Wurst, K.R. (1991). DEFARGE: A Real-Time Execution Monitor for a Case-Based Planner. In *Proceedings of the DARPA Case-Based Reasoning Workshop,* edited by E.R. Bareiss. San Francisco: Morgan Kaufmann Publishers.

Muñoz-Avila, H., and Hüllen, J. (1996). Feature Weighting by Explaining Case-Based Planning Episodes. In *Advances in Case-Based Reasoning,* edited by I. Smith and B. Faltings. Lecture Notes in Artificial Intelligence 1168. Berlin: Springer-Verlag.

Napoli, A., and Lieber, J. (1993). Finding Strategies in Organic Synthesis Planning with Case-Based Reasoning. In *Proceedings of EWCBR'93,* edited by M.M. Richter et al. Berlin: Springer-Verlag.

Oehlmann, R. (1996). Investigative Actions: Case-Based Planning of Laboratory Experiments. In *Proceedings of the Second U.K. Workshop on Case-Based Reasoning,* edited by I. Watson. Salford, UK: Salford University.

Pu, P., and Reschberger, M. (1991). Case-Based Assembly Planning. In *Proceedings of the DARPA Case-Based Reasoning Workshop,* edited by E.R. Bareiss. San Francisco: Morgan Kaufmann Publishers.

Sycara, K. (1988). Patching Up Old Plans. In *Proceedings of the Tenth Annual Conference of the Cognitive Science Society.* Northvale, NJ: Lawrence Erlbaum Associates.

Veloso, M.M., and Carbonell, J.G. (1993). Derivational Analogy in PRODIGY: Automating Case Acquisition, Storage, and Utilization. *Machine Learning,* 10(3), 249–278.

Veloso, M.M., and Carbonell, J.G. (1993). Towards Scaling Up Machine Learning: Case Study with Derivational Analogy in PRODIGY. In *Machine Learning Methods for Planning and Scheduling,* edited by S. Minton. San Francisco: Morgan Kaufmann Publishers.

Zarley, D.K. (1991). A Case-Based Process Planner for Small Assemblies. In *Proceedings of the DARPA Case-Based Reasoning Workshop,* edited by E.R. Bareiss. San Francisco: Morgan Kaufmann Publishers.

10.4.2.13 Problem Solving

This section contains papers that use CBR to solve problems in miscellaneous domains.

Aamodt, A. (1989). Towards Robust Expert Systems That Learn from Experience—An Architectural Framework. In *EKAW-89 Third European Knowledge Acquisition for Knowledge-Based Systems Workshop*, edited by J. Boose, B. Gaines, and J.-G. Ganascia, 311–326.

Aamodt, A. (1991). *A Knowledge-Intensive Approach to Problem Solving and Sustained Learning*. Ph.D. dissertation, University of Trondheim, Norwegian Institute of Technology, May 1991. (University Microfilms PUB 92-08460).

Bakhtari, S., and Oertel, W. (1995). DOM-Arc: An Active Decision Support System for Quality Assessment of Cases. In *Case-Based Reasoning Research and Development*, edited by M. Veloso and A. Aamodt. Lecture Notes in Artificial Intelligence 1010. Berlin: Springer-Verlag.

Barletta, R., and Mark, W. (1988). Explanation-Based Indexing of Cases. In *Proceedings of the DARPA Case-Based Reasoning Workshop*, edited by J.L. Kolodner. San Francisco: Morgan Kaufmann Publishers.

Berger, J. (1989). ROENTGEN: A Case-Based Approach to Radiation Therapy Planning. In *Proceedings of the DARPA Case-Based Reasoning Workshop*, edited by K.J. Hammond. San Francisco: Morgan Kaufmann Publishers.

Bichindaritz, I. (1995). A Case-Based Reasoner Adaptive to Different Cognitive Tasks. In *Case-Based Reasoning Research and Development*, edited by M. Veloso and A. Aamodt. Lecture Notes in Artificial Intelligence 1010. Berlin: Springer-Verlag.

Birnbaum, L., Collins, G., Brand, M., Freed, M., Krulwich, B., and Pryor, L. (1991). A Model-Based Approach to the Construction of Adaptive Case-Based Planning Systems. In *Proceedings of the DARPA Case-Based Reasoning Workshop*, edited by E.R. Bareiss. San Francisco: Morgan Kaufmann Publishers.

Bisio, R., and Malabocchia, F. (1995). Cost Estimation of Software Projects Through Case Base Reasoning. In *Case-Based Reasoning Research and Development*, edited by M. Veloso and A. Aamodt. Lecture Notes in Artificial Intelligence 1010, Berlin: Springer-Verlag.

Carbonell, J.G. (1986). Derivational Analogy: A Theory of Reconstructive Problem Solving and Expertise Acquisition. In *Machine Learning*, 2.

Carbonell, J.G., and Veloso, M.M. (1988). Integrating Derivational Analogy into a General Problem Solving Architecture. In *Proceedings of the DARPA Case-Based Reasoning Workshop*, edited by J.L. Kolodner. San Francisco: Morgan Kaufmann Publishers.

Cunningham, P., Smyth, B., and Hurley, N. (1995). On the Use of CBR in Optimisation Problems Such As the TSP. In *Case-Based Reasoning Research and Development*, edited by M. Veloso and A. Aamodt. Lecture Notes in Artificial Intelligence 1010. Berlin: Springer-Verlag.

Flinter, S., and Keane, M.T. (1995). On the Automatic Generation of Case Libraries by Chunking Chess Games. In *Case-Based Reasoning Research and Development*, edited by M. Veloso and A. Aamodt. Lecture Notes in Artificial Intelligence 1010. Berlin: Springer-Verlag.

Goel, A.K., Kolodner, J.L., Pearce, M., Billington, R., and Zimring, C. (1991). Towards a Case-Based Tool for Aiding Conceptual Design Problem Solving. In *Proceedings of the DARPA Case-Based Reasoning Workshop*, edited by E.R. Bareiss. San Francisco: Morgan Kaufmann Publishers.

Hammond, K.J. (1988). Opportunistic Memory: Storing and Recalling Suspended Goals. In *Proceedings of the DARPA Case-Based Reasoning Workshop*, edited by J.L. Kolodner. San Francisco: Morgan Kaufmann Publishers.

Hammond, K.J., Burke, R., and Schmitt, K. (1996). A Case-Based Approach to Knowledge Navigation. In *Case-Based Reasoning: Experiences, Lessons, & Future Directions*, edited by D.B. Leake. Cambridge, MA: AAAI Press / MIT Press.

Hammond, K.J., and Hurwitz, N. (1988). Extracting Diagnostic Features from Explanations. In *Proceedings of the DARPA Case-Based Reasoning Workshop*, edited by J.L. Kolodner. San Francisco: Morgan Kaufmann Publishers.

Hendler, J.A. (1988). Refitting Plans for Case-Based Reasoning. In *Proceedings of the DARPA Case-Based Reasoning Workshop*, edited by J.L. Kolodner. San Francisco: Morgan Kaufmann Publishers.

Hennessy, D., and Hinkle, D. (1991). Initial Results from Clavier: A Case-Based Autoclave Loading Assistant. In *Proceedings of the DARPA Case-Based Reasoning Workshop*, edited by E.R. Bareiss. San Francisco: Morgan Kaufmann Publishers.

Hinrichs, T.R. (1988). Towards an Architecture for Open World Problem Solving. In *Proceedings of the DARPA Case-Based Reasoning Workshop*, edited by J.L. Kolodner. San Francisco: Morgan Kaufmann Publishers.

Kolodner, J.L. (1987). Extending Problem Solving Capabilities Through Case-Based Inference. In *Proceedings of the Fourth Annual International Machine Learning Workshop*.

Macura, R.T., and Macura, K. (1995). MacRad: Radiology Image Resource with a Case-Based Retrieval System. In *Case-Based Reasoning Research and Development*, edited by M. Veloso and A. Aamodt. Lecture Notes in Artificial Intelligence 1010. Berlin: Springer-Verlag.

Marks, M., Hammond, K.J., and Converse, T. (1988). Planning in an Open World: A Pluralistic Approach. In *Proceedings of the DARPA Case-Based Reasoning Workshop*, edited by J.L. Kolodner. San Francisco: Morgan Kaufmann Publishers.

Navinchandra, D. (1988). Case-Based Reasoning in CYCLOPS, a Design Problem Solver. In *Proceedings of the DARPA Case-Based Reasoning Workshop*, edited by J.L. Kolodner. San Francisco: Morgan Kaufmann Publishers.

Owens, C. (1988). Domain-Independent Prototype Cases for Planning. In *Proceedings of the DARPA Case-Based Reasoning Workshop*, edited by J.L. Kolodner. San Francisco: Morgan Kaufmann Publishers.

Plaza, E., and Arcos, J.L. (1993). Reflection and Analogy in Memory-Based Learning. In *Proceedings of the Multi-Strategy Learning Workshop*, 42–49.

Rougegrez, S. (1995). Case-Based Reasoning for the Prediction of Process Behavior. In *Applications & Innovations in Expert Systems III*, edited by A. Macintosh and C. Cooper. Oxford: SGES Publications.

Sycara, K. (1988). Using Case-Based Reasoning for Plan Adaptation and Repair. In *Proceedings of the DARPA Case-Based Reasoning Workshop*, edited by J.L. Kolodner. San Francisco: Morgan Kaufmann Publishers.

Sycara, K., and Navinchandra, D. (1991). Influences: A Thematic Abstraction for Creative Use of Multiple Cases. In *Proceedings of the DARPA Case-Based Reasoning Workshop*, edited by E.R. Bareiss. San Francisco: Morgan Kaufmann Publishers.

Turner, R.M. (1988). Organising and Using Schematic Knowledge for Medical Diagnosis. In *Proceedings of the DARPA Case-Based Reasoning Workshop*, edited by J.L. Kolodner. San Francisco: Morgan Kaufmann Publishers.

Veloso, M.M., and Carbonell, J.G. (1991). Variable-Precision Case Retrieval in Analogical Problem Solving. In *Proceedings of the DARPA Case-Based Reasoning Workshop*, edited by E.R. Bareiss. San Francisco: Morgan Kaufmann Publishers.

10.4.2.14 Robot Navigation

Goel, A., and Callantine, T. (1992). An Experience-Based Approach to Navigational Path Planning. In *Proceedings of the IEEE International Conference on Robotics and Systems*. New York: IEEE Press.

Moorman, K., and Ram, A. (1992). A Case-Based Approach to Reactive Control for Autonomous Robots. In *Proceedings of the AAAI Fall Symposium on AI for Real-World Autonomous Robots*. Cambridge, MA: AAAI Press / MIT Press.

Ram, A., Arkin, R.C., Moorman, K., and Clark, R.J. (1993). *Case-Based Reactive Navigation: A Case-Based Method for On-Line Selection and Adaptation of Reactive Control Parameters in Autonomous Robotic Systems*. Technical Report No. GIT-CC92/57, College of Computing. Atlanta: Georgia Institute of Technology.

10.4.2.15 Scheduling

Koton, P. (1989). SMARTplan: A Case-Based Resource Allocation and Scheduling System. In *Proceedings of the DARPA Case-Based Reasoning Workshop*, edited by K.J. Hammond. San Francisco: Morgan Kaufmann Publishers.

Miyashita, K., and Sycara, K. (1993). Case-based incremental schedule revision. In *Knowledge-Based Scheduling*, edited by M. Fox and M. Zweben. San Francisco: Morgan Kaufmann Publishers.

10.4.2.16 Story Understanding and Explanation

Bareiss, E.R., and Slator, B.M. (1992). The Evolution of a Case-Based Approach to Knowledge Representation, Categorization, and Learning. In *Categorization and Category Learning by Humans and Machines*, edited by Medin, Nakamura, and Taraban. New York: Academic Press.

Ferguson, W., Bareiss, E.R., Birnbaum, L., and Osgood, R. (1992). ASK systems: An Approach to the Realization of Story-Based Teachers. *Journal of the Learning Sciences*, 2, 95–134.

Job, D., Shankararaman, V., and Cordingley, B. (1996). Using Natural Language Processing in Case-Base Systems. In *Research & Development in Expert Systems XIII*, edited by J.L. Nealon and J. Hunt. Oxford: SGES Publications.

Leake, D.B. (1989). The Effect of Explainer Goals on Case-Based Explanation. In *Proceedings of the DARPA Case-Based Reasoning Workshop*, edited by K.J. Hammond. San Francisco: Morgan Kaufmann Publishers.

Micarelli, A., and Sciarrone, F. (1996). A Case-Based System for Adaptive Hypermedia Navigation. In *Advances in Case-Based Reasoning*, edited by I. Smith and B. Faltings. Lecture Notes in Artificial Intelligence 1168. Berlin: Springer-Verlag.

Ram, A. (1989). Incremental Learning of Paradigmatic Cases. In *Proceedings of the DARPA Case-Based Reasoning Workshop*, edited by K.J. Hammond. San Francisco: Morgan Kaufmann Publishers.

Ram, A. (1993). Indexing, Elaboration and Refinement: Incremental Learning of Explanatory Cases. *Machine Learning*, 10(3), 201–248.

Ram, A., and Leake, D.B. (1991). Evaluation of Explanatory Hypotheses. In *Proceedings of the Thirteenth Annual Conference of the Cognitive Science Society*. Northvale, NJ: Lawrence Erlbaum Associates.

Turner, E. (1989). Using Dynamic Memory to Interpret Indirect Speech Acts. In *Proceedings of the DARPA Case-Based Reasoning Workshop*, edited by K.J. Hammond. San Francisco: Morgan Kaufmann Publishers.

10.4.2.17 Teaching

Aha, D.W., ed. (1997). *Artificial Intelligence Review* (special issue on Lazy Learning). Norwell, MA: Kluwer.

Aleven, V., and Ashley, K.D. (1992). Automated Generation of Examples for a Tutorial in Case-Based Argumentation. In *Proceedings, Second International Conference on Intelligent Tutoring Systems (ITS 92)*, edited by C. Frasson, G. Gauthier, and G.L. McCallan. Berlin: Springer-Verlag.

Aluisio, S.M., and de Oliveira, Jr., O.N. (1995). A Case-Based Approach for Developing Writing Tools Aimed at Non-Native Users of English. In *Case-Based Reasoning Research and Development*, edited by M. Veloso and A. Aamodt. Lecture Notes in Artificial Intelligence 1010. Berlin: Springer-Verlag.

Ashley, K.D., and Aleven, V. (1991). Computational Approach to Explaining Case-Based Concepts of Relevance in a Tutorial Context. In *Proceedings of the DARPA Case-Based Reasoning Workshop*, edited by E.R. Bareiss. San Francisco: Morgan Kaufmann Publishers.

Bareiss, E.R., Ferguson, W., and Fano, A. (1991). The Story Archive: A Memory for Case-Based Tutoring. In *Proceedings of the DARPA Case-Based Reasoning Workshop*, edited by E.R. Bareiss. San Francisco: Morgan Kaufmann Publishers.

Burke, R., and Kass, A. (1996). Retrieving Stories for Case-Based Teaching. In *Case-Based Reasoning: Experiences, Lessons, & Future Directions*, edited by D.B. Leake. Cambridge, MA: AAAI Press / MIT Press.

Edelson, D. (1991). Oh, the Stories I Could Tell: Managing an Aesopic Teaching Dialogue. In *Proceedings of the DARPA Case-Based Reasoning Workshop*, edited by E.R. Bareiss. San Francisco: Morgan Kaufmann Publishers.

Farrell, R. (1987). Intelligent case selection and presentation. In *Proceedings of the Tenth International Joint Conference on Artificial Intelligence, IJCAI-87*, 1, 74–76.

Farrell, R. (1988). Facilitating Self-Education by Questioning Assumptive Reasoning Using Paradigm Cases. In *Proceedings of the DARPA Case-Based Reasoning Workshop*, edited by J.L. Kolodner. San Francisco: Morgan Kaufmann Publishers.

Khan, T., and Yip, Y.J. (1995). Case-Based Curriculum Planning for Computer-Aided Instruction. In *Progress in Case-Based Reasoning*, edited by I. Watson. Lecture Notes in Artificial Intelligence 1020. Berlin: Springer-Verlag.

Khan, T., and Yip, Y.J. (1996). A Case-Based Approach to Guided Discovery. In *Proceedings of the Second U.K. Workshop on Case-Based Reasoning*, edited by I. Watson. Salford, UK: Salford University.

Schank, R. (1996). Goal-Based Scenarios: Case-Based Reasoning Meets Learning by Doing. In *Case-Based Reasoning: Experiences, Lessons, & Future Directions*, edited by D.B. Leake. Cambridge, MA: AAAI Press / MIT Press.

10.4.3 *Commercial Applications*

Acorn, T.L., and Walden, S.H. (1992). SMART: Support Management Cultivated Reasoning Technology for Compaq Customer Service. In *Innovative Applications of Artificial Intelligence 4, Proceedings of AAAI-92*, edited by S. Scott and P. Klahr. Cambridge, MA: AAAI Press / MIT Press.

Allen, B. (1994). Case-Based Reasoning: Business Applications. *Communications of the ACM*, 37(3), 40–42.

Althoff, K.-D., Auriol, E., Barletta, R., and Manago, M. (1995). *A Review of Industrial Case-Based Reasoning Tools*. Oxford: AI Intelligence.

Block, F., and Poynter, L. (1996). The Swiss Bank Corporation Know-How Project. In *Applications & Innovations in Expert Systems IV*, edited by A. Macintosh and C. Cooper. Oxford: SGES Publications.

Borron, J., Morales, D., and Klahr, P. (1996). Developing and Deploying Knowledge on a Global Scale. In *Innovative Applications of Artificial Intelligence 8, Proceedings of AAAI-96*. Cambridge, MA: AAAI Press / MIT Press.

Bouchet, J.-L., and Eichenbaum-Voline, C. (1996). Case-Based Reasoning Techniques Applied to Operation—Experience Feedback in Nuclear Power Plants. In *Advances in Case-Based Reasoning*, edited by I. Smith and B. Faltings. Lecture Notes in Artificial Intelligence 1168. Berlin: Springer-Verlag.

Brown, B., and Lewis, L. (1991). A Case-Based Reasoning Solution to the Problem of Redundant Resolutions of Nonconformances in Large Scale Manufacturing. In *Innovative Applications for Artificial Intelligence 3*, edited by R. Smith and C. Scott. Cambridge, MA: MIT Press.

Cordingley, B. (1996). The B-CBR-T Future: Fitting Case-Based Reasoning into BT in the Future. In *Advances in Case-Based Reasoning*, edited by I. Smith and B. Faltings. Lecture Notes in Artificial Intelligence 1168. Berlin: Springer-Verlag.

Curet, O., and Elliot, J. (1996). Using Transfer Pricing Cases in Multinationals—A Survey of Current Practice and the Applicability of Case-Based Systems. In *Proceedings of the Second U.K. Workshop on Case-Based Reasoning*, edited by I. Watson. Salford, UK: Salford University.

Curet, O., Jackson, M., and Killin, J. (1996). Implementing and Evaluating Case-Based Learning and Reasoning Applications: A Case Study. In *Proceedings of the Second U.K. Workshop on Case-Based Reasoning*, edited by I. Watson. Salford, UK: Salford University.

Dattani, I., Magaldi, R.V., and Bramer, M.A. (1996). A Review and Evaluation of the Application of Case-Based Reasoning (CBR) Technology in Aircraft Maintenance. In *Applications and Innovations in Expert Systems IV*, 189–203, edited by A. Macintosh and C. Cooper. Oxford: SGES Publications.

Dearden, A.M., and Bridge, D.G. (1993). Choosing a Reasoning Style for a Knowledge-Based System: Lessons from Supporting a Help Desk. *The Knowledge Engineering Review*, 8(3), 210–222.

Ellman, J. (1995). An Application of Case-Based Reasoning to Object Oriented Database Retrieval. In *Progress in Case-Based Reasoning*, edited by I. Watson. Lecture Notes in Artificial Intelligence 1020. Berlin: Springer-Verlag.

Georgin, E., Bordin, F., and McDonald, J. (1995). CBR Applied to Fault Diagnosis on Steam Turbines. In *Progress in Case-Based Reasoning*, edited by I. Watson. Lecture Notes in Artificial Intelligence 1020. Berlin: Springer-Verlag.

Heider, R. (1996). Troubleshooting CFM 56-3 Engines for the Boeing 737—Using CBR and Data-Mining. In *Advances in Case-Based Reasoning*, edited by I. Smith and B. Faltings. Lecture Notes in Artificial Intelligence 1168. Berlin: Springer-Verlag.

Hennessy, D., and Hinkle, D. (1991). Initial Results from CLAVIER: A Case-Based Autoclave Loading Assistant. In *Proceedings of the DARPA Case-Based Reasoning Workshop*, edited by E.R. Bareiss. San Francisco: Morgan Kaufmann Publishers.

Hennessy, D., and Hinkle, D. (1992). Applying Case-Based Reasoning to Autoclave Loading. *IEEE Expert* 7(5), 21–26.

Hinkle, D., and Toomey, C. (1994). CLAVIER: Applying Case-Based Reasoning to Composite Part Fabrication. In *Innovative Applications of Artificial Intelligence* 6, 54–62. Cambridge, MA: AAAI Press / MIT Press.

Jez, M., and Legendre, L. (1996). Capitalisation of Knowledge and Diagnosis Aid System. In *Advances in Case-Based Reasoning*, edited by I. Smith and B. Faltings. Lecture Notes in Artificial Intelligence 1168. Berlin: Springer-Verlag.

Kitano, H., and Shimazu, H. (1996). The Experience Sharing Architecture: A Case Study in Corporate-Wide Case-Based Software Quality Control. In *Case-Based Reasoning: Experiences, Lessons, & Future Directions*, edited by D.B. Leake. Cambridge, MA: AAAI Press / MIT Press.

Klahr, P. (1996). Global Case-Based Development and Deployment. In *Advances in Case-Based Reasoning*, 519–530, edited by I. Smith and B. Faltings. Lecture Notes in Artificial Intelligence 1168. Berlin: Springer-Verlag.

Laffey, J., Machiraju, R., and Chandhok, R. (1991). Integrated Support and Learning Systems for Augmenting Knowledge Workers: A Focus on Case-Based Retrieval. In *Proceedings of the World Congress on Expert Systems*, Orlando, Florida. Elmsford, NY: Pergamon Press.

Magaldi, R.V. (1994). CBR for Troubleshooting Aircraft on the Flight Line. In *Proceedings of the IEE Colloquium on Case-Based Reasoning: Prospects for Applications,* Digest No. 1994/057, 6/1–6/9.

Magaldi, R.V. (1994). Maintaining Aeroplanes in Time-Constrained Operational Situations Using Case-Based Reasoning. In *Advances in Case-Based Reasoning*, edited by J.-M. Haton, M. Keane, and M. Manago. Lecture Notes in Artificial Intelligence 984. Berlin: Springer-Verlag.

Magaldi, R.V., and Barr, J.M. (1996). Corporate Knowledge Management for the Millennium. In *Advances in Case-Based Reasoning,* edited by I. Smith and B. Faltings. Lecture Notes in Artificial Intelligence 1168. Berlin: Springer-Verlag.

Mark, W., Simoudis, E., and Hinkle, D. (1996). Case-Based Reasoning: Expectations and Results. In *Case-Based Reasoning: Experiences, Lessons, & Future Directions*, edited by D.B. Leake. Cambridge, MA: AAAI Press / MIT Press.

McCarthy, D. (1994). Automation of Help Desks Using Case-Based Reasoning. In *Proceedings of IEE Colloquium on Case-Based Reasoning: Prospects for Applications,* Digest No. 1994/057, 9/1–9/3.

Netten, B.D., and Vingerhoeds, R.A. (1995). Large-Scale Fault Diagnosis for On-Board Train Systems. In *Case-Based Reasoning Research and Development*, edited by M. Veloso and A. Aamodt. Lecture Notes in Artificial Intelligence 1010. Berlin: Springer-Verlag.

Nguyen, T., Czerwinski, M., and Lee, D. (1993). Compaq QuickSource: Providing the Consumer with the Power of Artificial Intelligence. In *Innovative Applications of Artificial Intelligence 5, Proceedings of AAAI-93,* edited by P. Klahr and D. Byrnes. Cambridge, MA: AAAI Press / MIT Press.

Nordbo, I., Skalle, P., Sveen, J., Aakvik, G., and Aamodt, A. (1992). *Reuse of Experience in Drilling—Phase I Report.* SINTEF DELAB and NTH, Div. of Petroleum Engineering, STF 40 RA92050 and IPT 12/92/PS/JS. Trondheim.

Price, C.J., and Pegler, I. (1995). Deciding Parameter Values with Case-Based Reasoning. In *Progress in Case-Based Reasoning*, edited by I. Watson. Lecture Notes in Artificial Intelligence 1020. Berlin: Springer-Verlag.

Simoudis, E. (1992). Using case-based reasoning for customer technical support. *IEEE Expert 7(5)*, 7–13.

Simoudis, E., and Miller, J.S. (1991). The Application of CBR to Help Desk Applications. In *Proceedings of the DARPA Workshop on Case-Based Reasoning,* edited by E.R. Bareiss. San Francisco: Morgan Kaufmann Publishers.

Waltz, D. (1996). Large-Scale Applications of CBR. In *Advances in Case-Based Reasoning,* edited by I. Smith and B. Faltings. Lecture Notes in Artificial Intelligence 1168. Berlin: Springer-Verlag.

10.5 Hybrid CBR

The following papers present combinations of different reasoning methods with CBR, including rules, analogical reasoning, deep causal reasoning, genetic algorithms, and neural nets.

Allen, J.R.C., Patterson, D., Mulvenna, M.D., and Hughes, J.G. (1995). Integration of Case-Based Retrieval with a Relational Database System in Aircraft Technical Support. In *Case-Based Reasoning Research and Development*, edited by M. Veloso and A. Aamodt. Lecture Notes in Artificial Intelligence 1010. Berlin: Springer-Verlag.

Auriol, E., Wess, S., Manago, M., Althoff, K.-D., and Traphoner, R. (1995). INRECA: A seamlessly integrated system based on inductive inference and case-based reasoning. In *Case-Based Reasoning Research and Development*, edited by M. Veloso and A. Aamodt. Lecture Notes in Artificial Intelligence 1010. Berlin: Springer-Verlag.

Avesani, P., Perini, A., and Ricci, F. (1993). Combining CBR and Constraint Reasoning in Planning Forest Fire Fighting. In *Proceedings of EWCBR'93*, edited by M.M. Richter et al. Berlin: Springer-Verlag.

Bartsch-Sporl, B. (1995). Towards the Integration of Case-Based, Schema-Based and Model-Based Reasoning for Supporting Complex Design Tasks. In *Case-Based Reasoning Research and Development*, edited by M. Veloso and A. Aamodt. Lecture Notes in Artificial Intelligence 1010. Berlin: Springer-Verlag.

Bichindaritz, I. (1995). Incremental Concept Learning and Case-Based Reasoning: For a Co-operative Approach. In *Progress in Case-Based Reasoning*, edited by I. Watson. Lecture Notes in Artificial Intelligence 1020. Berlin: Springer-Verlag.

Bradburn, C., Zelznikow, J., and Adams, A. (1993). Florence: Synthesis of Case-Based and Model-Based Reasoning in Nursing Care Planning System. *Computers in Nursing*, 11(1), 20–24.

Branting, L.K. (1988). Exploiting the Complementarity of Rules and Precedents with Reciprocity and Fairness. In *Proceedings of the DARPA Case-Based Reasoning Workshop*, edited by J.L. Kolodner. San Francisco: Morgan Kaufmann Publishers.

Brown, M., Watson, I., and Filer, N. (1995). Separating the Cases from the Data: Towards More Flexible Case-Based Reasoning. In *Case-Based Reasoning Research and Development*, edited by M. Veloso and A. Aamodt. Lecture Notes in Artificial Intelligence 1010. Berlin: Springer-Verlag.

Cunningham, P., and Slattery, S. (1993). Modelling of Engineering Thermal Problems—An Implementation Using CBR with Derivational Analogy. In *Proceedings of EWCBR'93*, edited by M.M. Richter et al. Berlin: Springer-Verlag.

Grolimund, S., and Ganascia, J.-G. (1995). Integrating Case-Based Reasoning and Tabu Search for Solving Optimisation Problems. In *Case-Based Reasoning Research and Development*, edited by M. Veloso and A. Aamodt. Lecture Notes in Artificial Intelligence 1010. Berlin: Springer-Verlag.

Huang, Y. (1996). An Evolutionary Agent Model of Case-Based Classification. In *Advances in Case-Based Reasoning,* edited by I. Smith and B. Faltings. Lecture Notes in Artificial Intelligence 1168. Berlin: Springer-Verlag.

Hunt, J. (1995). Evolutionary Case-Based Design. In *Progress in Case-Based Reasoning*, edited by I. Watson. Lecture Notes in Artificial Intelligence 1020. Berlin: Springer-Verlag.

Indurkhya, N., and Weiss, S.M. (1995). Using Case Data to Improve on Rule-based Function Approximation. In *Case-Based Reasoning Research and Development*, edited by M. Veloso and A. Aamodt. Lecture Notes in Artificial Intelligence 1010. Berlin: Springer-Verlag.

Karamouzis, T., and Feyock, S. (1992). An Integration of Case-Based and Model-Based Reasoning and its Application to Physical System Faults. In *Lecture Notes in Computer Science 604*, 100–108. Berlin: Springer-Verlag.

Lenz, M. (1993). CABAT—A Hybrid CBR System. In *Proceedings of EWCBR'93*, edited by M.M. Richter et al. Berlin: Springer-Verlag.

Liu, B., et al. (1994). Integrating Case-Based Reasoning, Knowledge-Based Approach and Dijkstra Algorithm for Route Finding. In *Proceedings of the Conference on Artificial Intelligence Applications,* 149–155.

Maher, M.L. (1994). Creative Design Using a Genetic Algorithm. *ASCE*, 2014–2021.

Munoz-Avila, H., and Hüllen, J. (1995). Retrieving Cases in Structured Domains by Using Goal Dependencies. In *Case-Based Reasoning Research and Development*, edited by M. Veloso and A. Aamodt. Lecture Notes in Artificial Intelligence 1010. Berlin: Springer-Verlag.

Musgrove, P.B., Davies, J., and Izzard, D. (1996). A Comparison of Nearest Neighbour, Rule Induction and Neural Networks for the Recommendation of Treatment at Anticoagulant Out-Patient Clinics. In *Proceedings of the Second U.K. Workshop on Case-Based Reasoning*, edited by I. Watson. Salford, UK: Salford University.

Nakhaeizadeh, G. (1993). Learning Prediction of Time Series: A Theoretical and Empirical Comparison of CBR with Some Other Approaches. In *Proceedings of EWCBR'93*, edited by M.M. Richter et al. Berlin: Springer-Verlag.

Pal, K., and Campbell, J.A. (1996). Suitability of Reasoning Methods in a Hybrid System. In *Proceedings of the Second U.K. Workshop on Case-Based Reasoning*, edited by I. Watson. Salford, UK: Salford University.

Pal, K., and Campbell, J.A. (1996). A Technique for Generating Partial Advice from a Rule Base or Hybrid Knowledge Base. In *Research & Development in Expert Systems XIII*, edited by J.L. Nealon and J. Hunt. Oxford: SGES Publications.

Portinale, L., and Torasso, P. (1995). ADAPtER: An Integrated Diagnostic System Combining Case-Based and Abductive Reasoning. In *Case-Based Reasoning Research and Development*, edited by M. Veloso and A. Aamodt. Lecture Notes in Artificial Intelligence 1010. Berlin: Springer-Verlag.

Purvis, L., and Pu, P. (1995). Adaptation Using Constraint Satisfaction Techniques. In *Case-Based Reasoning Research and Development*, edited by M. Veloso and A. Aamodt. Lecture Notes in Artificial Intelligence 1010. Berlin: Springer-Verlag.

Ram, A., and Francis, A.G. (1996). Multi-Plan Retrieval and Adaptation in an Experience-Based Agent. In *Case-Based Reasoning: Experiences, Lessons, & Future Directions,* edited by D.B. Leake. Cambridge, MA: AAAI Press / MIT Press.

Reategui, E., Campbell, J.A., and Borghetti, S. (1995). Using a Neural Network to Learn General Knowledge in a Case-Based System. In *Case-Based Reasoning Research and Development*, edited by M. Veloso and A. Aamodt. Lecture Notes in Artificial Intelligence 1010. Berlin: Springer-Verlag.

Rissland, E.L., Basu, C., Daniels, J.J., McCarthy, J., Rubinstein, B., and Skalak, D.B. (1991). A Blackboard-Based Architecture for CBR: An Initial Report. In *Proceedings of the DARPA Case-Based Reasoning Workshop*, edited by E.R. Bareiss. San Francisco: Morgan Kaufmann Publishers.

Schmalhofer, F., and Thoben, J. (1992). The Model-Based Construction of a Case-Oriented Expert System. *AI Communication* 5(1), 3–18.

Skalak, D.B. (1989). Options for Controlling Mixed Paradigm Systems. In *Proceedings of the DARPA Case-Based Reasoning Workshop*, edited by K.J. Hammond. San Francisco: Morgan Kaufmann Publishers.

Surma, J., and Vanhoof, K. (1995). Integrating Rules and Cases for the Classification Task. In *Case-Based Reasoning Research and Development*, edited by M. Veloso and A. Aamodt. Lecture Notes in Artificial Intelligence 1010. Berlin: Springer-Verlag.

Thrift, P. (1989). A Neural Network Model for Case-Based Reasoning. In *Proceedings of the DARPA Case-Based Reasoning Workshop*, edited by K.J. Hammond. San Francisco: Morgan Kaufmann Publishers.

Weber-Lee, R., Barcia, R.M., and Khator, S.K. (1995). Case-Based Reasoning for Cash Flow Forecasting Using Fuzzy Retrieval. In *Case-Based Reasoning Research and Development*, edited by M. Veloso and A. Aamodt. Lecture Notes in Artificial Intelligence 1010. Berlin: Springer-Verlag.

10.5.1 *CBR and Analogy*

CBR and analogous reasoning share similarities. CBR can be defined as intra-domain reasoning, whereas analogous reasoning is inter-domain. The following papers discuss this subject.

Brooks, L., Allen, S., and Norman, M. (1989). The Multiple and Variable Availability of Familiar Cases. In *Proceedings of the DARPA Case-Based Reasoning Workshop*, edited by K.J. Hammond. San Francisco: Morgan Kaufmann Publishers.

Burstein, M. (1989). Analogy vs. CBR: The Purpose of Mapping. In *Proceedings of the DARPA Case-Based Reasoning Workshop*, edited by K.J. Hammond. San Francisco: Morgan Kaufmann Publishers.

Eskridge, T.C. (1989). Continuous Analogical Reasoning: Summary of Current Research. In *Proceedings of the DARPA Case-Based Reasoning Workshop*, edited by K.J. Hammond. San Francisco: Morgan Kaufmann Publishers.

Gentner, D. (1989). Finding the Needle: Accessing and Reasoning from Prior Cases. In *Proceedings of the DARPA Case-Based Reasoning Workshop*, edited by K.J. Hammond. San Francisco: Morgan Kaufmann Publishers.

Haigh, K.Z., and Veloso, M. (1995). Route Planning by Analogy. In *Case-Based Reasoning Research and Development*, edited by M. Veloso and A. Aamodt. Lecture Notes in Artificial Intelligence 1010. Berlin: Springer-Verlag.

Liang, T.-P. (1993). Analogical Reasoning and Case-Based Learning in Model Management Systems. *Decision Support Systems,* 10, 137–160.

Ross, B. (1989). Some Psychological Results on Case-based Reasoning. In *Proceedings of the DARPA Case-Based Reasoning Workshop*, edited by K.J. Hammond. San Francisco: Morgan Kaufmann Publishers.

Seifert, C. (1989). Analogy and Case-Based Reasoning. In *Proceedings of the DARPA Case-Based Reasoning Workshop*, edited by K.J. Hammond. San Francisco: Morgan Kaufmann Publishers.

Seifert, C., and Hammond, K.J. (1989). Why There's No Analogical Transfer. In *Proceedings of the DARPA Case-Based Reasoning Workshop*, edited by K.J. Hammond. San Francisco: Morgan Kaufmann Publishers.

Shinn, H.S. (1988). Abstractional Analogy: A Model of Analogical Reasoning. In *Proceedings of the DARPA Case-Based Reasoning Workshop*, edited by J.L. Kolodner. San Francisco: Morgan Kaufmann Publishers.

Veloso, M.M., and Carbonell, J.G. (1989). Learning Analogies by Analogy— The Closed Loop of Memory Organization and Problem Solving. In *Proceedings of the DARPA Case-Based Reasoning Workshop*, edited by K.J. Hammond. San Francisco: Morgan Kaufmann Publishers.

10.6 Internet Information Sources

The Internet is becoming an increasingly valuable source of information. The following section presents sources that provide information via the Internet on CBR.

10.6.1 AI-CBR

This is *the* Internet site for CBR and is maintained by the author. This site is regularly updated (through forms, you can even add your own information), and it will contain more up-to-date information than is presented in this book. The site contains lists of links to researchers, projects, research labs, tools, vendors, consultants, conferences, and case-bases, as well as an extensive library. AI-CBR also includes a threaded discussion group where people can discuss topics of interest relating to CBR. The site:

> http://www.surveying.salford.ac.uk/ai-cbr/

In addition to the Web site, AI-CBR runs an Internet e-mail forum for broadcasting CBR news (e.g., calls for papers, jobs, bug fixes, etc.) and discussing all aspects of CBR research and practice. Membership is free, and members include academics, industrialists, and many of the CBR software vendors. To join the mailing list, send the following message to "mailbase@mailbase.ac.uk":

> join ai-cbr <first name> <last name>

If your name were Joan Smith, for example, your message would be as follows:

> To: mailbase@mailbase.ac.uk
> Subject: join ai-cbr Joan Smith

10.6.2 CBR-MED

The CBR-MED mailing list provides a forum for the discussion of CBR methods in medicine. The list brings together medical practitioners, health information specialists, and CBR researchers in the service of two goals:

1. To support the delivery of medical care by fostering the development of CBR software that performs health care–related tasks
2. To spur the development of CBR methods by focusing the efforts of researchers on the challenges (large databases, knowledge-representation problems, etc.) provided by medical and health information problems

To subscribe to CBR-MED, send a message that looks like this:

To: listproc@cs.uchicago.edu
Subject: subscribe CBR-MED <your first name> <your last name>

If your name were Joan Smith, for example, your subscription request would look like this:

To: listproc@cs.uchicago.edu
Subject: subscribe CBR-MED Joan Smith

Further information about CBR-MED may be obtained from Jeff Berger:

OWNER-CBR-MED@cs.uchicago.edu.

10.6.3 *The European CBR Newsletter*

The case-based reasoning electronic newsletter is delivered to members of the German AK-CBR and to the participants of the European CBR workshops. Thus, the *CBR Newsletter* addresses mainly a European readership. Its objective is to support an exchange of information, news, and opinions on CBR that relate to both scientific- and application-oriented issues. Submissions to and requests to receive the *CBR Newsletter* should be made to Dietmar Janetzko:

dietmar@cognition.iig.uni-freiburg.

10.6.4 *Other Internet Sites*

You also might consider looking at the following sites:

- David Aha's Machine Learning and Case-Based Reasoning Home Page:

www.aic.nrl.navy.mil/~aha/

- The Institute for Learning Sciences:

  www.ils.nwu.edu

- The Case-Based Reasoning Group at the University of Massachusetts:

  cbr-www.cs.umass.edu/

Index